DAX Patterns 2015

ALBERTO FERRARI
MARCO RUSSO

DAX Patterns 2015

Publisher: Loader
Editorial Production: SQLBI
Copyeditor: Lisa Maynard
Authors: Alberto Ferrari, Marco Russo
Cover Design: Daniele Perilli

Printed by CreateSpace, An Amazon.com Company

Available on Kindle and online stores
Available on iOS devices and iBooks Store

Download examples and resources at
http://www.daxpatterns.com

All the code in this book has been formatted with DAX Formatter
http://www.daxformatter.com

Contents at a Glance

Contents

Introduction

We are accustomed to sharing nearly all the DAX code we develop by writing blog posts, speaking at conferences, and teaching courses. Often, people ask us about a scenario we have solved in the past and, every time, we have to search through our own blogs for the solution.

After four years of DAX coding, we had collected a good library of patterns and we decided to publish them on the http://www.daxpatterns.com website, sharing its content with all of our readers. As we reviewed the patterns, we took time to optimize the code, looking for the best solutions. Once we have published a solution on the web, we can easily find it when we need it again, freeing up our own minds (we have very active brain garbage collectors: DAX Patterns is our long-term DAX memory).

We have received many appreciations for the website, and several readers asked for a printed version of its content, so we did it! You are reading the printed version of the content of the DAX Patterns website as of December 2014.

All the patterns included in this book are also available for free on http://www.daxpatterns.com. We added only the first two chapters: DAX Fundamentals and Time Intelligence Functions, which are not patterns by themselves but can be useful to many readers.

Why should you pay for a book when its content is also available for free? Several reasons come to mind—a printed set of the patterns is generally faster to scan, it is available on a plane with no Wi-Fi, and studying "offline" generally leads to a better understanding of a topic.

You still need to access the website for the sample files. In fact, each chapter of this book contains a link to the corresponding article on http://www.daxpatterns.com, where you will find sample workbooks for both Excel 2010 and 2013. If needed, you can easily create a corresponding Analysis Services Tabular project starting from the Excel 2013 file.

We hope that you will find these patterns useful in your daily work and that you will improve your DAX knowledge by studying them. We had a lot of fun writing—now it is your time to enjoy reading!

If you have any feedback, share it with us by using comments on http://www.daxpatterns.com.

Alberto Ferrari
Marco Russo

CHAPTER 1

DAX Fundamentals

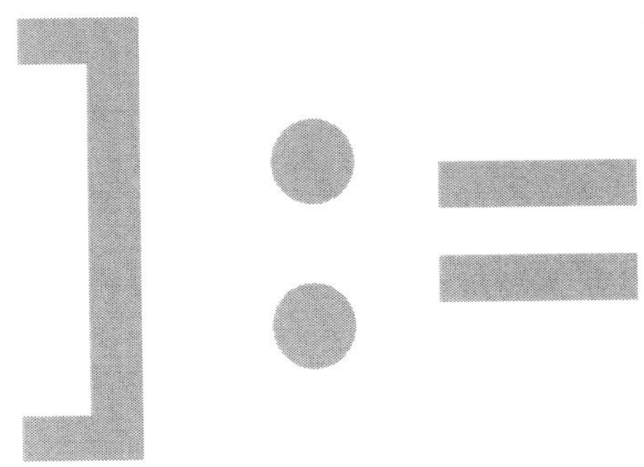

The Data Analysis Expression (DAX) language is a functional language used by PowerPivot for Excel and Analysis Services Tabular to define calculations within the data model and to query the data model itself. DAX has its roots in Microsoft Excel expressions and inherits a similar syntax and a functional approach, but it also extends its scope in order to handle calculations on data stored in multiple tables.

This chapter offers a summary of the DAX syntax and the important evaluation context behavior, which is fundamental knowledge for those hoping to master the language. Many of the patterns in this book are based on manipulating both the filter and the row context. Even if you can apply the patterns in your data model without a full understanding of the internal calculation behavior, the knowledge of evaluation context allows you to manipulate these patterns with full control.

DAX Syntax

A DAX expression returns either a table or a scalar value. A table in a DAX expression can have one or more columns and zero or more rows. A scalar value can be in any of the data types handled by the language. You can write DAX expressions to define calculated columns and measures (also known as calculated fields in Excel 2013), and as parts of a DAX query.

DAX Data Types

DAX supports the following data types:

- Integer
- Real
- Currency
- Date (datetime)
- TRUE/FALSE (Boolean)
- String
- BLOB (binary large object)

Usually type conversion happens automatically, and you do not have to call conversion functions in your expressions, even if in certain cases you might want to do that to force a particular behavior or to make your statement more readable and explicit about intentions.

The Currency data type is a fixed-point decimal number that is very useful in financial calculations. The datetime data type internally stores the value using a floating-point number, wherein the integer corresponds to the number of days (starting from December 30, 1899), and the decimal identifies the fraction of the day (hours, minutes, and seconds are converted to decimal fractions of a day). Thus, the expression

```
= NOW() + 0.5
```

increases a date by 12 hours (exactly half a day). You should, however, consider using specific DAX functions such as DATEADD whenever possible to make your code more readable. If you need only the date part of a DATETIME, always remember to use TRUNC to get rid of the decimal part.

DAX Operators

Table 1-1 shows a list of operators available in the DAX language.

Operator Type	Symbol	Use	Example
Parenthesis	( )	Precedence order and grouping of arguments	(5 + 2) * 3
Arithmetic	+	Addition	4 + 2
	-	Subtraction/negation	5 – 3
	*	Multiplication	4 * 2
	/	Division	4 / 2
Comparison	=	Equal to	[Country] = "USA"
	<>	Not equal to	[Country] <> "USA"
	>	Greater than	[Quantity] > 0
	>=	Greater than or equal to	[Quantity] >= 100
	<	Less than	[Quantity] < 0
	<=	Less than or equal to	[Quantity] <= 100

<table>
<tr><th>Operator Type</th><th>Symbol</th><th>Use</th><th>Example</th></tr>
<tr><td>Text concatenation</td><td>&</td><td>Concatenation of strings</td><td>"Value is " & [Amount]</td></tr>
<tr><td rowspan="2">Logical</td><td>&&</td><td>AND condition between two Boolean expressions</td><td>[Country] = "USA" && [Quantity] > 0</td></tr>
<tr><td>||</td><td>OR condition between two Boolean expressions</td><td>[Country] = "USA" || [Quantity] > 0</td></tr>
</table>

TABLE 1-1 Operators

Because of the compatibility with Excel syntax, the logical operators are also available as DAX functions. For example, you can write

```
AND ( [Country] = "USA", [Quantity] > 0 )
OR ( [Country] = "USA", [Quantity] > 0 )
```

which correspond, respectively, to these:

```
[Country] = "USA" && [Quantity] > 0
[Country] = "USA" || [Quantity] > 0
```

DAX Values

In a DAX expression, you can use scalar values such as "USA" or 0, which are called **literals**, or you can refer to the value of a column in a table. When you reference a column in order to get its value, you use the following basic syntax:

```
'Table Name'[Column Name]
```

Here is an example:

```
'Products'[ListPrice]
```

The table name precedes the column name. You can omit the single quote character that encloses the table name whenever the table name is a single name without spaces or other special characters and does not correspond to a reserved word. For example, in the following formula you can omit the quotes:

```
Products[ListPrice]
```

The square brackets that enclose the column name are mandatory. Even if the table name is optional, it is a best practice always to include it when you reference a column and to omit it when you reference a measure (which you access with the same syntax of a column name).

Empty or Missing Values

In DAX, BLANK represents any missing or empty value. You can obtain a blank value in DAX by calling the BLANK function, which has no arguments. Such a value is useful only as result of a DAX expression, because you cannot use it in a comparison statement (see ISBLANK for that in the "Conditional Statements" section later in this chapter). In a numeric expression, a blank is automatically converted into 0, whereas in a string expression, a blank is automatically converted into an empty string--with certain exceptions in which BLANK is retained in the expression result (such as a product, numerator in a division, or sum of blanks). In the following examples, you can see how DAX handles BLANK in different operations involving numbers, string, and Boolean data types:

```
BLANK() + BLANK()      = BLANK()
10 * BLANK()           = BLANK()
BLANK() / 3            = BLANK()
BLANK() / BLANK()      = BLANK()
BLANK() || BLANK()     = FALSE
BLANK() && BLANK()     = FALSE
BLANK() - 10           = -10
18 + BLANK()           = 18
4 / BLANK()            = Infinity
0 / BLANK()            = NaN
FALSE || BLANK()       = FALSE
```

```
FALSE && BLANK()       = FALSE
TRUE || BLANK()        = TRUE
TRUE && BLANK()        = FALSE
```

Usually, you will use BLANK as a result for an expression assigned to a measure or to a calculated column. However, it is useful to understand how BLANK propagates (and does not propagate) in DAX expressions, because this is the behavior you handle when a column reference or another sub-expression returns blank.

Conditional Statements

DAX is a functional language, and classical conditional statements are available as functions. The first and most used conditional statement is IF, which has three arguments: the first is the condition to test, the second is the value returned if the first argument evaluates to TRUE, and the third is the value returned otherwise. If you omit the third argument, it defaults to BLANK. Here you can see a few examples of expressions using the IF function:

```
IF ( 20 < 30, "second", "third" ) = "second"
IF ( 20 < 15, "second", BLANK() ) = BLANK()
IF ( 20 < 15, "second" )          = BLANK()
```

You might use nested IF statements to check different values for an expression. For example, you might decode the single-letter Status column of the Customer table into a more meaningful description using the following nested IF calls:

```
IF ( Customer[Status] = "A", "Platinum",
    IF ( Customer[Status] = "B", "Gold",
        IF ( Customer[Status] = "C", "Silver",
            IF ( Customer[Status] = "D", "White", "None" )
        )
    )
)
```

However, you can obtain much more readable code by using the SWITCH function--in fact, you can rewrite the previous expression in this way:

```
SWITCH (
    Customer[Status],
    "A", "Platinum",
    "B", "Gold",
    "C", "Silver",
    "D", "White",
    "None"
)
```

The SWITCH syntax is much more readable, but internally it generates exactly the same code as the nested IF statements and the performance is the same. In this syntax, you can see that the first argument is the expression evaluated once, and the following arguments are in pairs: if the first argument in the pair matches the result of the first expression, the SWITCH function returns the value of the second expression in the pair. The last argument is the expression value to return if there are no matches.

You can also use SWITCH to test different, unrelated conditions instead of matching the value returned by a single expression. You can obtain that by passing TRUE() as the first argument, and then writing the logical expression of each condition you want to test. For example, you can write the following SWITCH statement:

```
SWITCH (
    TRUE (),
    Products[UnitPrice] < 10, "LOW",
    Products[UnitPrice] < 50, "MEDIUM",
    Products[UnitPrice] < 100, "HIGH",
    "VERY HIGH"
)
```

This corresponds to these equivalent nested IF calls:

```
IF ( Products[UnitPrice] < 10, "LOW",
    IF ( Products[UnitPrice] < 50, "MEDIUM",
        IF ( Products[UnitPrice] < 100, "HIGH", "VERY HIGH" )
    )
)
```

You can check whether an expression is blank by using the ISBLANK function. A common usage is defining a default value for an expression in case it evaluates to BLANK, as in the following example:

```
IF ( ISBLANK ( Sales[Quantity] ), 1, Sales[Quantity] )
```

You can also detect the presence of an error in an expression by using the ISERROR function. For example, if you want to avoid the propagation of an error in a statement, you can write an expression like this:

```
IF ( ISERROR ( SQRT ( Test[Omega] ) ), BLANK(), SQRT ( Test[Omega] ) )
```

When you implement the preceding pattern, returning a value in case of an error, you can avoid duplicating the same expression by using IFERROR, which automatically returns the expression passed as first argument if it raises an error:

```
IFERROR ( SQRT ( Test[Omega] ), BLANK() )
```

Keep in mind that the use of ISERROR and IFERROR might be expensive. It is always better to anticipate the condition for an error. For example, if the concern for the square root in the previous example is the presence of negative numbers, you should use this expression instead:

```
IF ( Test[Omega] >= 0, SQRT ( Test[Omega] ), BLANK() )
```

A common test is to check the value of the denominator of a ratio. In such a case, you should use the DIVIDE function. So, instead of writing this,

```
IF ( Sales[Quantity] = 0, BLANK(), Sales[SalesAmount] / Sales[Quantity] )
```

you would write this:

```
DIVIDE ( Sales[SalesAmount], Sales[Quantity] )
```

The DIVIDE argument also has a third optional argument, which is the value to return in case the denominator is zero and defaults to BLANK. For example, the following expressions are equivalent (please note the boldfaced corresponding arguments in the two versions):

```
IF ( Sales[Quantity] = 0, Sales[SalesAmount], Sales[SalesAmount] / Sales[Quantity] )
```

```
DIVIDE ( Sales[SalesAmount], Sales[Quantity], Sales[SalesAmount] )
```

You should always use DIVIDE whenever possible to protect your expressions against division-by-zero errors, because this offers better performance than the IF-based approach.

DAX Calculations

You use DAX expressions to define calculated columns, measures, and queries. It is important that you know the difference between calculated columns and measures.

Calculated Columns

You define calculated columns within tables in the data model by adding new columns. The expression assigned to a calculated column is evaluated for every row of the table, and its result is stored in the table like any other column value. Refreshing the table content produces the evaluation of all the calculated columns for all the rows of the table, regardless of the portion of the modified table. Thus, all calculated columns occupy space in memory and are computed once, during table processing.

The DAX expression defined for a calculated column operates in the context of the current row of the table it belongs to. Any reference to a column returns the value of that column in the current row. You cannot access directly the values of other rows.

When you define a calculated column, you specify only the expression in the user interface, and you define the name of the column in the table header. To make the text more readable, we use a syntax whereby the name of the column precedes the assignment operator. Thus, the following syntax defines the GrossMargin calculated column as the difference between SalesAmount and TotalProductCost in the Sales table:

```
Sales[GrossMargin] = Sales[SalesAmount] - Sales[TotalProductCost]
```

The actual expression you enter as a calculated column formula does not include the table and column names and directly starts with the assignment operator:

```
= Sales[SalesAmount] - Sales[TotalProductCost]
```

However, in this text you will always see the complete form, including the assigned column name. The name of a calculated column has to be unique in the table, but you can have columns with the same name in different tables of the same data model.

Measures

A **measure** is a DAX expression that is evaluated in a context made by a set of rows of the data model. Functions used in a DAX query generate different filter contexts used to evaluate DAX expressions defined in measures or locally defined in the query itself. Moreover, every cell of a pivot table defines an implicit set of filters that is different for every cell of the pivot table itself. The cell context depends on the user selections in the pivot table. So when you use SUM([SalesAmount]) in a measure, you mean the sum of all the rows that are aggregated under this cell; whereas when you use [SalesAmount] in a calculated column, you mean the value of the column SalesAmount in the current row.

In Excel 2013, measures are called "calculated fields", whereas in Excel 2010 the name "measures" was used by the PowerPivot add-on. However, the name "measures" is more appropriate in DAX and is used by the user interface in Visual Studio. Hence, we will use the term "measure" in this book when referring to these.

The syntax of a measure is similar to that of a calculated column, but it uses := instead of = as an assignment operator. For example, the following expression defines a measure named Total Sales that sums the value of the SalesAmount column in the Sales table for all the rows included in the current filter context:

```
[Total Sales] := SUM ( Sales[SalesAmount] )
```

A measure cannot reference the value of a single row in a direct way. A reference to a column always has to be included in an aggregation function (SUM, COUNT, and so on) or by using an iteration function (FILTER, SUMX, and so on).

You define a measure within a table, but this simply defines the table under which the measure will be displayed to the end user in a PivotTable. The name of a measure must be unique in the entire data model, so you cannot use the same name for two measures, even if they are defined in different tables. Usually, it is not important to define in which table a measure is defined, but in case this would be relevant in a pattern description, the following syntax might appear in the text--preceding the measure name with the table name:

```
Sales[Total Sales] := SUM ( Sales[SalesAmount] )
```

A measure name is enclosed in square brackets, just as a calculated column. Because it is important to discriminate between columns and measures, the best practice to disambiguate the syntax reading a DAX formula is the following:

- Always specify the table name when referencing a column.
- Always omit the table name when referencing a measure.

Following this simple best practice, you can say that the DAX expression

```
= Orders[Price] * [Quantity]
```

will multiply the value of the Price column in the current row of the Orders table by the value returned by the measure Quantity, which could aggregate more rows returning a simple scalar value.

Another reason why it is important to identify measures in a DAX expression is that a measure implies a context transition (a row context is transformed into a filter context). You want to recognize this behavior when reading a DAX expression.

Aggregation Functions

DAX provides several functions that aggregate data over sets of rows, returning a scalar value. These functions operate according to the filter context, covered later in this chapter, but it is important that you anticipate the functions' syntax.

The simplest aggregation functions apply an aggregation over a single numeric column in a table, which is the only argument of the following functions:

- AVERAGE, AVERAGEA
- MAX, MAXA
- MIN, MINA
- STDEV.S, STDEV.P
- SUM
- VAR.S, VAR.P

TIP Function names that include the A suffix exist only for maintaining the Excel syntax, even if in PowerPivot they work only on numeric columns, whereas in Excel these functions can be used for columns containing text. The only difference is that, if applied to a non-numeric column, functions with the A suffix return 0 instead of raising an error. From a practical point of view, you may ignore any function with the A suffix.

All of these functions use the following syntax:

```
<FunctionName> ( Table[Column] )
```

You can pass only one column as an argument. If you need to aggregate the results of a more complex expression, you need to use one of the **X** iteration functions, which use the following syntax:

```
<FunctionName>X ( Table, <expression> )
```

The expression passed as a second argument is evaluated for each row of the table passed as the first argument, and the result will be aggregated according to the aggregation function used. The expression behaves as a temporary calculated column during its evaluation. All the syntax rules that are valid for calculated columns also apply to that argument.

Most (but not all) of the simple aggregation's functions have a corresponding **X** counterpart:

- AVERAGEX
- MAXX
- MINX
- STDEVX.S, STDEVX.P
- SUMX
- VARX.S, VARX.P

You can rewrite every simple aggregation using the corresponding iterative function. For example, instead of writing the following expression,

```
SUM ( Sales[SalesAmount] )
```

you can write this one:

```
SUMX ( Sales, Sales[SalesAmount] )
```

But if you want to use a more complex expression, you have to use the SUMX function:

```
SUMX ( Sales, Sales[OrderQuantity] * Sales[UnitPrice] )
```

There are no performance differences between using SUM or a corresponding SUMX in the same expression.

Counting Values

If you want to count the number of rows in a table, the number of rows with a relevant value in a certain column, or the number of distinct values in a column, you can use the following functions:

- COUNT, COUNTA
- COUNTX, COUNTAX
- COUNTBLANK
- COUNTROWS
- DISTINCTCOUNT

TIP The COUNTA function can be used to count how many rows have a non-blank value in a column regardless of its data type, whereas COUNT does the same but works only on numeric columns. From a practical point of view, you might consider always using COUNTA instead of COUNT.

The COUNTROWS function has only one argument, which must be a table. Its result corresponds to the sum of COUNTA and COUNTBLANK of any column of the same table. You can assume this:

```
COUNTROWS ( Table ) = COUNTA ( Table[Column] ) + COUNTBLANK ( Table[Column] )
```

The DISTINCTCOUNT function returns the number of distinct value in a column and corresponds to calling COUNTROWS on the result of DISTINCT for the same column. You can assume this:

```
DISTINCTCOUNT ( Table[Column] ) = COUNTROWS ( DISTINCT ( Table[Column] ) )
```

You should use DISTINCTCOUNT instead of COUNTROWS / DISTINCT, because the former is more readable and might be faster as well.

Evaluation Context

The evaluation of a DAX expression considers the context in which the formula operates, so that the same DAX expression will return different values, depending on the existing context. For example, every cell of a PivotTable in Excel defines a different filter context.

The evaluation context is composed of the following:

- **Filter Context**, which always exists and defines a set of active rows in a calculation
- **Row Context**, which is the current row in table iterations and exists only during a table iteration

We describe these concepts in more detail in the following sections.

Filter Context

When a DAX expression is evaluated, a set of filters over the tables in the data model define the set of active rows that will be used for the calculation. This set of filters is a filter context. The filter context corresponds to a subset of all the rows made visible, including the special cases of the entire set of all the rows (no filters at all) and of the empty set (the filters exclude all the rows).

For example, every cell in a PivotTable defines a different filter context that depends on the current selection of slicers, filters, rows, and columns. The same formula of a DAX measure is executed in a different filter context for each cell of a PivotTable, and for this reason returns a different result for every cell.

When a filter context is applied to a table, the filter also propagates to other related tables, following any relationship along the one-to-many direction. For example, consider the data model in Figure 1-1.

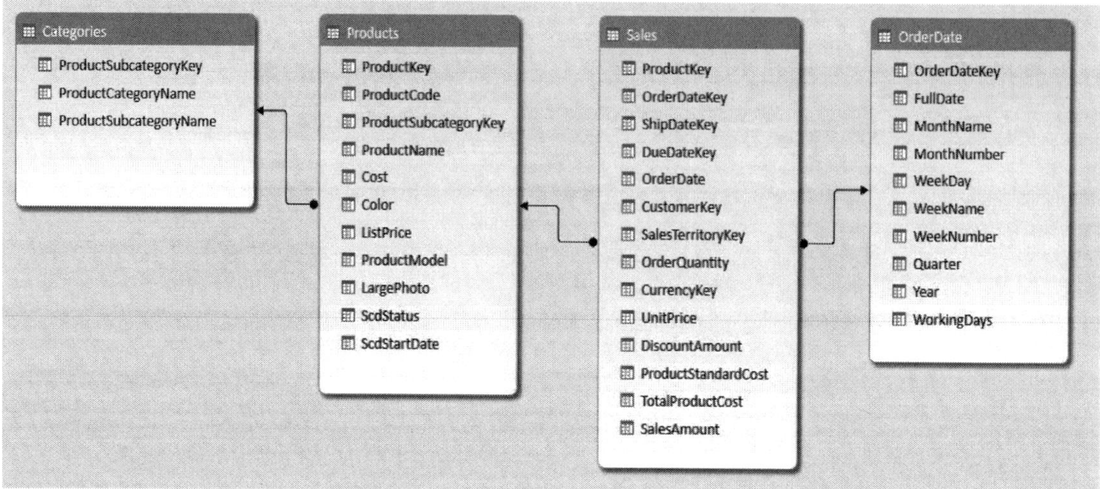

FIGURE 1-1 The filter context propagates following relationships defined in the data model.

If you apply a filter to Categories[ProductCategoryName], which is the ProductCategoryName column of the Categories table, you implicitly apply a filter to the Products table as well. Only the rows in Products that correspond to the selected category name will be active in the filter context. The filter context also propagates to the Sales table, filtering only the sales that correspond to one of the filtered products. The filter context stops its propagation at the Sales table. The relationship between Sales to OrderDate is a many-to-one relationship, and the filter context does not propagate in such a direction. If a filter is applied to OrderDate[Year], which is the Year column of the OrderDate table, the OrderDate table will have a filter context that includes all the days of such a year. This filter context also propagates to the Sales table, filtering only the rows related to selected days. Since there are two filter contexts propagated to the Sales table (one from Categories and one from OrderDate), the resulting filter applied to the Sales table is the intersection of both. In other words, filter contexts sum their effects to target tables by filtering only the rows that satisfy all of the filters, resulting in a logical AND condition between all the applied filters.

If you filter the Sales[UnitPrice] column, such a filter is combined with other filters coming from other tables (such as Categories, Products, and OrderDate in this example), but it does not propagate itself to other tables because of the direction of the relationship. Filter context propagates to other tables following only one-to-many relationships and does not propagate in the opposite many-to-one direction of the same relationships.

FILTER Function

Any DAX expression automatically applies the existing filter context to any operation, including aggregation functions. For example, the following expression returns the sum of the SalesAmount column in the Sales table, considering only the rows active in the filter context existing when the SUMX is called:

```
SUMX ( Sales, Sales[SalesAmount] )
```

Instead of a table, such as in the first parameter of the previous SUMX function, you can use any DAX expression returning a table. By using the name of a table, you include all the rows active in the current filter context. You can pass a different set of rows by using a function that returns a table. The FILTER function, for example, receives a table as a first argument and returns all the rows that satisfy the logical condition passed as a second argument, which is evaluated for each row of the table it receives. For example, if you want to calculate the sum of SalesAmount only for the rows having a UnitPrice value greater than 10, you can use the following expression:

```
SUMX (
    FILTER ( Sales, Sales[UnitPrice] > 10 ),
    Sales[SalesAmount]
)
```

This expression does not alter the existing filter context. Thus, the filter on UnitPrice does not replace any existing filter active in the filter context. If you want to replace existing filters, you have to use other functions, such as ALL and CALCULATE, which are described later in the chapter.

Row Context

The row context is conceptually close to the notion of current row. Any reference to a column in a DAX expression requires a row context in order to retrieve the value of such a column. For this reason, you receive an error if you try to reference a column in a DAX expression executed without a row context. The row context is available only to DAX expressions defined in calculated columns or passed as arguments to DAX functions that iterate over a table (such as SUMX, FILTER, ADDCOLUMNS, and many others).

For example, the following calculated column for the table Sales has a row context for the same table and makes this definition valid:

```
Sales[GrossMargin] = Sales[SalesAmount] - Sales[TotalProductCost]
```

RELATED Function

If you try to access a row from a lookup table (a table accessible through a many-to-one relationship from the current one), you get an error. The following definition in the Sales table is not valid because there is no active row context for the Products table:

```
Sales[ListAmount] = Sales[OrderQuantity] * Products[ListPrice]
```

To propagate the row context through the many-to-one relationship existing between two tables, you use the RELATED function, which traverses any number of many-to-one relationships until it reaches the table containing the column specified as RELATED argument. The following formula fixes the previous error:

```
Sales[ListAmount] = Sales[OrderQuantity] * RELATED ( Products[ListPrice] )
```

RELATEDTABLE Function

If you want to traverse one or more one-to-many relationships to retrieve the set of rows that are related to the current row context in a given table, you can use RELATEDTABLE. The use of this function in a scalar expression (such as a measure or a calculated column) requires some aggregation or computation over the table returned by RELATEDTABLE. For example, the following calculated columns in the Products table return the number of orders and the list amount of those orders for each product, respectively:

```
Products[NumberOrders] = COUNTROWS ( RELATEDTABLE ( Sales ) )
```

```
Products[ListAmount] =
SUMX (
    RELATEDTABLE ( Sales ),
    Sales[OrderQuantity] * Products[ListPrice]
)
```

The ListAmount calculated column uses the row context defined for the Products table and uses another row context defined during the iteration of the related rows in the Sales table. Thus, the expression evaluated by SUMX uses two active row contexts. Since these row contexts refer to different tables, there are neither ambiguities nor overrides.

EARLIER Function

A new row context on a table that already has an active row context produces an override of the existing row context. To access a row context hidden by a new one, you have to use the EARLIER function. For example, the following PriceRanking calculated column in the Products table accesses the ListPrice column through the row context defined by the FILTER function over Products, and then it compares this value with the ListPrice column of the current row context provided by the calculated column itself:

```
Products[PriceRanking] =
COUNTROWS (
    FILTER (
        Products,
        Products[ListPrice] > EARLIER ( Products[ListPrice] )
    )
)
```

The EARLIER function has a second optional argument that allows you to obtain a previous row context doing more than one hop (the second argument specifies how many row contexts to skip in the stack of nested row contexts--the default is 1). The EARLIEST function applies the outermost row context regardless of the number of nested row contexts.

CALCULATE Function

To manipulate the filter context and execute calculation on different filters (for example, the total of the category to which a product belongs, or the total of the current year) you can use the CALCULATE function.

The syntax of CALCULATE is as follows:

```
CALCULATE (
    <expression>,
    <filter1>,
    ...
    <filterN>
)
```

The <expression> is the only mandatory argument. You can add one or more filter expressions, which will modify the filter context in which the <expression> is evaluated. The filter expressions can be one of the following:

- A logical expression containing just a single column reference: in this case, any existing filter over that column is replaced by the new filter condition.
- A table expression that returns one or more columns: in this case, all the filters on the columns returned by the table expression are replaced by the new filter conditions.

For example, the following expression calculates the sum of SalesAmount for only the year 2006, keeping filters on other columns such as month and quarter:

```
[Sales2006] :=
CALCULATE (
    SUM ( Sales[SalesAmount] ),
    OrderDate[Year] = 2006
)
```

ALL Function

In reality, the previous Sales2006 measure is internally rewritten in this way:

```
[Sales2006] :=
CALCULATE (
    SUM ( Sales[SalesAmount] ),
    FILTER ( ALL ( OrderDate[Year] ), OrderDate[Year] = 2006 )
)
```

The ALL function returns all the values of a column or of a table, depending on the argument passed to the function call. If you want to eliminate the filters on any other column of the Date table, you must explicitly write the FILTER condition specifying the entire Date table in the ALL function call:

```
[Sales2006Complete] :=
CALCULATE (
    SUM ( Sales[SalesAmount] ),
    FILTER ( ALL ( OrderDate ), OrderDate[Year] = 2006 )
)
```

As an alternative that may be faster, you can remove the filter on other columns of the same table by adding an ALL condition over that table. All the conditions in the same CALCULATE statement are considered in a logical AND condition:

```
[Sales2006Complete] :=
CALCULATE (
    SUM ( Sales[SalesAmount] ),
    OrderDate[Year] = 2006,
    ALL ( OrderDate )
)
```

VALUES Function

If you do not want to remove the existing filter context over a column or a table, you can use VALUES instead of ALL as an argument of the FILTER call used in a CALCULATE filter argument. For example, the following measure considers only data from year 2006 if it is part of the current selection:

```
[Sales2006ifSelected] :=
CALCULATE (
    SUM ( Sales[SalesAmount] ),
    FILTER ( VALUES ( OrderDate[Year] ), OrderDate[Year] = 2006 )
)
```

The VALUES function returns a table made by a single column containing all the values active in the current filter context.

DISTINCT Function

When you apply VALUES to a column of a lookup table, the result includes an empty value in case there are rows in the related table that do not have a valid correspondence in the lookup table itself. For example, the Products table might contain products with a missing or invalid value for the ProductSubcategoryKey column. In this case, the empty row virtually added to the lookup table makes it possible to browse these rows. If you want to ignore such a row in the VALUES result, you should use the DISTINCT function, which has the same syntax of VALUES but does not return the empty row generated for non-matching rows in a related table.

You can see the difference in the PivotTable shown in Figure 1-2, where the number of rows returned by DISTINCT does not include the blank value, which is included in the number of rows returned by VALUES. In fact, the Products table has 209 rows that do not have a value defined in the ProductSubcategoryKey column.

		DISTINCT	VALUES
Row Labels	NumOfProducts	NumOfCategories	NumOfCategoriesIncludingMissing
Accessories	35	1	1
Bikes	125	1	1
Clothing	48	1	1
Components	189	1	1
(blank)	209		1
Grand Total	**606**	**4**	**5**

FIGURE 1-2 The DISTINCT function does not return the empty row returned by VALUES.

Here are the definitions of the three measures used in Figure 1-2:

```
NumOfProducts := COUNTROWS ( Products )

NumOfCategories := COUNTROWS ( DISTINCT ( Categories[ProductCategoryName] ) )

NumOfCategoriesIncludingMissing := COUNTROWS ( VALUES ( Categories[ProductCategoryName] ) )
```

Because you will usually use VALUES and DISTINCT as arguments of iterators such as FILTER and SUMX, you will probably need VALUES more than DISTINCT, unless you explicitly want to exclude from the calculation the same rows that would be excluded by an INNER JOIN condition between related tables in a SQL query.

CHAPTER 2

Time Intelligence Functions

There are many time-related calculations that you probably need in your reports. You can write simple time-related calculations using a group of DAX "time intelligence" functions. However, these functions work only on standard calendars. If you need a custom calendar, such as an ISO 8601 week calendar, you will need to use more complex DAX expressions.

Any time-related calculation is based on changing the date filter during a calculation. In this chapter, we introduce the common time intelligence functions in DAX.

In the following chapter, we show alternative time patterns, which are variations of the filter applied to the calendar table and are not based on DAX time intelligence functions.

Time Intelligence Functions

All the time intelligence functions available in DAX require a date table in the data model. This table must contain a column with the date data type. You use this column to mark the table as a date table. The date table must contain all the days in each year you want to consider. You can have many date tables in the data model: in this case, you specify the table to use in each DAX calculation (there is no default date table in the data model).

Aggregating and Comparing over Time

You have a set of DAX functions to aggregate and compare data over time. For example, you might want to calculate the aggregated value of a measure from the beginning of the year up to the period you are selecting. (This is known as year-to-date aggregation.) You might also want to compare the sales of this year with the sales of the previous year. Both aggregations and comparisons change the date filter, modifying the initial selection into a different one that corresponds to the desired calculation.

Year-to-Date, Quarter-to-Date, and Month-to-Date

The calculation of year-to-date (YTD), quarter-to-date, (QTD) and month-to-date (MTD) are all very similar. Each of these calculations extends the current selection from the beginning of the period (year, quarter, and month, respectively). For example, the month-to-date calculation computes the measure from the beginning of the month until the day selected. As you can see in Figure 2-1, the SalesMTD column restarts its incremental sum every first day of the month.

Year	Quarter	MonthName	Date	Values Sales	SalesMTD
⊟2006	⊟Q1	⊟January	1/28/2006	15,508.00	536,583.59
			1/29/2006	11,255.63	547,839.21
			1/30/2006	27,145.18	574,984.40
			1/31/2006	21,762.16	596,746.56
		⊟February	2/1/2006	18,590.45	18,590.45
			2/2/2006	18,590.45	37,180.90
			2/3/2006	24,844.61	62,025.51
			2/4/2006	16,410.37	78,435.88
			2/5/2006	20,884.78	99,320.66

FIGURE 2-1 The SalesMTD column computes the month-to-date sum of Sales.

The Sales measure used in the example is the sum of the Sales Amount column of the Sales table. The SalesMTD measure uses the TOTALMTD function. TOTALMTD requires an expression to compute ([Sales] in our example) and a reference to the date column in the date table as the second argument.

```
[Sales] := SUM( Sales[Sales Amount] )

[SalesMTD] := TOTALMTD ( [Sales], 'Date'[Date] )
```

Figure 2-2 shows the quarter-to-date and year-to-date calculation in the SalesQTD and SalesYTD columns, respectively. Their definition is the following:

```
[SalesQTD] := TOTALQTD ( [Sales], 'Date'[Date] )

[SalesYTD] := TOTALYTD ( [Sales], 'Date'[Date] )
```

Year	Quarter	MonthName	Sales	SalesQTD	SalesYTD
2006	Q1	January	596,746.56	596,746.56	596,746.56
		February	550,816.69	1,147,563.25	1,147,563.25
		March	644,135.20	1,791,698.45	1,791,698.45
	Q1 Total		**1,791,698.45**	**1,791,698.45**	**1,791,698.45**
	Q2	April	663,692.29	663,692.29	2,455,390.74
		May	673,556.20	1,337,248.48	3,128,946.94
		June	676,763.65	2,014,012.13	3,805,710.59
	Q2 Total		**2,014,012.13**	**2,014,012.13**	**3,805,710.59**
	Q3	July	500,365.16	500,365.16	4,306,075.74
		August	546,001.47	1,046,366.63	4,852,077.21
		September	350,466.99	1,396,833.62	5,202,544.20
	Q3 Total		**1,396,833.62**	**1,396,833.62**	**5,202,544.20**
	Q4	October	415,390.23	415,390.23	5,617,934.44
		November	335,095.09	750,485.32	5,953,029.53
		December	577,314.00	1,327,799.32	6,530,343.53
	Q4 Total		**1,327,799.32**	**1,327,799.32**	**6,530,343.53**
2006 Total			**6,530,343.53**	**1,327,799.32**	**6,530,343.53**

FIGURE 2-2 The SalesQTD and SalesYTD columns compute the quarter-to-date and year-to-date sums of Sales, respectively.

You can write the calculations obtained by TOTALMTD, TOTALQTD, and TOTALYTD with a CALCULATE function call, using the results of DATESMTD, DATESQTD, and DATESYTD, respectively. This is an alternative way of writing SalesMTD, SalesQTD, and SalesYTD.

```
[SalesMTD] := CALCULATE ( [Sales], DATESMTD ( 'Date'[Date] ) )

[SalesQTD] := CALCULATE ( [Sales], DATESQTD ( 'Date'[Date] ) )

[SalesYTD] := CALCULATE ( [Sales], DATESYTD ( 'Date'[Date] ) )
```

The version with CALCULATE is more flexible, because you can add other filters to the CALCULATE statement. It also makes more evident the internal behavior of the time-related aggregation functions; you will see a more detailed explanation of that behavior in a later section.

To calculate a year-to-date measure over a fiscal year that does not end on December 31, you need to use an optional parameter that specifies the last day of the fiscal year. For example, you can calculate the fiscal year-to-date for Sales by using one of the following measure definitions:

```
[Fiscal SalesYTD] := TOTALYTD ( [Sales], 'Date'[Date], "06-30" )

[Fiscal SalesYTD] := CALCULATE ( [Sales], DATESYTD ( 'Date'[Date], "06-30" ) )
```

The last parameter corresponds to June 30 being the end of the fiscal year. Several time intelligence functions accept a last, optional YE_Date parameter for this purpose. They are: STARTOFYEAR, ENDOFYEAR, PREVIOUSYEAR, NEXTYEAR, DATESYTD, TOTALYTD, OPENINGBALANCEYEAR, and CLOSINGBALANCEYEAR.

Values from Previous Periods

Many times you will need to perform a comparison of values between different periods. A common case is to compute a value from the same period in the previous year (PY), quarter (PQ), or month (PM). The following DAX expressions calculate such values:

```
[PY Sales] := CALCULATE ( [Sales], DATEADD ( 'Date'[Date], -1, YEAR ) )

[PQ Sales] := CALCULATE ( [Sales], DATEADD ( 'Date'[Date], -1, QUARTER ) )

[PM Sales] := CALCULATE ( [Sales], DATEADD ( 'Date'[Date], -1, MONTH ) )
```

Figure 2-3 shows an example of these three measures. In PM Sales, each month has the value of the previous month (and BLANK in case there were no sales in the previous month). The quarter and year totals represent the sum of the shifted months. In PQ Sales the values are shifted by one quarter, and in PY Sales they are shifted by one year.

Year	Quarter	MonthName	Sales	PY Sales	PQ Sales	PM Sales
2005	Q3	July	473,388.16			
		August	506,191.69			473,388.16
		September	473,943.03			506,191.69
	Q3 Total		**1,453,522.89**			**979,579.85**
	Q4	October	513,329.47		473,388.16	473,943.03
		November	543,993.41		506,191.69	513,329.47
		December	755,527.89		473,943.03	543,993.41
	Q4 Total		**1,812,850.77**		**1,453,522.89**	**1,531,265.91**
2005 Total			**3,266,373.66**		**1,453,522.89**	**2,510,845.77**
2006	Q1	January	596,746.56		513,329.47	755,527.89
		February	550,816.69		543,993.41	596,746.56
		March	644,135.20		755,527.89	550,816.69
	Q1 Total		**1,791,698.45**		**1,812,850.77**	**1,903,091.14**
	Q2	April	663,692.29		596,746.56	644,135.20
		May	673,556.20		550,816.69	663,692.29
		June	676,763.65		644,135.20	673,556.20
	Q2 Total		**2,014,012.13**		**1,791,698.45**	**1,981,383.69**
	Q3	July	500,365.16	473,388.16	663,692.29	676,763.65
		August	546,001.47	506,191.69	673,556.20	500,365.16
		September	350,466.99	473,943.03	676,763.65	546,001.47
	Q3 Total		**1,396,833.62**	**1,453,522.89**	**2,014,012.13**	**1,723,130.28**
	Q4	October	415,390.23	513,329.47	500,365.16	350,466.99
		November	335,095.09	543,993.41	546,001.47	415,390.23
		December	577,314.00	755,527.89	350,466.99	335,095.09
	Q4 Total		**1,327,799.32**	**1,812,850.77**	**1,396,833.62**	**1,100,952.31**
2006 Total			**6,530,343.53**	**3,266,373.66**	**7,015,394.98**	**6,708,557.42**

FIGURE 2-3 PY Sales, PQ Sales, and PM Sales show the Sales value shifted by one year, quarter, and month, respectively.

The DATEADD function transforms the current selection of days to a corresponding set of days after the translation applied by the second and third arguments. You can move the date forward by using a positive value in the second argument, or backward by using a negative value. The third argument can be YEAR, QUARTER, MONTH, or DAY.

You can obtain the value of the previous year in an alternative and more readable way by using the function SAMEPERIODLASTYEAR, which is a specialized version of the DATEADD function. Internally, the same DATEADD call is made, using -1 and YEAR as the second and third arguments. For example, you can define the same PY Sales measure in this way:

```
[PY Sales] := CALCULATE( [Sales], SAMEPERIODLASTYEAR( 'Date'[Date] ) )
```

NOTE The DATEADD function returns a table made by one column and a number of rows that depends on the number of days active in the current filter context. For example, when the pivot table shows a cell with sales for one month, the current filter includes all the days in that month. If you move back to a different month, the number of days can be different. This detection works automatically, looking at the active days in the filter. For example, if the filter contains all 30 days in September, the result will include all 31 days in August. However, if there are only 29 days in September, because one day is not active in the filter, only 29 correspondent days in August will be returned, not including the missing day translated in August and August 31.

If you need the value of an entire period translated in time, you can also use the PARALLELPERIOD function, which is similar to DATEADD but returns the full period specified in the third parameter instead of the partial period returned by DATEADD. You can define the PY Total Sales measure that calculates the total of sales for the previous year in this way:

```
[PY Total Sales] := CALCULATE( [Sales], PARALLELPERIOD( 'Date'[Date], -1, YEAR ) )
```

Such a value is usually compared with the year-to-date value, so you can obtain a percentage like the YTD Over Total PY measure by defining it in this way:

```
[YTD Over Total PY]:= DIVIDE ( [SalesYTD], [PY Total Sales] )
```

You can see in Figure 2-4 that the sales in June 2006 reached more than 100% of the total sales in 2005.

Year	Quarter	MonthName	Sales	SalesYTD	PY Total Sales	YTD Over Total PY
			Values			
2005	Q3	July	473,388.16	473,388.16		
		August	506,191.69	979,579.85		
		September	473,943.03	1,453,522.89		
	Q3 Total		**1,453,522.89**	**1,453,522.89**		
	Q4	October	513,329.47	1,966,852.36		
		November	543,993.41	2,510,845.77		
		December	755,527.89	3,266,373.66		
	Q4 Total		**1,812,850.77**	**3,266,373.66**		
2005 Total			**3,266,373.66**	**3,266,373.66**		
2006	Q1	January	596,746.56	596,746.56	3,266,373.66	18.27 %
		February	550,816.69	1,147,563.25	3,266,373.66	35.13 %
		March	644,135.20	1,791,698.45	3,266,373.66	54.85 %
	Q1 Total		**1,791,698.45**	**1,791,698.45**	**3,266,373.66**	**54.85 %**
	Q2	April	663,692.29	2,455,390.74	3,266,373.66	75.17 %
		May	673,556.20	3,128,946.94	3,266,373.66	95.79 %
		June	676,763.65	3,805,710.59	3,266,373.66	116.51 %
	Q2 Total		**2,014,012.13**	**3,805,710.59**	**3,266,373.66**	**116.51 %**
	Q3	July	500,365.16	4,306,075.74	3,266,373.66	131.83 %
		August	546,001.47	4,852,077.21	3,266,373.66	148.55 %
		September	350,466.99	5,202,544.20	3,266,373.66	159.28 %
	Q3 Total		**1,396,833.62**	**5,202,544.20**	**3,266,373.66**	**159.28 %**
	Q4	October	415,390.23	5,617,934.44	3,266,373.66	171.99 %
		November	335,095.09	5,953,029.53	3,266,373.66	182.25 %
		December	577,314.00	6,530,343.53	3,266,373.66	199.93 %
	Q4 Total		**1,327,799.32**	**6,530,343.53**	**3,266,373.66**	**199.93 %**
2006 Total			**6,530,343.53**	**6,530,343.53**	**3,266,373.66**	**199.93 %**

FIGURE 2-4 The PY Total Sales displays the same value (total of previous year) at any level (year, quarter, and month).

If you need to perform this comparison with the corresponding year-to-date value of the previous year, you need to combine different date filters. You can use any function that filters dates as an argument of other functions that filter dates. This allows you to combine these functions in nested calls. For example, instead of passing the Date[Date] parameter to SAMEPERIODLASTYEAR, which corresponds to the list of dates that are active in the current filter context, you can use the DATESYTD function to transform these dates, defining the year-to-date group first. However, you can also invert the order of these calls without affecting the result. In fact, the two following definitions of PY YTD Sales are equivalent:

```
[PY YTD Sales] :=
CALCULATE (
    [Sales],
    SAMEPERIODLASTYEAR ( DATESYTD ( 'Date'[Date] ) )
)
```

```
[PY YTD Sales] :=
CALCULATE(
    [Sales],
    DATESYTD ( SAMEPERIODLASTYEAR ( 'Date'[Date] ) )
)
```

Figure 2-5 shows the results of the PY YTD Sales measure, which displays the values of SalesYTD shifted by one year.

			Values			
Year	Quarter	MonthName	Sales	SalesYTD	PY YTD Sales	YTD Over PY
2007	Q1	January	438,865.17	438,865.17	596,746.56	73.54 %
		February	489,090.34	927,955.51	1,147,563.25	80.86 %
		March	485,574.79	1,413,530.30	1,791,698.45	78.89 %
	Q1 Total		**1,413,530.30**	**1,413,530.30**	**1,791,698.45**	**78.89 %**
	Q2	April	506,399.27	1,919,929.57	2,455,390.74	78.19 %
		May	562,772.56	2,482,702.13	3,128,946.94	79.35 %
		June	554,799.23	3,037,501.36	3,805,710.59	79.81 %
	Q2 Total		**1,623,971.06**	**3,037,501.36**	**3,805,710.59**	**79.81 %**
	Q3	July	886,668.84	3,924,170.20	4,306,075.74	91.13 %
		August	847,413.51	4,771,583.71	4,852,077.21	98.34 %
		September	1,010,258.13	5,781,841.84	5,202,544.20	111.13 %
	Q3 Total		**2,744,340.48**	**5,781,841.84**	**5,202,544.20**	**111.13 %**
	Q4	October	1,080,449.58	6,862,291.42	5,617,934.44	122.15 %
		November	1,196,981.11	8,059,272.53	5,953,029.53	135.38 %
		December	1,731,787.77	9,791,060.30	6,530,343.53	149.93 %
	Q4 Total		**4,009,218.46**	**9,791,060.30**	**6,530,343.53**	**149.93 %**
2007 Total			**9,791,060.30**	**9,791,060.30**	**6,530,343.53**	**149.93 %**

FIGURE 2-5 The PY YTD Sales measure reports the SalesYTD of the year 2006 (not visible in the pivot table).

Another common calculation used in time comparison is the moving annual total (MAT), which always aggregates the last 12 months to de-emphasize seasonal changes in sales. For example, the value of MAT Sales for March 2007 is calculated by summing the range of dates from April 2006 to March 2007. Consider the following MAT Sales measure definition, which calculates the moving annual total for Sales:

```
[MAT Sales] :=
    CALCULATE (
        [Sales],
        DATESBETWEEN (
            'Date'[Date],
```

```
            NEXTDAY ( SAMEPERIODLASTYEAR ( LASTDATE( 'Date'[Date] ) ) ),
            LASTDATE ( 'Date'[Date] )
        )
    )
```

The implementation of this measure requires some attention. You need to use the DATESBETWEEN function, which returns the dates from a column included between two specified dates. Because this calculation is always made at the day level, even if you are querying data at the month level, you must calculate the first day and the last day of the desired interval. You can obtain the last day by calling the LASTDATE function, which returns the last date of a given column (always considering the current filter context). Starting from this date, you can get the first day of the interval by requesting the following day (by calling NEXTDAY) of the corresponding last date one year earlier. (You can do this by using SAMEPERIODLASTYEAR, as we did before.)

An alternative way to define the MAT Sales measure is using the DATESINPERIOD function, which returns all the days included in the period with the offset specified relative to the date passed as a second argument, as shown in the following definition:

```
[MAT Sales] :=
    CALCULATE (
        [Sales],
        DATESINPERIOD (
            'Date'[Date],
            LASTDATE ( 'Date'[Date] ),
            -1,
            YEAR
        )
    )
```

In Figure 2-6, you can see a pivot table showing the moving annual total calculation. In 2005, the values of MAT Sales and SalesYTD are identical, because this is the first year of sales in our data. However, in 2006 the SalesYTD restarts its incremental sum in January, whereas the MAT Sales continues to increase; in July, it corresponds to the sum of the months between August 2005 and July 2006.

Year	Quarter	MonthName	Sales	MAT Sales	SalesYTD
2005	Q3	July	473,388.16	473,388.16	473,388.16
		August	506,191.69	979,579.85	979,579.85
		September	473,943.03	1,453,522.89	1,453,522.89
	Q3 Total		**1,453,522.89**	**1,453,522.89**	**1,453,522.89**
	Q4	October	513,329.47	1,966,852.36	1,966,852.36
		November	543,993.41	2,510,845.77	2,510,845.77
		December	755,527.89	3,266,373.66	3,266,373.66
	Q4 Total		**1,812,850.77**	**3,266,373.66**	**3,266,373.66**
2005 Total			**3,266,373.66**	**3,266,373.66**	**3,266,373.66**
2006	Q1	January	596,746.56	3,863,120.21	596,746.56
		February	550,816.69	4,413,936.91	1,147,563.25
		March	644,135.20	5,058,072.11	1,791,698.45
	Q1 Total		**1,791,698.45**	**5,058,072.11**	**1,791,698.45**
	Q2	April	663,692.29	5,721,764.40	2,455,390.74
		May	673,556.20	6,395,320.59	3,128,946.94
		June	676,763.65	7,072,084.24	3,805,710.59
	Q2 Total		**2,014,012.13**	**7,072,084.24**	**3,805,710.59**
	Q3	July	500,365.16	7,099,061.24	4,306,075.74
		August	546,001.47	7,138,871.02	4,852,077.21
		September	350,466.99	7,015,394.98	5,202,544.20
	Q3 Total		**1,396,833.62**	**7,015,394.98**	**5,202,544.20**
	Q4	October	415,390.23	6,917,455.73	5,617,934.44
		November	335,095.09	6,708,557.42	5,953,029.53
		December	577,314.00	6,530,343.53	6,530,343.53
	Q4 Total		**1,327,799.32**	**6,530,343.53**	**6,530,343.53**
2006 Total			**6,530,343.53**	**6,530,343.53**	**6,530,343.53**

FIGURE 2-6 The moving annual total (MAT Sales) vs. year-to-date calculation (SalesYTD).

NOTE If sales information is incomplete for the previous 12 months, you may want to return blank for the MAT Sales calculation. For example, in Figure 2-6 you might return a blank value until May 2006, starting to return the calculation only from June 2006. You can implement this control in this way:

```
MAT Sales Checked :=
CALCULATE (
    IF (
        COUNTROWS (
            FILTER ( VALUES ( 'Date'[MonthName] ), [Sales] > 0 )
        ) = 12,
        [Sales]
    ),
    DATESINPERIOD (
```

```
            'Date'[Date],
            LASTDATE ( 'Date'[Date] ),
            -1,
            YEAR
        )
    )
```

In case the number of months with Sales greater than zero is not 12, the result of the IF statement is BLANK. You can adapt the check condition to your requirements.

Difference over Previous Year

You can show the difference between a measure and its value in a previous period (for example, the previous year) as an absolute value or by using a percentage. You have already seen how to obtain the value for the prior year with the PY Sales measure:

```
[PY Sales] := CALCULATE ( [Sales], SAMEPERIODLASTYEAR ( 'Date'[Date] ) )
```

The absolute difference of Sales over the previous year (year-over-year, or YOY) is a simple subtraction. You can define a YOY Sales measure with the following expression:

```
[YOY Sales] := [Sales] - [PY Sales]
```

The analogous calculation for comparing the year-to-date measure with a corresponding value in the prior year is a simple subtraction of two measures, SalesYTD and PY SalesYTD, which you saw in the previous section (shown here as a reminder):

```
[SalesYTD] := TOTALYTD ( [Sales], 'Date'[Order Date] )

[PY SalesYTD] := CALCULATE ( [Sales], SAMEPERIODLASTYEAR ( DATESYTD ( 'Date'[Date] ) ) )

[YOY SalesYTD] := [SalesYTD] - [PY SalesYTD]
```

Most of the time, the year-over-year difference is better expressed as a percentage in a report. You can define this calculation by dividing YOY Sales by the PY Sales. In this way, the difference uses the prior read value as a reference for the percentage difference (100% corresponds to a value that doubled in one year). In the following expression that defines the YOY Sales% measure, the DIVIDE call avoids a divide-by-zero error in case there is no corresponding data in the prior year:

```
[YOY Sales%] := DIVIDE ( [YOY Sales], [PY Sales] )
```

You can make a similar calculation to display the percentage difference of a year-over-year comparison for the year-to-date aggregation. You can define YOY SalesYTD% using the following formula:

```
[YOY SalesYTD%] := DIVIDE ( [YOY SalesYTD], [PY SalesYTD] )
```

In Figure 2-7, you can see the results of these measures in a pivot table.

			Values							
Year	Quarter	MonthName	Sales	PY Sales	YOY Sales	YOY Sales%	SalesYTD	PY SalesYTD	YOY SalesYTD	YOY SalesYTD%
2007	Q1	January	438,865.17	596,746.56	-157,881.39	-26.46 %	438,865.17	596,746.56	-157,881.39	-26.46 %
		February	489,090.34	550,816.69	-61,726.36	-11.21 %	927,955.51	1,147,563.25	-219,607.74	-19.14 %
		March	485,574.79	644,135.20	-158,560.41	-24.62 %	1,413,530.30	1,791,698.45	-378,168.15	-21.11 %
	Q1 Total		**1,413,530.30**	**1,791,698.45**	**-378,168.15**	**-21.11 %**	**1,413,530.30**	**1,791,698.45**	**-378,168.15**	**-21.11 %**
	Q2	April	506,399.27	663,692.29	-157,293.02	-23.70 %	1,919,929.57	2,455,390.74	-535,461.17	-21.81 %
		May	562,772.56	673,556.20	-110,783.63	-16.45 %	2,482,702.13	3,128,946.94	-646,244.81	-20.65 %
		June	554,799.23	676,763.65	-121,964.42	-18.02 %	3,037,501.36	3,805,710.59	-768,209.23	-20.19 %
	Q2 Total		**1,623,971.06**	**2,014,012.13**	**-390,041.08**	**-19.37 %**	**3,037,501.36**	**3,805,710.59**	**-768,209.23**	**-20.19 %**
	Q3	July	886,668.84	500,365.16	386,303.69	77.20 %	3,924,170.20	4,306,075.74	-381,905.54	-8.87 %
		August	847,413.51	546,001.47	301,412.04	55.20 %	4,771,583.71	4,852,077.21	-80,493.51	-1.66 %
		September	1,010,258.13	350,466.99	659,791.14	188.26 %	5,781,841.84	5,202,544.20	579,297.63	11.13 %
	Q3 Total		**2,744,340.48**	**1,396,833.62**	**1,347,506.86**	**96.47 %**	**5,781,841.84**	**5,202,544.20**	**579,297.63**	**11.13 %**
	Q4	October	1,080,449.58	415,390.23	665,059.35	160.10 %	6,862,291.42	5,617,934.44	1,244,356.98	22.15 %
		November	1,196,981.11	335,095.09	861,886.02	257.21 %	8,059,272.53	5,953,029.53	2,106,243.00	35.38 %
		December	1,731,787.77	577,314.00	1,154,473.77	199.97%	9,791,060.30	6,530,343.53	3,260,716.77	49.93 %
	Q4 Total		**4,009,218.46**	**1,327,799.32**	**2,681,419.14**	**201.94 %**	**9,791,060.30**	**6,530,343.53**	**3,260,716.77**	**49.93 %**
2007 Total			**9,791,060.30**	**6,530,343.53**	**3,260,716.77**	**49.93 %**	**9,791,060.30**	**6,530,343.53**	**3,260,716.77**	**49.93 %**

FIGURE 2-7 The year-over-year (YOY) measures used in a pivot table.

Semi-Additive Measures

A semi-additive measure does not aggregate data over all attributes like a regular additive measure. For example, semi-additive measures like balance account and product inventory units can be aggregated over any attribute but time. Instead of considering the period selected (for example, one month) you consider only a particular moment in time related to the period selected. It could be the first day, the last day, the last day that had transactions, and so on.

This condition is typical for tables containing snapshots over time, such as products inventory or accounts balance. In the following table, you can see an excerpt of a Product Inventory table. Each product has a Units Balance value for each date. You cannot sum such a column for two different dates (you might want to calculate the average over different dates). If you want to calculate the value of Units Balance for July 2001, you need to filter the rows for the last day in the month, ignoring rows for all the other days.

Product Name	Date Key	Units In	Units Out	Units Balance
...	...	...	...	...
Road-650 Red, 44	20050630	0	0	170
Road-650 Red, 44	20050701	0	103	67
Road-650 Red, 44	20050702	102	0	169
Road-650 Red, 62	20050630	0	0	185
Road-650 Red, 62	20050701	0	135	50
Road-650 Red, 62	20050702	129	0	179
...	...	...	...	...

To implement a semi-additive measure in DAX, you use a technique that is similar to the one used to compute aggregations and comparisons over time. You change the filter over the date in a CALCULATE statement, but in this case you limit the range of dates selected instead of extending it (like year-to-date) or moving it (like prior year). You can use LASTDATE to get the last day active in the current filter context for a particular date column passed as an argument. The result is a table of one column and one value that you can use as a filter argument in a CALCULATE statement, as in the following definition:

```
Units LastDate := CALCULATE ( SUM ( Inventory[UnitsBalance] ), LASTDATE ( 'Date'[Date] ) )
```

The result in Figure 2-8 shows that the total for each quarter corresponds to the value of the last month in the quarter (for example, Q1 value is the same as March). Each month value corresponds to the value of the last day in that month.

Units LastDate			ProductName		
Year	Quarter	MonthName	Road-650 Red, 44	Road-650 Red, 62	Grand Total
2006	Q1	January	163	185	348
		February	172	170	342
		March	164	180	344
	Q1 Total		**164**	**180**	**344**
	Q2	April	170	173	343
		May	184	165	349
		June	185	170	355
	Q2 Total		**185**	**170**	**355**
	Q3	July	179	165	344
		August	183	158	341
		September	175	176	351
	Q3 Total		**175**	**176**	**351**
	Q4	October	173	175	348
		November	187	173	360
		December	179	166	345
	Q4 Total		**179**	**166**	**345**
2006 Total			**179**	**166**	**345**

FIGURE 2-8 The Units LastDate measure returns the value for the last date of the period in each row.

The Units LastDate calculation assumes that there are data for every year in every month. If the inventory is daily, this is not an issue, but it could become a problem if the inventory is stored only for working days—if a month ends on a Saturday, you would not see any value for the entire month. The problem is evident for future dates. Figure 2-9 shows what happens using Units LastDate with an Inventory table that has rows until December 15, 2007: you do not see the total for year 2007, for Q4, or for December!

Units LastDate			ProductName		
Year	Quarter	MonthName	Road-650 Red, 44	Road-650 Red, 62	Grand Total
2007	Q1	January	183	159	342
		February	191	174	365
		March	190	174	364
	Q1 Total		**190**	**174**	**364**
	Q2	April	186	171	357
		May	173	168	341
		June	184	159	343
	Q2 Total		**184**	**159**	**343**
	Q3	July	184	159	343
		August	184	159	343
		September	184	159	343
	Q3 Total		**184**	**159**	**343**
	Q4	October	184	159	343
		November	184	159	343

FIGURE 2-9 The Units LastDate for 2007 displays data only until November, because December is not complete.

The reason for the missing data in December is that the LASTDATE formula operates on all dates available in the filter context and the date table contains all the days for the year 2007. This is required for correct behavior of time intelligence functions. However, there are no inventory data on December 31, which would be the day required to display data for December, Q4, and 2007. You can use another DAX function, LASTNONBLANK, which returns the last date that satisfies a non-blank condition for an expression passed as the second argument.

```
Units LastNonBlank :=
    CALCULATE (
        SUM ( Inventory[UnitsBalance] ),
        LASTNONBLANK (
            'Date'[Date],
            CALCULATE ( SUM ( Inventory[UnitsBalance] ) )
        )
    )
```

It is important that the second argument of the LASTNONBLANK statement applies the context transition using an implicit or explicit CALCULATE function—otherwise you would apply the expression without filtering by each date in the period and the result would be identical to LASTDATE. You can see the result in Figure 2-10, where December, Q4, and the total for 2007 are all now displayed.

Units LastNonBlank			ProductName		
Year	Quarter	MonthName	Road-650 Red, 44	Road-650 Red, 62	Grand Total
2007	Q1	January	183	159	342
		February	191	174	365
		March	190	174	364
	Q1 Total		**190**	**174**	**364**
	Q2	April	186	171	357
		May	173	168	341
		June	184	159	343
	Q2 Total		**184**	**159**	**343**
	Q3	July	184	159	343
		August	184	159	343
		September	184	159	343
	Q3 Total		**184**	**159**	**343**
	Q4	October	184	159	343
		November	184	159	343
		December	184	159	343
	Q4 Total		**184**	**159**	**343**
2007 Total			**184**	**159**	**343**

FIGURE 2-10 The Units LastNonBlank measure displays data of December 15 for December, Q4, and 2007.

If you need the first date of a period instead of the last one, you can use FIRSTDATE. Or you can use FIRSTNONBLANK to get the first date having some data, similar to how you use LASTNONBLANK for the last date having some data. All these functions return a table of one column and one row: for this reason, you can use them in a filter argument of a CALCULATE call. A common mistake is assuming that LASTDATE and MAX would produce the same result. While this is true from a logical point of view, there is an important syntactic difference. For example, you cannot write the following expression:

```
Units MaxDate :=
    CALCULATE (
        SUM ( Inventory[UnitsBalance] ),
        MAX ( 'Date'[Date] )
    )
```

The MAX function returns a scalar value and the filter argument of a CALCULATE function requires a table expression or a logical condition referencing only one column. Thus, you use MAX instead of LASTDATE by using the following definition:

```
Units MaxDate :=
    CALCULATE (
        SUM ( Inventory[UnitsBalance] ),
        FILTER (
            ALL( 'Date'[Date] ),
            'Date'[Date] = MAX ( 'Date'[Date] )
        )
    )
```

The best practice is to use LASTDATE when you write a filter expression and MAX when you write a logical expression in a row context, because LASTDATE implies a context transition that hides the external filter context. You can find more information about this difference in the following blog post: http://sql.bi/MaxLastDate.

Other time intelligence functions are useful in semi-additive measure for getting the first and last date of a period (year, quarter, or month). For example, looking at the month level (which may be displayed in rows), you might want to display also the value of the end of the quarter and the end of the year in the same row, as you can see in Figure 2-11.

ProductName Road-65...ed, 44

Year	Quarter	MonthName	OpeningMonth	ClosingMonth	OpeningQuarter	ClosingQuarter	OpeningYear	ClosingYear
2006	Q1	January	171	163	171	164	171	179
		February	163	172	171	164	171	179
		March	172	164	171	164	171	179
	Q1 Total		**171**	**164**	**171**	**164**	**171**	**179**
	Q2	April	164	170	164	185	171	179
		May	170	184	164	185	171	179
		June	184	185	164	185	171	179
	Q2 Total		**164**	**185**	**164**	**185**	**171**	**179**
	Q3	July	185	179	185	175	171	179
		August	179	183	185	175	171	179
		September	183	175	185	175	171	179
	Q3 Total		**185**	**175**	**185**	**175**	**171**	**179**
	Q4	October	175	173	175	179	171	179
		November	173	187	175	179	171	179
		December	187	179	175	179	171	179
	Q4 Total		**175**	**179**	**175**	**179**	**171**	**179**
2006 Total			**171**	**179**	**171**	**179**	**171**	**179**

FIGURE 2-11 The Opening... and Closing... measures display the values of the first and the last date in the corresponding period, respectively.

The ClosingMonth, ClosingQuarter, ClosingYear, OpeningMonth, OpeningQuarter, and OpeningYear measures used in Figure 2-11 are defined as follows:

```
ClosingMonth := CLOSINGBALANCEMONTH ( SUM ( Inventory[UnitsBalance] ), 'Date'[Date]  )

ClosingQuarter := CLOSINGBALANCEQUARTER ( SUM ( Inventory[UnitsBalance] ), 'Date'[Date]  )

ClosingYear := CLOSINGBALANCEYEAR ( SUM ( Inventory[UnitsBalance] ), 'Date'[Date]  )

OpeningMonth := OPENINGBALANCEMONTH ( SUM ( Inventory[UnitsBalance] ), 'Date'[Date]  )

OpeningQuarter := OPENINGBALANCEQUARTER ( SUM ( Inventory[UnitsBalance] ), 'Date'[Date]  )

OpeningYear := OPENINGBALANCEYEAR ( SUM ( Inventory[UnitsBalance] ), 'Date'[Date]  )
```

The measures above correspond to the measures below, which are defined using CALCULATE and the filter provided by ENDOFMONTH, ENDOFQUARTER, ENDOFYEAR, as in the following definitions:

```
ClosingEOM := CALCULATE ( SUM ( Inventory[UnitsBalance] ), ENDOFMONTH ( 'Date'[Date] ) )

ClosingEOQ := CALCULATE ( SUM ( Inventory[UnitsBalance] ), ENDOFQUARTER ( 'Date'[Date] ) )

ClosingEOY := CALCULATE ( SUM ( Inventory[UnitsBalance] ), ENDOFYEAR ( 'Date'[Date] ) )

StartingSOM :=
CALCULATE (
    SUM ( Inventory[UnitsBalance] ),
    DATEADD ( STARTOFMONTH ( 'Date'[Date] ), -1, DAY )
)

StartingSOQ :=
CALCULATE (
    SUM ( Inventory[UnitsBalance] ),
```

```
    DATEADD ( STARTOFQUARTER ( 'Date'[Date] ), -1, MONTH )
)

StartingSOY :=
CALCULATE (
    SUM ( Inventory[UnitsBalance] ),
    DATEADD ( STARTOFYEAR ( 'Date'[Date] ), -1, YEAR )
)
```

These functions, like LASTDATE, work on the date table and do not perform the NONBLANK condition, leading to unwanted results when there is no data in the date they compute. Figure 2-12 shows the behavior of the previous closing measures for the year 2007, where data is available only until December 15: ClosingQuarter for Q4, October, and November is blank.

ProductName Road-65 ed, 44

Year	Quarter	MonthName	ClosingMonth	ClosingQuarter	ClosingYear
2007	Q1	January	183	190	
		February	191	190	
		March	190	190	
	Q1 Total		**190**	**190**	
	Q2	April	186	184	
		May	173	184	
		June	184	184	
	Q2 Total		**184**	**184**	
	Q3	July	184	184	
		August	184	184	
		September	184	184	
	Q3 Total		**184**	**184**	
	Q4	October	184		
		November	184		

FIGURE 2-12 If you have data only through December 15, and you use standard CLOSING functions, some values are blank.

To display the correct values, instead of OPENING and CLOSING functions you should use the FIRSTNONBLANK and LASTNONBLANK functions as filter in a CALCULATE statement, applying an extension of the considered period using the PARALLELPERIOD function. Here are the corresponding definitions:

```
OpeningMonthNonBlank :=
    CALCULATE (
        SUM ( Inventory[UnitsBalance] ),
        CALCULATETABLE (
            FIRSTNONBLANK ( 'Date'[Date], CALCULATE ( SUM ( Inventory[UnitsBalance] ) ) ),
            PARALLELPERIOD ( 'Date'[Date], 0, MONTH )
        )
    )

OpeningQuarterNonBlank :=
    CALCULATE (
        SUM ( Inventory[UnitsBalance] ),
        CALCULATETABLE (
            FIRSTNONBLANK ( 'Date'[Date], CALCULATE ( SUM ( Inventory[UnitsBalance] ) ) ),
            PARALLELPERIOD ( 'Date'[Date], 0, QUARTER )
        )
    )

OpeningYearNonBlank :=
    CALCULATE (
        SUM ( Inventory[UnitsBalance] ),
        CALCULATETABLE (
            FIRSTNONBLANK ( 'Date'[Date], CALCULATE ( SUM ( Inventory[UnitsBalance] ) ) ),
            PARALLELPERIOD ( 'Date'[Date], 0, YEAR )
        )
    )

ClosingMonthNonBlank :=
    CALCULATE (
        SUM ( Inventory[UnitsBalance] ),
        CALCULATETABLE (
            LASTNONBLANK ( 'Date'[Date], CALCULATE ( SUM ( Inventory[UnitsBalance] ) ) ),
            PARALLELPERIOD ( 'Date'[Date], 0, MONTH )
        )
    )
```

```
ClosingQuarterNonBlank :=
    CALCULATE (
        SUM ( Inventory[UnitsBalance] ),
        CALCULATETABLE (
            LASTNONBLANK ( 'Date'[Date], CALCULATE ( SUM ( Inventory[UnitsBalance] ) ) ),
            PARALLELPERIOD ( 'Date'[Date], 0, QUARTER )
        )
    )

ClosingYearNonBlank :=
    CALCULATE (
        SUM ( Inventory[UnitsBalance] ),
        CALCULATETABLE (
            LASTNONBLANK ( 'Date'[Date], CALCULATE ( SUM ( Inventory[UnitsBalance] ) ) ),
            PARALLELPERIOD ( 'Date'[Date], 0, YEAR )
        )
    )
```

Figure 2-13 shows the final result of using these measures for year 2007.

ProductName Road-65…ed, 44

Year	Quarter	MonthName	ClosingMonthNonBlank	ClosingQuarterNonBlank	ClosingYearNonBlank
2007	Q1	January	183	190	184
		February	191	190	184
		March	190	190	184
	Q1 Total		**190**	**190**	**184**
	Q2	April	186	184	184
		May	173	184	184
		June	184	184	184
	Q2 Total		**184**	**184**	**184**
	Q3	July	184	184	184
		August	184	184	184
		September	184	184	184
	Q3 Total		**184**	**184**	**184**
	Q4	October	184	184	184
		November	184	184	184
		December	184	184	184
	Q4 Total		**184**	**184**	**184**
2007 Total			**184**	**184**	**184**

FIGURE 2-13 The ClosingMonth, ClosingQuarter, and ClosingYear measures display data of December 15 for December, Q4, and 2007, because their definition looks for the last non-blank date in the period.

The filter calculation might be different according to the logic you want to implement, but the pattern for a semi-additive measure is to filter a single date based on the initial selection of dates in the filter context. Such logic is usually in a filter argument of a CALCULATE function call, unless a special time intelligence function is used, hiding the internal calculation that is always applied on a CALCULATE statement.

Internal Behavior

All of the time intelligence calculations seen so far work only when a table marked as a date table exists in the data model. In order to write custom time intelligence calculations that compute correct results, you need to understand why this table is so important, and how DAX uses it.

Every time intelligence function in DAX requires you to specify a date column as one of its parameters. DAX time intelligence functions replace **any other existing filter** in the table marked as the date table with the set of dates they compute, such as all the days since January 1 for the year to date. If you think carefully about it, you should not expect this behavior.

Let us investigate why with an example from the Products table. When you filter a single product by name, you do not remove existing filters on other columns of the same table, such as color or price. For instance, consider a measure that calculates sales for the product Road-650 Red, 44:

```
SalesRoad650Red44 :=
    CALCULATE (
        SUM ( Sales[SalesAmount] ),
        Products[ProductName] = "Road-650 Red, 44"
    )
```

If you evaluate this measure in a context where you filter by color, any selection not including Red will result in a BLANK value, as shown in Figure 2-14. You can see that the value is visible only for the Red color because, in other cells, the calculation puts the filter for the color (e.g., Blue) in a logical AND with the filter for the product name, resulting in an empty set.

Row Labels	SalesRoad650Red44
Black	
Blue	
Grey	
Multi	
NA	
Red	$54,529.66
Silver	
Silver/Black	
White	
Yellow	
Grand Total	**$54,529.66**

FIGURE 2-14 The measure SalesRoad650Red44 is visible only for color Red.

To display the same value for the measure SalesRoad650Red44 regardless of any filter in other columns of the Products table, you have to add an ALL statement in the CALCULATE function, to remove existing filters from other columns.

```
SalesOnlyRoad650Red44 :=
    CALCULATE (
        SUM ( Sales[SalesAmount] ),
        Products[ProductName] = "Road-650 Red, 44",
        ALL ( Products )
    )
```

In Figure 2-15, you can see that the SalesOnlyRoad650Red44 measure always displays the same value, regardless of the color selection.

Row Labels	SalesRoad650Red44	SalesOnlyRoad650Red44
Black		$54,529.66
Blue		$54,529.66
Grey		$54,529.66
Multi		$54,529.66
NA		$54,529.66
Red	$54,529.66	$54,529.66
Silver		$54,529.66
Silver/Black		$54,529.66
White		$54,529.66
Yellow		$54,529.66
Grand Total	**$54,529.66**	**$54,529.66**

FIGURE 2-15 The measure SalesOnlyRoad650Red44 is visible for any color, because the color filter is ignored.

DAX time intelligence functions behave in a different way. Consider the following measures and their results in Figure 2-16. In SalesYTD, we used the canonical time intelligence pattern, passing the date column from the calendar table, whereas in SalesYTDwrong we made an intentional mistake, passing the Sales[OrderDate] column as the date parameter.

```
Sales := SUM ( Sales[SalesAmount] )
SalesYTD := CALCULATE ( [Sales], DATESYTD ( 'Date'[Date] ) )
SalesYTDwrong := CALCULATE ( [Sales], DATESYTD ( Sales[OrderDate] ) )
```

		Values		
Year	Month	Sales	SalesYTD	SalesYTDwrong
2006	January	596,746.56	596,746.56	596,747
	February	550,816.69	1,147,563.25	550,817
	March	644,135.20	1,791,698.45	644,135
	April	663,692.29	2,455,390.74	663,692
	May	673,556.20	3,128,946.94	673,556
	June	676,763.65	3,805,710.59	676,764
	July	500,365.16	4,306,075.74	500,365
	August	546,001.47	4,852,077.21	546,001
	September	350,466.99	5,202,544.20	350,467
	October	415,390.23	5,617,934.44	415,390
	November	335,095.09	5,953,029.53	335,095
	December	577,314.00	6,530,343.53	577,314
2006 Total		**6,530,343.53**	**6,530,343.53**	**6,530,344**
Grand Total		**6,530,343.53**	**6,530,343.53**	**6,530,344**

FIGURE 2-16 The SalesYTD column partially overrides the filter applied by the month on the rows, whereas the SalesYTDwrong measure is filtered by the month on the rows.

DATESYTD returns a list of values from the Date column it receives as a parameter, but it works only when Date[Date] is used, and not with Sales[OrderDate]. If you think about the previous example (the one on the Products table), the behavior of SalesYTDwrong is the correct one. The filter on month in the row is intersected (logical AND) with the list of days returned by DATESYTD. Thus, only the days in the corresponding month survive the filter. The result is that SalesYTDwrong produces the same result as the Sales measure. At this point, the question is: why doesn't SalesYTDwrong work (it does, in reality) whereas SalesYTD works as expected? It seems to override the filter of the month in the rows, resulting in a correct calculation. This seems to contradict our understanding of filter context interaction. Why is this behavior different from what you have seen in the SalesOnlyRoad650Red44 measure?

The reason is that when you mark a table as a date table, DAX automatically adds ALL (Date) to the CALCULATE function when a filter is applied on the date column of the table. This behavior makes the formula more intuitive to write, but requires some attention. Even if you define a measure in this way:

```
SalesYTD := CALCULATE ( [Sales], DATESYTD ( 'Date'[Date] ) )
```

Internally, DAX rewrites it in this way:

```
SalesYTD := CALCULATE ( [Sales], DATESYTD ( 'Date'[Date] ), ALL ( 'Date' ) )
```

If the column that defines the relationship with a date table is a datetime data type, then marking the table as a date table is not necessary. However, if the Sales table has a relationship with the date table through a column of another data type, such as an integer value, then you cannot use it in time intelligence functions. Instead, you will use the date column used to mark the calendar dimension as a date table, and not the column used in the relationship, because it is not a datetime data type. In this case, the ALL (Date) filter is automatically added as a filter argument of the CALCULATE function whenever the date column is used in a filter argument of the CALCULATE function itself. For this reason, marking a table as a date table is always a best practice, because you can assume that the ALL (Date) filter will always be added to the CALCULATE function, regardless of the relationship used to connect the date table to other tables in the data model.

There is one more reason why it is a best practice to mark the date column of a table as a date table in all time intelligence functions. All of these functions can only return existing values in the column that you specify. By using Sales[Date] as was done in the SalesYTDwrong measure, you cannot obtain dates for which there are no sales. Because DAX time intelligence functions handle special conditions in a particular way (such as changing the number of days returned in different months), it is very important that the date column belongs to a table that has all the days of each year you want to consider.

Custom Calendar

DAX time intelligence functions have an embedded business logic to handle months of different lengths and leap years, and the content of the date table itself is not relevant, with the exception of the date column. There is an implicit assumption that each day corresponds to the "natural" month and quarter of the calendar. However, when you have special calendars based on weeks, such as ISO 8601, this assumption is no longer true: a date can belong to a different month, quarter, and year. In that case, you cannot use the time intelligence functions, but must write an explicit DAX calculation that leverages information included in other columns of the date table, as you can see in the following chapter about time patterns.

CHAPTER 3

Time Patterns

The DAX time patterns are used to implement time-related calculations without relying on DAX time intelligence functions. This is useful whenever you have custom calendars, such as an ISO 8601 week calendar, or when you are using an Analysis Services Tabular model in DirectQuery mode.

Basic Pattern Example

Suppose you want to provide the user with a calculation of year-to-date sales without relying on DAX time intelligence functions. You need a relationship between the Date and Sales tables, as shown in Figure 3-1.

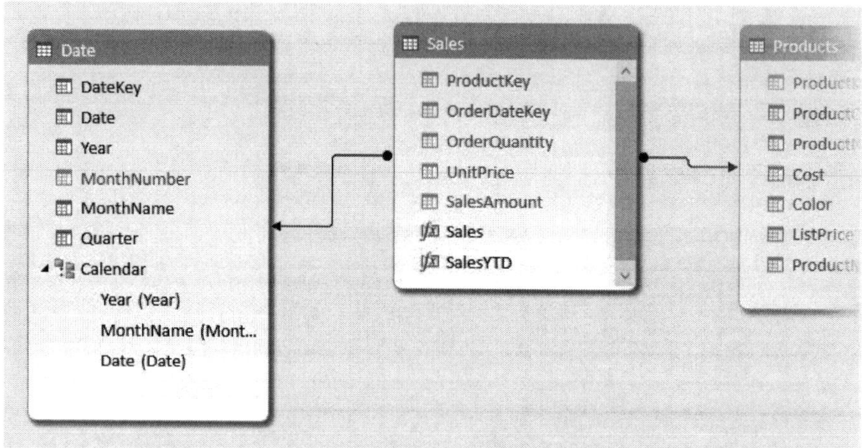

FIGURE 3-1 The Date table is marked as a date table using the Date column.

The Sales measure simply calculates the sum of the SalesAmount column:

```
Sales := SUM ( Sales[SalesAmount] )
```

The year-to-date calculation must replace the filter over the Date table, using a filter argument in a CALCULATE function. You can use a FILTER that iterates all the rows in the Date table, applying a logical condition that returns only the days that are less than or equal to the maximum date present in the current filter context, and that belong to the last selected year.

You define the SalesYTD measure as follows:

```
[SalesYTD] :=
CALCULATE (
    [Sales],
    FILTER (
        ALL ( 'Date' ),
        'Date'[Year] = MAX ( 'Date'[Year] )
            && 'Date'[Date] <= MAX ( 'Date'[Date] )
    )
)
```

You can see the result of Sales and SalesYTD in Figure 3-2.

Year	MonthName	Values Sales	SalesYTD
2006	January	596,746.56	596,746.56
	February	550,816.69	1,147,563.25
	March	644,135.20	1,791,698.45
	April	663,692.29	2,455,390.74
	May	673,556.20	3,128,946.94
	June	676,763.65	3,805,710.59
	July	500,365.16	4,306,075.74
	August	546,001.47	4,852,077.21
	September	350,466.99	5,202,544.20
	October	415,390.23	5,617,934.44
	November	335,095.09	5,953,029.53
	December	577,314.00	6,530,343.53
2006 Total		**6,530,343.53**	**6,530,343.53**
Grand Total		**6,530,343.53**	**6,530,343.53**

FIGURE 3-2 The SalesYTD measure computes the sum of Sales for all the days since the beginning of the year.

You can apply the same pattern for different time intelligence calculations by modifying the logical condition of the FILTER function.

IMPORTANT If you are not using time intelligence functions, the presence of ALL ('Date') in the calculate filter automatically produces the same effect as a table marked as a date table in the data model. In fact, filtering in a CALCULATE function the date column used to mark a date table would implicitly add the same ALL ('Date') that you see explicitly defined in this pattern. However, when you implement custom time-related calculations, it is always a good practice to mark a table as a date table, even if you do not use the DAX time intelligence functions.

Use Cases

You can use the Time Intelligence pattern whenever using the standard DAX time intelligence functions is not an option (for example, if you need a custom calendar). The pattern is very flexible and moves the business logic of the time-related calculations from the DAX predefined functions to the content of the Date table. The following is a list of some interesting use cases.

Week-Based and ISO 8601 Calendars

The time intelligence functions in DAX (such as TOTALYTD, SAMEPERIODLASTYEAR, and many others) assume that every day in a month belongs to the same quarter regardless of the year. This assumption is not valid for a week-based calendar, in which each quarter and each year might contain days that are not "naturally" related. For example, in an ISO 8601 calendar, January 1 and January 2 of 2011 belong to week 52 of year 2010, and the first week of 2011 starts on January 3. This approach is common in the retail and manufacturing industries, where the 4-4-5 calendar, 5-4-4 calendar, and 4-5-4 calendar are used. By using 4-4-5 weeks in a quarter, you can easily compare uniform numbers between quarters, mainly because you have the same number of working days and weekends in each quarter. You can find further information about these calendars on Wikipedia (see the **4-4-5 calendar** and **ISO week date** pages: http://en.wikipedia.org/wiki/4-4-5_calendar and http://en.wikipedia.org/wiki/ISO_week_date). The Time Intelligence pattern can handle any type of custom calendar.

DirectQuery

When you use the DirectQuery feature in an Analysis Services Tabular model, DAX queries are converted into SQL code sent to the underlying SQL Server data source, but the DAX time intelligence functions are not available. You can use the Time Intelligence pattern to implement time-related calculations using DirectQuery.

Complete Pattern

The Date table must contain all the attributes used in the calculation, in a numeric format. For example, the fiscal calendar shown in Figure 3-3 has strings for visible columns (Year, Month, Quarter, and Week Day), along with corresponding numeric values in other columns (YearNumber, MonthNumber, QuarterNumber, and WeekDayNumber). You will hide the numeric values from client tools in the data model but use them to implement time intelligence calculations in DAX and to sort the string columns.

DateKey	Date	YearNumber	Year	MonthNumber	Month	QuarterNumber	Quarter	WeekDayNumber	Week Day
20051226	12/26/2005	2006	FY 2006	6	December	2	Q2	2	Monday
20051227	12/27/2005	2006	FY 2006	6	December	2	Q2	3	Tuesday
20051228	12/28/2005	2006	FY 2006	6	December	2	Q2	4	Wednesday
20051229	12/29/2005	2006	FY 2006	6	December	2	Q2	5	Thursday
20051230	12/30/2005	2006	FY 2006	6	December	2	Q2	6	Friday
20051231	12/31/2005	2006	FY 2006	6	December	2	Q2	7	Saturday
20060101	1/1/2006	2006	FY 2006	7	January	3	Q3	1	Sunday
20060102	1/2/2006	2006	FY 2006	7	January	3	Q3	2	Monday
20060103	1/3/2006	2006	FY 2006	7	January	3	Q3	3	Tuesday
20060104	1/4/2006	2006	FY 2006	7	January	3	Q3	4	Wednesday
20060105	1/5/2006	2006	FY 2006	7	January	3	Q3	5	Thursday

FIGURE 3-3 The Date table in PowerPivot showing strings and corresponding numeric values for various time periods.

In order to support comparison between periods and other calculations, the Date table also contains:

- A sequential number of days within the current year, quarter, and month.
- A sequential number of quarters and months elapsed since a reference date (which could be the beginning of the calendar).
- The total number of days in the current quarter and month.

These additional columns are visible in Figure 3-4.

Day	YearDayNumber	QuarterDayNumber	MonthDayNumber	YearMonthNumber	MonthDays	YearQuarterNumber	QuarterDays
day	1	1	1	7	31	3	90
ay	2	2	2	7	31	3	90
day	3	3	3	7	31	3	90
day	4	4	4	7	31	3	90
nesday	5	5	5	7	31	3	90
sday	6	6	6	7	31	3	90
y	7	7	7	7	31	3	90
day	8	8	8	7	31	3	90
ay	9	9	9	7	31	3	90

FIGURE 3-4 Columns that support advanced calculation in the Date table.

Aggregation Pattern

Any aggregation over time filters the Date table to include all the dates in the period considered. The only difference in each formula is the condition that checks whether the date belongs to the considered aggregation or not.

The general formula will be:

```
[AggregationOverTime] :=
CALCULATE (
    [OriginalMeasure],
    FILTER (
        ALL ( 'Date' ),
        <check whether the date belongs to the aggregation>
    )
)
```

When you define an aggregation, usually you extend the period considered to include all the days elapsed since a particular day in the past. However, it is best to not make any assumption about the calendar structure, instead writing a condition that entirely depends on the data in the table. For example, you can write the year-to-date in this way:

```
[YTD] :=
CALCULATE (
    [OriginalMeasure],
    FILTER (
        ALL ( 'Date' ),
        'Date'[Year] = MAX ( 'Date'[Year] )
            && 'Date'[Date] <= MAX ( 'Date'[Date] )
    )
)
```

However, a calculation of the last 12 months would be more complicated, because there could be leap years (with February having 29 days instead of 28) and the year might not start on January 1.

A calculated column can have information that simplifies the condition. For example, the SequentialDayNumber column contains the running total of days in the Date table, excluding February 29. This is the formula used to define such a calculated column:

```
= COUNTROWS (
    FILTER (
        ALL ( Date ),
        'Date'[Date] <= EARLIER ( 'Date'[Date] )
        && NOT ( MONTH ( 'Date'[Date] ) = 2 && DAY ( 'Date'[Date] ) = 29 )
    )
)
```

When the formula is written in this way, February 29 will have always the same SequentialDayNumber as February 28. You can write the moving annual total (the total of the last 12 months) as the total of the last 365 days. Since the test is based on SequentialDayNumber, February 29 will be automatically included in the range, which will consider 366 days instead of 365.

```
[MAT Sales] :=
CALCULATE (
    [Sales],
    FILTER (
        ALL ( 'Date' ),
        'Date'[SequentialDayNumber] > MAX ( 'Date'[SequentialDayNumber] ) - 365
            && 'Date'[SequentialDayNumber] <= MAX ( 'Date'[SequentialDayNumber] )
    )
)
```

A complete list of calculations is included in the More Patterns section.

Period Comparison Pattern

You can write the calculation for an aggregation by simply using the date, even if the SequentialDayNumber column is required to handle leap years. The period comparison can be more complex, because it requires detection of the current selection in order to apply the correct filter on dates to get a parallel period. For example, to calculate the year-over-year difference, you need the value of the same selection in the previous year. This analysis complicates the DAX formula required, but it is necessary if you want a behavior similar to the DAX time intelligence functions for your custom calendar.

The following implementation assumes that the calendar month drives the logic to select a corresponding comparison period. If the user selects all the days in a month, that entire month will be selected in a related period (a month, quarter, or year back in time) for the comparison. If instead she selects only a few days in a month, then only the corresponding days in the same month will be selected in the related period. You can implement a different logic (based on weeks, for example) by changing the filter expression that selects the days to compare with.

For example, the month-over-month calculation (MOM) compares the current selection with the same selection one month before.

```
[MOM Sales] := [Sales] - [PM Sales]

[MOM% Sales] := DIVIDE ( [MOM Sales], [PM Sales] )
```

The complex part is the calculation of the corresponding selection for the previous month (PM Sales). The formula iterates the YearMonthNumber column, which contains a unique value for each month and year.

```
SUMX (
    VALUES ( 'Date'[YearMonthNumber] ),
    <calculation for the month>
)
```

The calculation is different depending on whether all the days of the month are included in the selection or not. So the first part of the calculation performs this check.

```
IF (
    CALCULATE ( COUNTROWS ( VALUES ( 'Date'[Date] ) ) )
        = CALCULATE ( VALUES ( 'Date'[MonthDays] ) ),
    <calculation for all days selected in the month>,
    <calculation for partial selection of the days in the month>
)
```

If the number of days selected is equal to the number of days in the month (stored in the MonthDays column), then the filter selects all the days in the previous month (by subtracting one from the YearMonthNumber column).

```
CALCULATE (
    [Sales],
    ALL ( 'Date' ),
    FILTER (
        ALL ( 'Date'[YearMonthNumber] ),
        'Date'[YearMonthNumber]
            = EARLIER ( 'Date'[YearMonthNumber] ) - 1
    )
)
```

Otherwise, the filter also includes the days selected in the month iterated (MonthDayNumber column); such a filter is highlighted in the following formula.

```
CALCULATE (
    [Sales],
    ALL ( 'Date' ),
    CALCULATETABLE ( VALUES ( 'Date'[MonthDayNumber] ) ),
    FILTER (
        ALL ( 'Date'[YearMonthNumber] ),
        'Date'[YearMonthNumber]
            = EARLIER ( 'Date'[YearMonthNumber] ) - 1
    )
)
)
```

The complete formula for the sales in the previous month is as follows.

```
[PM Sales] :=
SUMX (
    VALUES ( 'Date'[YearMonthNumber] ),
    IF (
        CALCULATE ( COUNTROWS ( VALUES ( 'Date'[Date] ) ) )
            = CALCULATE ( VALUES ( 'Date'[MonthDays] ) ),
        CALCULATE (
            [Sales],
            ALL ( 'Date' ),
            FILTER (
                ALL ( 'Date'[YearMonthNumber] ),
                'Date'[YearMonthNumber]
                    = EARLIER ( 'Date'[YearMonthNumber] ) - 1
            )
        ),
        CALCULATE (
            [Sales],
            ALL ( 'Date' ),
            CALCULATETABLE ( VALUES ( 'Date'[MonthDayNumber] ) ),
            FILTER (
                ALL ( 'Date'[YearMonthNumber] ),
                'Date'[YearMonthNumber]
                    = EARLIER ( 'Date'[YearMonthNumber] ) - 1
            )
        )
    )
)
```

The other calculations for previous quarter and previous year simply change the number of months subtracted in the filter on YearMonthNumber column. The complete formulas are included in the More Pattern Examples section.

Semi-Additive Pattern

Semi-additive measures require a particular calculation when you compare data over different periods. The simple calculation requires the LASTDATE function, which you can use also with custom calendars:

```
[Balance] :=
CALCULATE (
    [Inventory Value],
    LASTDATE ( 'Date'[Date] )
)
```

However, if you want to avoid any time intelligence calculation due to incompatibility with DirectQuery mode, you can use the following syntax:

```
[Balance DirectQuery] :=
CALCULATE (
    [Inventory Value],
    FILTER (
        'Date'[Date],
        'Date'[Date] = MAX ( 'Date'[Date] )
    )
)
```

You do not need to compute aggregations over time for semi-additive measures because of their nature: you need only the last day of the period and you can ignore values in other days. However, a different calculation is required if you want to compare a semi-additive measure over different periods. For example, if you want to compare the last day in two different month-based periods, you need a more complex logic to identify the last day because the months may have different lengths. A simple solution is to create a calculated column for each offset you want to handle, directly storing the corresponding date in the previous month, quarter, or year. For example, you can obtain the corresponding "last date" in the previous month with this calculated column:

```
'Date'[PM Date] =
CALCULATE (
    MAX  ( 'Date'[Date] ),
    ALL ( 'Date' ),
    FILTER (
        ALL ( 'Date'[MonthDayNumber] ),
        'Date'[MonthDayNumber] <= EARLIER ( 'Date'[MonthDayNumber] )
            || EARLIER ( 'Date'[MonthDayNumber] ) = EARLIER ( 'Date'[MonthDays] )
    ),
    FILTER (
        ALL ( 'Date'[YearMonthNumber] ),
        'Date'[YearMonthNumber]
            = EARLIER ( 'Date'[YearMonthNumber] ) - 1
    )
)
```

The logic behind the formula is that you consider the last available date in the previous month, so that if it has fewer days than the current month, you get the last available one. For example, for March 30, you will get February 28 or 29. However, if the previous month has more days than the current month, you still get the last day available, thanks to the condition that does not filter any MonthDayNumber if it is equal to MonthDays, which is the number of days in the current month. For example, for September 30, you will obtain August 31 as a result. You will just change the comparison to YearMonthNumber if you want to get the previous quarter or year, using 3 or 12, respectively, instead of 1 in this filter of [PQ Date] and [PY Date] calculated columns:

```
'Date'[PQ Date] =
...
        'Date'[YearMonthNumber]
            = EARLIER ( 'Date'[YearMonthNumber] ) - 3
...

'Date'[PY Date] =
...
        'Date'[YearMonthNumber]
            = EARLIER ( 'Date'[YearMonthNumber] ) - 12
...
```

Having an easy way to get the corresponding last date of the previous month, you can now write a short definition of the previous month Balance measure, by just using MAX (Date[PM Date]) to filter the date:

```
[PM Balance] :=
CALCULATE (
    Inventory[Inventory Value],
    FILTER (
        ALL ( 'Date' ),
        'Date'[Date] = MAX ( 'Date'[PM Date] )
    )
)
```

You can define the measures for the previous quarter and previous year just by changing the measure used in the MAX function, using [PQ Date] and [PY Date], respectively. These columns are useful also for implementing the comparison of aggregations over periods, such as Month Over Month To Date, as shown in the More Pattern Examples section.

More Pattern Examples

This section shows the time patterns for different types of calculations that you can apply to a custom monthly-based calendar without relying on DAX time intelligence functions. The measures defined will use the following naming convention:

Acronym	Description	Shift Period	Aggregation	Comparison
YTD	Year To Date		X	
QTD	Quarter To Date		X	
MTD	Month To Date		X	
MAT	Moving Annual Total		X	

Acronym	Description	Shift Period	Aggregation	Comparison
PY	Previous Year	X		
PQ	Previous Quarter	X		
PM	Previous Month	X		
PP	Previous Period (automatically selects year, quarter, or month)	X		
PMAT	Previous Year Moving Annual Total	X	X	
YOY	Year Over Year			X
QOQ	Quarter Over Quarter			X
MOM	Month Over Month			X
POP	Period Over Period (automatically selects year, quarter, or month)			X
AOA	Moving Annual Total Over Moving Annual Total	X	X	
PYTD	Previous Year To Date	X	X	
PQTD	Previous Quarter To Date	X	X	
PMTD	Previous Month To Date	X	X	
YOYTD	Year Over Year To Date	X	X	X
QOQTD	Quarter Over Quarter To Date	X	X	X
MOMTD	Month Over Month To Date	X	X	X

Complete Period Comparison Patterns

The formulas in this section define the different aggregations over time.

Additive Measures

```
[PY Sales] :=
SUMX (
    VALUES ( 'Date'[YearMonthNumber] ),
    IF (
        CALCULATE (
            COUNTROWS (
                VALUES ( 'Date'[Date] )
            )
        )
            = CALCULATE (
                VALUES ( 'Date'[MonthDays] )
            ),
        CALCULATE (
            [Sales],
            ALL ( 'Date' ),
            FILTER (
                ALL ( 'Date'[YearMonthNumber] ),
                'Date'[YearMonthNumber]
                    = EARLIER ( 'Date'[YearMonthNumber] ) - 12
            )
        ),
        CALCULATE (
            [Sales],
            ALL ( 'Date' ),
            CALCULATETABLE (
                VALUES ( 'Date'[MonthDayNumber] )
            ),
            FILTER (
                ALL ( 'Date'[YearMonthNumber] ),
                'Date'[YearMonthNumber]
                    = EARLIER ( 'Date'[YearMonthNumber] ) - 12
            )
        )
    )
)
```

```
[PQ Sales] :=
SUMX (
    VALUES ( 'Date'[YearMonthNumber] ),
    IF (
        CALCULATE (
            COUNTROWS (
                VALUES ( 'Date'[Date] )
            )
        )
            = CALCULATE (
                VALUES ( 'Date'[MonthDays] )
            ),
        CALCULATE (
            [Sales],
            ALL ( 'Date' ),
            FILTER (
                ALL ( 'Date'[YearMonthNumber] ),
                'Date'[YearMonthNumber]
                    = EARLIER ( 'Date'[YearMonthNumber] ) - 3
            )
        ),
        CALCULATE (
            [Sales],
            ALL ( 'Date' ),
            CALCULATETABLE (
                VALUES ( 'Date'[MonthDayNumber] )
            ),
            FILTER (
                ALL ( 'Date'[YearMonthNumber] ),
                'Date'[YearMonthNumber]
                    = EARLIER ( 'Date'[YearMonthNumber] ) - 3
            )
        )
    )
)
```

```
[PM Sales] :=
SUMX (
    VALUES ( 'Date'[YearMonthNumber] ),
    IF (
        CALCULATE (
            COUNTROWS (
                VALUES ( 'Date'[Date] )
            )
        )
            = CALCULATE (
                VALUES ( 'Date'[MonthDays] )
            ),
        CALCULATE (
            [Sales],
            ALL ( 'Date' ),
            FILTER (
                ALL ( 'Date'[YearMonthNumber] ),
                'Date'[YearMonthNumber]
                    = EARLIER ( 'Date'[YearMonthNumber] ) - 1
            )
        ),
        CALCULATE (
            [Sales],
            ALL ( 'Date' ),
            CALCULATETABLE (
                VALUES ( 'Date'[MonthDayNumber] )
            ),
            FILTER (
                ALL ( 'Date'[YearMonthNumber] ),
                'Date'[YearMonthNumber]
                    = EARLIER ( 'Date'[YearMonthNumber] ) - 1
            )
        )
    )
)
```

```
[PP Sales] :=
SWITCH (
    TRUE,
    ISFILTERED ( 'Date'[Month] ), [PM Sales],
    ISFILTERED ( 'Date'[Quarter] ), [PQ Sales],
    ISFILTERED ( 'Date'[Year] ), [PY Sales],
    BLANK ()
)

[YOY Sales] :=
[Sales] - [PY Sales]

[QOQ Sales] :=
[Sales] - [PQ Sales]

[MOM Sales] :=
[Sales] - [PM Sales]

[POP Sales] :=
[Sales] - [PP Sales]

[YOY% Sales] :=
DIVIDE ( [YOY Sales], [PY Sales] )

[QOQ% Sales] :=
DIVIDE ( [QOQ Sales], [PQ Sales] )

[MOM% Sales] :=
DIVIDE ( [MOM Sales], [PM Sales] )

[POP% Sales] :=
DIVIDE ( [POP Sales], [PP Sales] )
```

Semi-Additive Measures

```
[Balance] :=
CALCULATE (
    Inventory[Inventory Value],
    FILTER (
        ALL ( 'Date'[Date] ),
        'Date'[Date] = MAX ( 'Date'[Date] )
    )
)

[PY Balance] :=
CALCULATE (
    Inventory[Inventory Value],
    FILTER (
        ALL ( 'Date' ),
        'Date'[Date] = MAX ( 'Date'[PY Date] )
    )
)

[PQ Balance] :=
CALCULATE (
    Inventory[Inventory Value],
    FILTER (
        ALL ( 'Date' ),
        'Date'[Date] = MAX ( 'Date'[PQ Date] )
    )
)

[PM Balance] :=
CALCULATE (
    Inventory[Inventory Value],
    FILTER (
        ALL ( 'Date' ),
        'Date'[Date] = MAX ( 'Date'[PM Date] )
    )
)
```

```
[PP Balance] :=
CALCULATE (
    Inventory[Inventory Value],
    FILTER (
        ALL ( 'Date' ),
        'Date'[Date] = MAX ( 'Date'[PP Date] )
    )
)

[YOY Balance] :=
[Balance] - [PY Balance]

[QOQ Balance] :=
[Balance] - [PQ Balance]

[MOM Balance] :=
[Balance] - [PM Balance]

[POP Balance] :=
[Balance] - [PP Balance]

[YOY% Balance] :=
DIVIDE ( [YOY Balance], [PY Balance] )

[QOQ% Balance] :=
DIVIDE ( [QOQ Balance], [PQ Balance] )

[MOM% Balance] :=
DIVIDE ( [MOM Balance], [PM Balance] )

[POP% Balance] :=
DIVIDE ( [POP Balance], [PP Balance] )
```

Complete Aggregation Patterns

The formulas in this section define the different aggregations over time.

Simple Aggregation for Additive Measures

```
[Sales] :=
SUM ( Sales[SalesAmount] )

[YTD Sales] :=
CALCULATE (
    [Sales],
    FILTER (
        ALL ( DATE ),
        'Date'[YearNumber] = MAX ( 'Date'[YearNumber] )
            && 'Date'[Date] <= MAX ( 'Date'[Date] )
    )
)

[QTD Sales] :=
CALCULATE (
    [Sales],
    FILTER (
        ALL ( DATE ),
        'Date'[YearQuarterNumber] = MAX ( 'Date'[YearQuarterNumber] )
            && 'Date'[Date] <= MAX ( 'Date'[Date] )
    )
)

[MTD Sales] :=
CALCULATE (
    [Sales],
    FILTER (
        ALL ( DATE ),
```

```
            'Date'[YearMonthNumber] = MAX ( 'Date'[YearMonthNumber] )
                && 'Date'[Date] <= MAX ( 'Date'[Date] )
        )
)
```

```
[MAT Sales] :=
CALCULATE (
    [Sales],
    FILTER (
        ALL ( 'Date' ),
        'Date'[SequentialDayNumber] > MAX ( 'Date'[SequentialDayNumber] ) - 365
            && 'Date'[SequentialDayNumber] <= MAX ( 'Date'[SequentialDayNumber] )
    )
)
```

Combined Aggregation and Period Comparison for Additive Measures

The measures that combine aggregation and period comparison are implemented using the calculated columns (in the Date table) that return the corresponding date in a previous period (year, quarter, and month).

```
[PYTD Sales] :=
CALCULATE (
    [Sales],
    FILTER (
        ALL ( DATE ),
        'Date'[YearNumber] = MAX ( 'Date'[YearNumber] ) - 1
            && 'Date'[Date] <= MAX ( 'Date'[PY Date] )
    )
)
```

```
[PQTD Sales] :=
CALCULATE (
    [Sales],
    FILTER (
```

```
        ALL ( DATE ),
        'Date'[YearQuarterNumber] = MAX ( 'Date'[YearQuarterNumber] ) - 1
            && 'Date'[Date] <= MAX ( 'Date'[PQ Date] )
    )
)
```

[PMTD Sales] :=

```
CALCULATE (
    [Sales],
    FILTER (
        ALL ( DATE ),
        'Date'[YearMonthNumber] = MAX ( 'Date'[YearMonthNumber] ) - 1
            && 'Date'[Date] <= MAX ( 'Date'[PM Date] )
    )
)
```

[PMAT Sales] :=

```
CALCULATE (
    [Sales],
    FILTER (
        ALL ( 'Date' ),
        'Date'[SequentialDayNumber] > MAX ( 'Date'[SequentialDayNumber] ) - 730
            && 'Date'[SequentialDayNumber] <= MAX ( 'Date'[SequentialDayNumber] ) - 365
    )
)
```

[YOYTD Sales] :=

```
[YTD Sales] - [PYTD Sales]
```

[QOQTD Sales] :=

```
[QTD Sales] - [PQTD Sales]
```

[MOMTD Sales] :=

```
[MTD Sales] - [PMTD Sales]
```

```
[AOA Sales] :=
[MAT Sales] - [PMAT Sales]

[YOYTD% Sales] :=
DIVIDE ( [YOYTD Sales], [PYTD Sales] )

[QOQTD% Sales] :=
DIVIDE ( [QOQTD Sales], [PQTD Sales] )

[MOMTD% Sales] :=
DIVIDE ( [MOMTD Sales], [PMTD Sales] )

[AOA% Sales] :=
DIVIDE ( [AOA Sales], [PMAT Sales] )
```

Download sample workbooks for both Excel 2010 and 2013 on
http://www.daxpatterns.com/time-patterns

Note that you can easily create a corresponding SQL Server Analysis Services Tabular project starting from the Excel 2013 file

CHAPTER 4

Cumulative Total

The Cumulative Total pattern allows you to perform calculations such as running totals, and you can use it to implement warehouse stock and balance sheet calculations using the original transactions instead of using snapshots of data over time. For example, in order to create an Inventory table that shows the stock of each product for every month, you can make the same calculation using the original warehouse movements table, without processing and consolidating data in advance.

Basic Pattern Example

Suppose you want to calculate the monthly cumulative sum of the transaction quantities. The data model has a Date table that is marked as a Date table. In Figure 4-1, the Transactions table has a relationship with the Date table. You might have more relationships between the tables, but this would not change the DAX measure for this pattern.

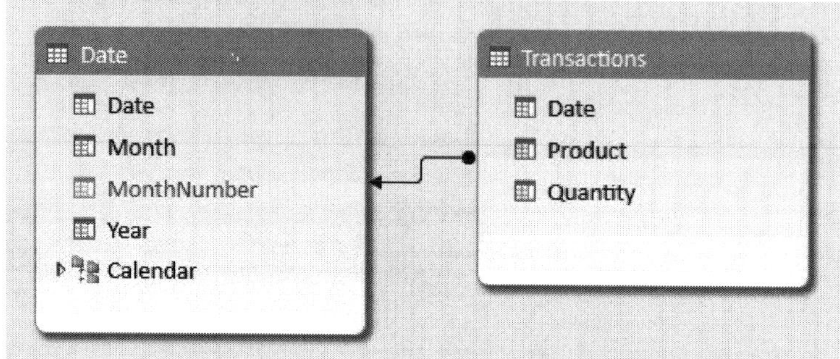

FIGURE 4-1 The Transactions table has a relationship with the Date table.

Figure 4-2 shows a sample Transactions table, with a few transactions for every month.

Date	Product	Quantity
12/20/2012	Shirt	1
12/20/2012	Bike	1
1/15/2013	Bike	1
1/15/2013	Shirt	2
2/15/2013	Bike	2
2/15/2013	Bike	1
3/15/2013	Shirt	3
3/15/2013	Bike	1
4/15/2013	Shirt	1
4/15/2013	Shirt	2

FIGURE 4-2 Sample data in a Transactions table.

As shown in Figure 4-3, you compute the cumulative quantity, which is similar to a running total of the Sum of Quantity measure.

Row Labels	Sum of Quantity	Cumulative Quantity
2012	**2**	**2**
Dec	2	2
2013	**13**	**15**
Jan	3	5
Feb	3	8
Mar	4	12
Apr	3	15
Grand Total	**15**	**15**

FIGURE 4-3 The Cumulative Quantity measure produces a running total of the Sum of Quantity.

At any given date, the Cumulative Quantity measure displays the Sum of Quantity for all the transactions made on a date that is less than or equal to the selected date. For example, the Cumulative Quantity of February 2013 corresponds to the sum of December 2012, January 2013, and February 2013.

You define the Cumulative Quantity measure as follows:

```
Cumulative Quantity :=
CALCULATE (
    SUM ( Transactions[Quantity] ),
    FILTER (
        ALL ( 'Date'[Date] ),
        'Date'[Date] <= MAX ( 'Date'[Date] )
    )
)
```

The FILTER function returns the list of all the dates that are less than or equal to the last date in the current selection. Every cell of the PivotTable in Figure 4-3 has a different selection of dates. You apply the filter to the Date column of the Date table, which must be marked as a Date table in the data model.

Use Cases

You can use the Cumulative Total pattern whenever you want to show the total of a measure up to a certain date, considering all the previous operations (even those earlier than the current selection of dates). You might solve similar problems by creating a snapshot table, which calculates the value of a certain entity at a particular point in time. Moving this calculation at query time saves memory, but you might have a slower response at that time. The granularity of the Cumulative Total pattern is always the same as that of the Transactions table, without requiring additional storage. You have to evaluate the convenience of the Cumulative Total pattern on a case-by-case basis.

Inventory Stock

Providing inventory stock information usually requires a snapshot table that persistently holds the stock availability for each product and each day. In order to save space, you might have a different granularity of the snapshot table, defined at weekly or monthly level instead of daily. You can implement the Inventory Stock calculation as a dynamic calculation in DAX, using the Movements table as a Transactions table in the Cumulative Total pattern.

Balance Sheet

You can evaluate the numbers in balance sheet accounts (assets, liabilities, equity) by aggregating all the transactions using the Cumulative Total pattern. Most transactional systems already have a built-in calculation for these accounts that saves the updated cumulative value to the accounts involved in each transaction. You can use the Cumulative Total pattern to rebuild the historical or predicted behavior at any given granularity.

Cumulative Balance

It is common to implement the cumulative balance as a year-to-date calculation. In some cases, however, you might want to calculate the cumulative balance without year boundaries—for example, if you want to display trends and forecast analysis beyond the limit of the year. You can use or adapt the Cumulative Quantity pattern to this purpose.

Complete Pattern

You apply the Cumulative Total pattern to models that have a table marked as a Date table in the data model. The calculation extends the period to include all the dates before the period selected. To ensure correct results, choose the date column from the correct table (the one marked as a Date table).

Figure 4-4 shows a data model where the relationship between the Transactions table and the Date table is defined using an integer column (DateKey). The Date table is marked as a Date table in the data model by use of the Date column.

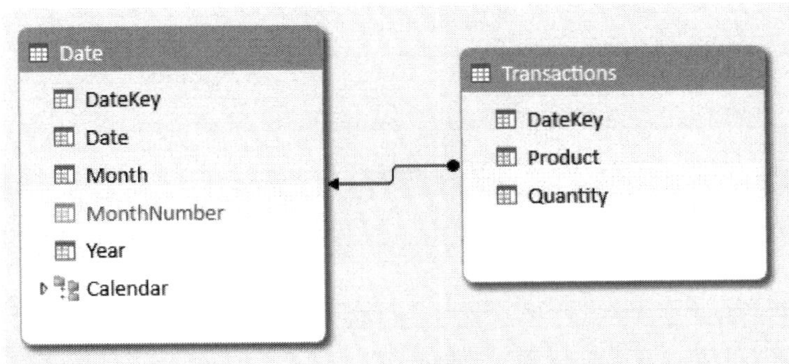

FIGURE 4-4 The DateKey column (in both tables) is an integer value, whereas the Date column in the Date table has a datetime data type.

In order to avoid displaying a value when the selected period is greater than any date in the Transactions table, you can apply a conditional statement that checks this condition. In the following

Cumulative Quantity measure, you compare the minimum DateKey value of the selected period with the maximum value of the DateKey in the entire Transactions table.

```
Cumulative Quantity :=
IF (
    MIN ( 'Date'[DateKey] )
        <= CALCULATE ( MAX ( Transactions[DateKey] ), ALL ( Transactions ) ),
    CALCULATE (
        SUM ( Transactions[Quantity] ),
        FILTER (
            ALL ( 'Date'[Date] ),
            'Date'[Date] <= MAX ( 'Date'[Date] )
        )
    )
)

Cumulative Quantity Unchecked :=
CALCULATE (
    SUM ( Transactions[Quantity] ),
    FILTER (
        ALL ( 'Date'[Date] ),
        'Date'[Date] <= MAX ( 'Date'[Date] )
    )
)
```

In this pattern, you compare the two columns that define the relationship between the tables; you will adapt this comparison to the columns used in your data model. Thanks to this check, you avoid the propagation of the last value in periods that are later than the last transactions in your data. In Figure 4-5, you can see that the unchecked calculation propagates the April 2013 value to all the following months, whereas the checked version returns blank when there are no more transactions available.

Row Labels	Cumulative Quantity Unchecked	Cumulative Quantity
2012	**2**	**2**
Dec	2	2
2013	**15**	**15**
Jan	5	5
Feb	8	8
Mar	12	12
Apr	15	15
May	15	
Jun	15	
Jul	15	
Aug	15	
Sep	15	
Oct	15	
Nov	15	
Dec	15	
Grand Total	**15**	**15**

FIGURE 4-5 The checked version of the Cumulative Quantity measure displays blank values when the period is later than the last transaction available.

More Pattern Examples

You can easily apply the Cumulative Total pattern to the examples described earlier. The following section discusses the Inventory Stock calculation in more detail.

Inventory Valuation

You can apply the general Cumulative Total pattern to the Inventory Stock calculation. The Movements table corresponds to the Transactions table. If you want to calculate an inventory valuation, you need to calculate the unit price for each product at any given point in time. If you create a snapshot table containing the unit price for each product on each day, you probably will use the same table to store the inventory stock. Thus, you will use the Cumulative Total pattern only when you can dynamically calculate in a DAX expression the product unit price for any given day.

Consider the data model in Figure 4-6: every row in the Movements table has a Quantity and a UnitCost. Negative values in Quantity identify sales, whereas positive values in Quantity identify purchases. The related UnitCost in the same row is either the sale or purchase price, respectively.

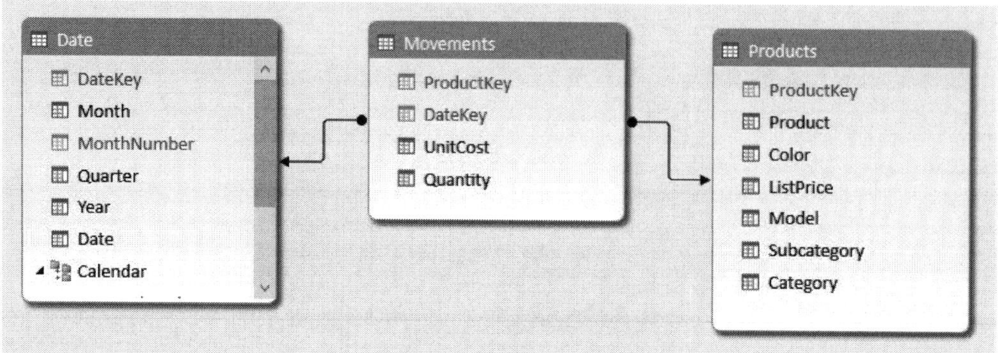

FIGURE 4-6 The UnitCost in the Movements table represents the sale or purchase price.

You have to calculate the inventory value product by product, because each product might have a different price. Industries that share the same price for categories of products might apply a different calculation granularity. In order to obtain an aggregated value, you have to implement the following measure:

```
Value :=
SUMX (
    VALUES ( Products[ProductKey] ),
    [ProductPrice] * [UnitsInStock]
)
```

The SUMX function iterates over all the products selected. It is important to iterate over the ProductKey column in the Products table, instead of using the ProductKey column in the Movements table, because the latter would ignore products without transactions in the considered period. For each product, you multiply two other measures: UnitsInStock and ProductPrice.

You can implement the UnitsInStock measure by applying the Cumulative Total pattern:

```
UnitsInStock :=
IF (
    MIN ( 'Date'[DateKey] ) <= CALCULATE ( MAX ( Movements[DateKey] ), ALL ( Movements ) ),
    CALCULATE (
        SUM ( Movements[Quantity] ),
        FILTER (
            ALL( 'Date'[Date] ),
            'Date'[Date] <= MAX ( 'Date'[Date] )
        )
    )
)
```

The ProductPrice implementation depends on the inventory valuation method that you want to apply. For example, you can calculate the last buy price with the following measure:

```
LastBuyPrice :=
IF (
    HASONEVALUE ( Products[ProductKey] ),
    AVERAGEX (
        CALCULATETABLE (
            TOPN (
                1,
                Movements,
                Movements[DateKey]
            ),
            Movements[Quantity] > 0,
            FILTER (
                ALL ( 'Date'[Date] ),
                'Date'[Date] <= MAX ( 'Date'[Date] )
            )
        ),
        Movements[UnitCost]
    )
)
```

The LastBuyPrice measure works if only one product is selected. It calculates the average value of UnitCost for the rows in the Movements table of the selected product in the last day of movement until the selected period. The TOPN function returns all the movements of the product in the last day available, and the AVERAGEX function returns an average of the UnitCost if there are more rows in the same day. Quantity is filtered to consider only purchases, which are positive numbers in Movements. In a similar way, you can implement the LastSellPrice by changing the filter for Quantity and considering only negative values, as shown in the following example:

```
LastSellPrice :=
IF (
    HASONEVALUE ( Products[ProductKey] ),
    AVERAGEX (
        CALCULATETABLE (
            TOPN (
                1,
                Movements,
                Movements[DateKey]
            ),
            Movements[Quantity] < 0,
            FILTER (
                ALL ( 'Date'[Date] ),
                'Date'[Date] <= MAX ( 'Date'[Date] )
            )
        ),
        Movements[UnitCost]
    )
)
```

The sample workbook contains two measures (ValueBuy and ValueSell) that implement the Value measure by replacing ProductPrice with LastBuyPrice and LastSellPrice, respectively.

In Figure 4-7, you can see the result using a sample set of data loaded from the AdventureWorks database. The Buy and Sell values are different (although the difference is not realistic due to the particular AdventureWorks data set used).

Row Labels	UnitsInStock	ValueBuy	ValueSell
2005	**262,638**	**$23,116,514.73**	**$23,113,304.67**
2006	**261,884**	**$22,913,283.56**	**$22,932,876.94**
2007	**259,344**	**$22,720,825.60**	**$22,760,927.97**
2008	**258,981**	**$22,786,964.64**	**$22,836,931.71**
Q1	**259,533**	**$22,812,516.54**	**$22,849,342.71**
Q2	**258,803**	**$22,763,526.70**	**$22,813,364.53**
April	258,979	$22,664,149.99	$22,713,391.15
May	259,076	$22,703,665.80	$22,765,251.65
June	258,803	$22,763,526.70	$22,813,364.53
Q3	**258,981**	**$22,786,964.64**	**$22,836,931.71**
July	258,917	$22,786,297.38	$22,836,265.52
August	258,981	$22,786,964.64	$22,836,931.71
Grand Total	**258,981**	**$22,786,964.64**	**$22,836,931.71**

FIGURE 4-7 The inventory valuation obtained with two different algorithms (last buy price and last sell price).

A more detailed analysis of the Inventory Stock calculation is available in this article on the SQLBI website: http://sql.bi/DaxInventoryStock. The article compares size and performance between a classic snapshot-based calculation and an equivalent implementation based on the Cumulative Total pattern. Choosing between these approaches depends on data volume and distribution and must be evaluated on a case-by-case basis.

Download sample workbooks for both Excel 2010 and 2013 on
http://www.daxpatterns.com/cumulative-total

Note that you can easily create a corresponding SQL Server Analysis Services Tabular project starting from the Excel 2013 file

CHAPTER 5

Related Distinct Count

The Related Distinct Count pattern allows you to apply the distinct count calculation to any column in any table in the data model. Instead of just counting the number of distinct count values in the entire table using only the DISTINCTCOUNT function, the pattern filters only those values related to events filtered in another table. For example, you can calculate the number of distinct products bought in a particular period, but you can also count the number of distinct categories bought in a period, even if the category is in a column of a table different from the one containing the sales, which defines who bought what and when.

Basic Pattern Example

Suppose you want to provide a distinct count measure over a column in a table, considering only the rows that are referenced by a related table. The data model must contain at least one relationship between two tables, and the column you want to count should be in the lookup table (on the "one" side of the one-to-many relationship). In Figure 5-1, Products is the lookup table and Sales is the related table.

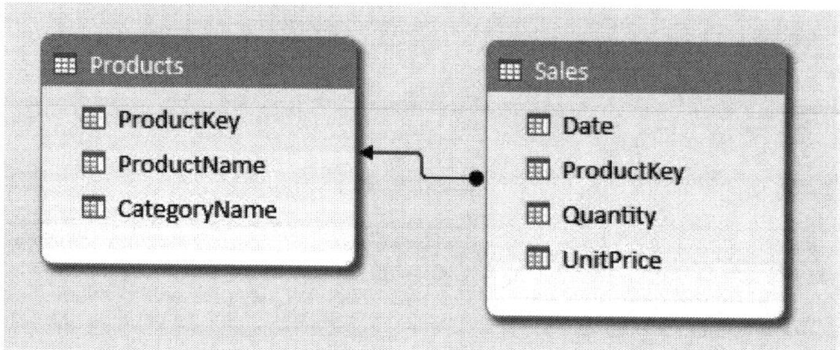

FIGURE 5-1 The target of the distinct count calculation is the columns in the Products table (the lookup table).

Considering the Products and Sales tables shown in Figure 5-2, you want to count how many distinct products and categories have been sold every day.

ProductKey	ProductName	CategoryName
1	Bike Sport	Bikes
2	Bike Road	Bikes
3	Mountain Bike	Bikes
4	Shirt Black	Clothing
5	Shirt Whte	Clothing
6	Shirt Red	Clothing
7	Mountain Tire Tube	Accessories
8	Road Tire Tube	Accessories
9	Front Brakes	Components

Date	ProductKey	Quantity	UnitPrice
8/1/2013	3	1	560
8/1/2013	4	1	30
8/1/2013	7	3	15
8/2/2013	3	1	560
8/2/2013	4	1	30
8/2/2013	5	1	25
8/2/2013	6	1	30
8/3/2013	2	1	950
8/3/2013	3	1	540
8/3/2013	7	2	15
8/3/2013	8	2	20
8/3/2013	6	1	30

FIGURE 5-2 The content of the Products and Sales tables.

As shown in Figure 5-3, you compute the number of distinct products and categories sold for every day and as a grand total for the entire table.

	Column Labels			
Values	8/1/2013	8/2/2013	8/3/2013	Grand Total
SoldProducts	3	4	5	7
SoldCategories	3	2	3	3

FIGURE 5-3 The SoldProducts and SoldCategories measures compute the distinct count for sales made in every day and in the entire Sales table.

You define the SoldProducts and SoldCategories measures as follows:

```
SoldProducts := DISTINCTCOUNT ( Sales[ProductKey] )

SoldCategories :=
CALCULATE (
    DISTINCTCOUNT ( Products[CategoryName] ),
    Sales
)
```

Only the SoldCategories measure uses the Related Distinct Count pattern. The SoldProduct measure uses a simple DISTINCTCOUNT function, because it uses the ProductKey column in the Sales table, which is the same table that contains the events you want to use as filter on the distinct count calculation.

The important part of the pattern is that the DISTINCTCOUNT function is included within a CALCULATE function that receives the related table as a filter argument. In this way, any filter active on Sales (the related table) propagates to the lookup table, so the DISTINCTCOUNT function only considers those products used by rows filtered in the Sales table.

In order to understand the importance of the pattern, compare the previous results with the ListProducts and ListCategories measures, defined as follows:

```
ListProducts := DISTINCTCOUNT ( Products[ProductKey] )

ListCategories := DISTINCTCOUNT ( Products[CategoryName] )
```

You can see their results in Figure 5-4: the total for each day and the grand total always calculate to the same value, because the filters active on the Sales table do not propagate to the Products table.

	Column Labels			
Values	8/1/2013	8/2/2013	8/3/2013	Grand Total
ListProducts	9	9	9	9
ListCategories	4	4	4	4

FIGURE 5-4 The ListProducts and ListCategories measures ignore filters on columns of related tables.

Use Cases

You can use the Related Distinct Count pattern whenever you want to calculate the number of distinct occurrences in a column of a table that has a relationship with a table containing events you are filtering from other tables. This is very common when you have a relational model such as a star schema or a snowflake schema.

Distinct Count on Dimension Attribute

When you extract data from a data mart modeled as a star schema or snowflake schema, the tables containing qualitative information are called **dimensions**. Different types of dimensions differ in the way they handle changes of attributes over time. Regardless of dimension type, you can always apply the Related Distinct Count pattern to slowly changing dimensions in star and snowflake schemas, adapting the pattern to your data model.

Complete Pattern

Whenever you have tables with relationships between them, you can apply the Related Distinct Count pattern if the calculation is on a column of a lookup table. In order to filter the distinct count calculation on a lookup table to consider only the values connected to rows filtered in the related table, you write the DISTINCTCOUNT expression in a CALCULATE statement that contains the related table in its filter argument.

The diagram in Figure 5-5 shows a data model where you can filter the Sales table by date, product, subcategory, and category. The columns in the Products table represent a star schema, whereas those in the Subcategories table represent a snowflake schema.

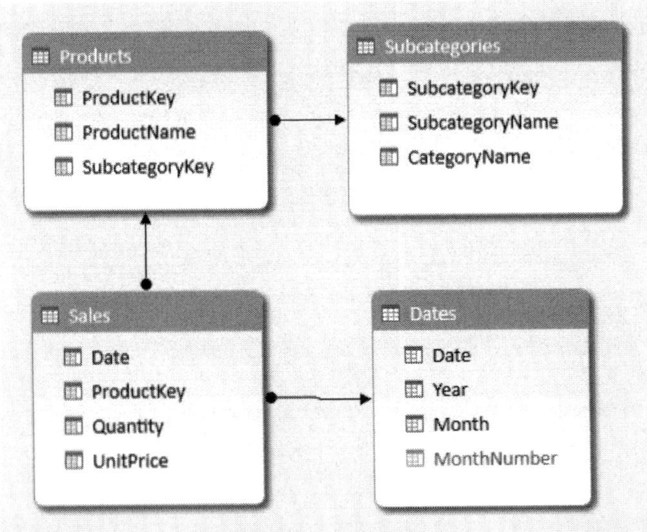

FIGURE 5-5 The Sales table is the fact table of a snowflake schema, having two levels of relationships connecting to the Subcategories table.

Regardless of the structure represented, you always use the same DAX pattern to obtain the distinct count of categories or subcategories. You can apply the same CALCULATE pattern to categories and subcategories, as shown below.

```
SoldSubcategories :=
CALCULATE (
    DISTINCTCOUNT ( Products[SubcategoryKey] ),
    Sales
)

SoldCategories :=
CALCULATE (
    DISTINCTCOUNT( Subcategories[CategoryName] ),
    Sales
)
```

The filter argument of the CALCULATE function contains the Sales table, which extends its filter to all its lookup tables, including Products, Subcategories, and Dates. All lookup tables are part of the extended filter, regardless of the number of relationships traversed. By passing the Sales table (which is the equivalent of a fact table in a star or snowflake schema), you apply this extended filter to the existing filter context. For example, you might have a filter on a CategoryName and you want to calculate how many distinct subcategories have been sold.

More Pattern Examples

In this section, you see a few examples of the Related Distinct Count pattern.

Simple Distinct Count

You do not need to use the Related Distinct Count pattern if you want to calculate the distinct count on a column in a table containing events that you already filter. You only need the Related Distinct Count pattern when you apply the calculation to a column in a lookup table, not when you apply it to a column in the related table. For example, no column of the Sales table needs the Related Distinct Count pattern, because it is already implicit in the current filter context.

```
SoldProducts := DISTINCTCOUNT ( Sales[ProductKey] )

DaysWithSales := DISTINCTCOUNT ( Sales[Date] )
```

If you apply the Related Distinct Count pattern, you will obtain the same results. However, it is unnecessary to apply the pattern when the table specified in the filter argument of the CALCULATE function is the same table to which the column passed to the DISTINCTCOUNT function belongs. For example, in the definitions below, the Sales table has the columns used as an argument for DISTINCTCOUNT as well as being the second argument for CALCULATE.

```
SoldProducts :=
CALCULATE (
    DISTINCTCOUNT ( Sales[ProductKey] ),
    Sales
)

DaysWithSales :=
CALCULATE (
    DISTINCTCOUNT ( Sales[Date] ),
    Sales
)
```

Thus, there is no need to use the CALCULATE function for the Related Distinct Count pattern if you write a simple distinct count calculation.

Distinct Count on Attribute in a Star Schema

Use the Related Distinct Count pattern whenever you apply a distinct count on an attribute that is included in a table that has a direct relationship to the table that contains events that you want to filter.

For example, Products and Dates tables in Figure 5-5 have a relationship with the Sales table, which contains the transactions executed. If you want to calculate the number of months in which you had at least one sale for a given product, or how many product subcategories had at least one sale in a given period, you have to include the Sales table in the filter argument of the CALCULATE function, as shown in the following examples:

```
MonthsWithSales :=
CALCULATE (
    DISTINCTCOUNT ( Dates[MonthNumber] ),
    Sales
)

SoldSubcategories :=
CALCULATE (
    DISTINCTCOUNT ( Products[SubcategoryKey] ),
    Sales
)
```

The filter argument used in CALCULATE is always a related table from the point of view of the column you specify as the argument of DISTINCTCOUNT.

Distinct Count on Attribute in a Snowflake Schema

Use the Related Distinct Count pattern whenever you apply a distinct count on an attribute that is included in a table that has more than one relationship to the table that contains events that you want to consider as filter.

For example, the Subcategory table in Figure 5-5 has a relationship to the Products table, which has a relationship to the Sales table. If you want to calculate how many product categories had at least one sale in a given period, you have to include the Sales table in the filter argument of the CALCULATE function, as shown in the following example:

```
SoldCategories :=
CALCULATE (
    DISTINCTCOUNT ( Subcategories[CategoryName] ),
    Sales
)
```

The filter argument used in CALCULATE is always a related table from the point of view of the column you specify as an argument of DISTINCTCOUNT. Such a related table usually only has lookup tables and does not have cascading related tables. For example, it would be an error to write the following expression:

```
WrongCalculation :=
CALCULATE (
    DISTINCTCOUNT ( Subcategories[CategoryName] ),
    Products
)
```

The WrongCalculation above calculates how many distinct categories are included in the current selection of Products, regardless of the current selection of Sales. In Figure 5-6, you can see that WrongCalculation always returns the same number for any date, because the date filters the Sales table and not the Products table. The Sales table must be included as a filter in the CALCULATE arguments in order to apply a filter to the lookup tables (including Products and Subcategories).

Row Labels	WrongCalculation	SoldCategories
8/1/2013	4	3
8/2/2013	4	2
8/3/2013	4	3
Grand Total	**4**	**3**

FIGURE 5-6 The WrongCalculation always returns the same number regardless of the day in the rows.

Distinct Count on Slowly Changing Dimension Type 2

A **slowly changing dimension** is a table that contains several rows for the same entity, because you have different versions of it. In Figure 5-7, you see on the left a Customers table where a customer

(Sophia Turner) has two rows, describing two different cities in which she lived; on the right you see that Sophia bought products when she lived in New York (CustomerKey is 2) and then when she lived in Boston (CustomerKey is 3).

CustomerKey	CustomerCode	CustomerName	City
1	C102	Eddie Romero	Seattle
2	C363	Sophia Turner	New York
3	C363	Sophia Turner	Boston
4	C762	Barbara Yuan	Los Angeles

Date	ProductKey	CustomerKey	Quantity	UnitPrice
8/1/2013	3	1	1	560
8/1/2013	4	2	1	30
8/1/2013	7	4	3	15
8/2/2013	3	1	1	560
8/2/2013	4	1	1	30
8/2/2013	5	1	1	25
8/2/2013	6	4	1	30
8/3/2013	2	3	1	950
8/3/2013	3	4	1	540
8/3/2013	7	3	2	15
8/3/2013	8	3	2	20
8/3/2013	6	4	1	30

FIGURE 5-7 The Customers table contains one row for each version of the customer. The CustomerKey column in the Sales table shows the version of the customer who made the transaction.

In Figure 5-8, you see that the Customers table has a relationship with the Sales table through the CustomerKey column. You should not use such a column in a DISTINCTCOUNT calculation, however.

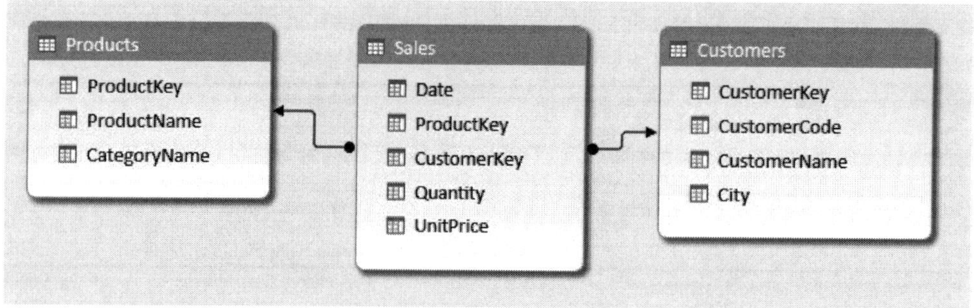

FIGURE 5-8 The Customers table has a relationship with the Sales table using CustomerKey.

Using the DISTINCTCOUNT function on the CustomerKey column in the Sales table would return the number of distinct versions of customers, and not the number of distinct customers that made a purchase. The following expression is syntactically correct, but returns 4 customers who made transactions in the entire Sales table, whereas the right number should be 3.

```
WrongCustomers := DISTINCTCOUNT ( Sales[CustomerKey] )
```

In order to calculate the right number of distinct customers, you have to use the CustomerCode column in the Customers table as an argument of the DISTINCTCOUNT function. Since that column is in a lookup table, you have to apply the Related Distinct Count pattern as shown in the following expression:

```
UniqueCustomers :=
CALCULATE (
    DISTINCTCOUNT ( Customers[CustomerCode] ),
    Sales
)
```

Download sample workbooks for both Excel 2010 and 2013 on
http://www.daxpatterns.com/distinct-count

Note that you can easily create a corresponding SQL Server Analysis Services Tabular project starting from the Excel 2013 file

CHAPTER 6

Statistical Patterns

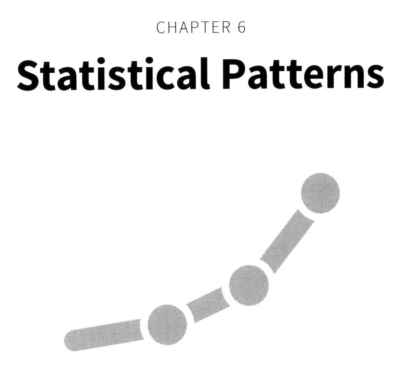

DAX includes a few statistical aggregation functions, such as average, variance, and standard deviation. Other typical statistical calculations require you to write longer DAX expressions. Excel, from this point of view, has a much richer language. The Statistical Patterns are a collection of common statistical calculations: median, mode, moving average, percentile, and quartile. We would like to thank Colin Banfield, Gerard Brueckl, and Javier Guillén, whose blogs inspired some of the following patterns.

Basic Pattern Example

The formulas in this pattern are the solutions to specific statistical calculations.

Average

You can use standard DAX functions to calculate the mean (arithmetic average) of a set of values.

- **AVERAGE:** returns the average of all the numbers in a numeric column.
- **AVERAGEA:** returns the average of all the numbers in a column, handling both text and non-numeric values (non-numeric and empty text values count as 0).
- **AVERAGEX:** calculate the average on an expression evaluated over a table.

Moving Average

The moving average is a calculation to analyze data points by creating a series of averages of different subsets of the full data set. You can use many DAX techniques to implement this calculation. The simplest technique is using AVERAGEX, iterating a table of the desired granularity and calculating for each iteration the expression that generates the single data point to use in the average. For example, the following formula calculates the moving average of the last 7 days, assuming that you are using a Date table in your data model.

```
Moving AverageX 7 Days :=
AVERAGEX (
    DATESINPERIOD (
        'Date'[Date],
        LASTDATE ( 'Date'[Date] ),
        -7,
```

```
        DAY
    ),
    [Total Amount]
)
```

Using AVERAGEX, you automatically calculate the measure at each granularity level. When using a measure that can be aggregated (such as SUM), then another approach—based on CALCULATE—may be faster. You can find this alternative approach in the complete pattern of Moving Average.

Variance

You can use standard DAX functions to calculate the variance of a set of values.

- VAR.S: returns the variance of values in a column representing a sample population.
- VAR.P: returns the variance of values in a column representing the entire population.
- VARX.S: returns the variance of an expression evaluated over a table representing a sample population.
- VARX.P: returns the variance of an expression evaluated over a table representing the entire population.

Standard Deviation

You can use standard DAX functions to calculate the standard deviation of a set of values.

- STDEV.S: returns the standard deviation of values in a column representing a sample population.
- STDEV.P: returns the standard deviation of values in a column representing the entire population.

- **STDEV.S:** returns the standard deviation of an expression evaluated over a table representing a sample population.
- **STDEV.P:** returns the standard deviation of an expression evaluated over a table representing the entire population.

Median

The median is the numerical value separating the higher half of a population from the lower half. If there is an odd number of rows, the median is the middle value (sorting the rows from the lowest value to the highest value). If there is an even number of rows, it is the average of the two middle values. The formula ignores blank values, which are not considered part of the population. The result is identical to the MEDIAN function in Excel.

```
Median :=
(
    MINX (
        FILTER (
            VALUES ( Data[Value] ),
            CALCULATE (
                COUNT ( Data[Value] ),
                Data[Value]
                    <= EARLIER ( Data[Value] )
            )
                > COUNT ( Data[Value] ) / 2
        ),
        Data[Value]
    )
        + MINX (
            FILTER (
                VALUES ( Data[Value] ),
                CALCULATE (
                    COUNT ( Data[Value] ),
                    Data[Value]
```

```
                        <= EARLIER ( Data[Value] )
                )
                    > ( COUNT ( Data[Value] ) - 1 ) / 2
            ),
            Data[Value]
        )
) / 2
```

Figure 6-1 shows a comparison between the result returned by Excel and the corresponding DAX formula for the median calculation.

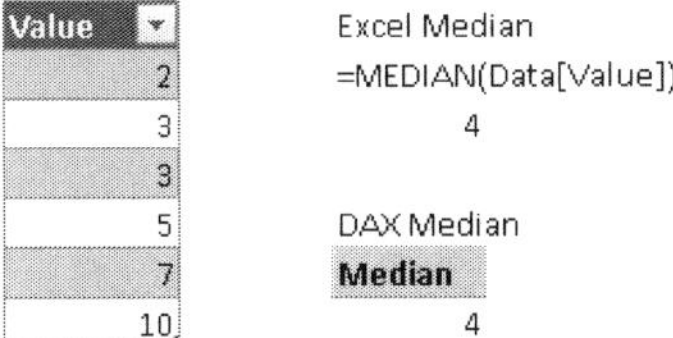

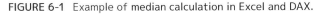

FIGURE 6-1 Example of median calculation in Excel and DAX.

Mode

The mode is the value that appears most often in a set of data. The formula ignores blank values, which are not considered part of the population. The result is identical to the MODE and MODE.SNGL functions in Excel, which return only the minimum value when there are multiple modes in the set of values considered. The Excel function MODE.MULT would return all of the modes, but you cannot implement it as a measure in DAX.

```
Mode :=
MINX (
    TOPN (
        1,
        ADDCOLUMNS (
            VALUES ( Data[Value] ),
            "Frequency", CALCULATE ( COUNT ( Data[Value] ) )
        ),
```

```
            [Frequency],
            0
        ),
        Data[Value]
  )
```

Figure 6-2 compares the result returned by Excel with the corresponding DAX formula for the mode calculation.

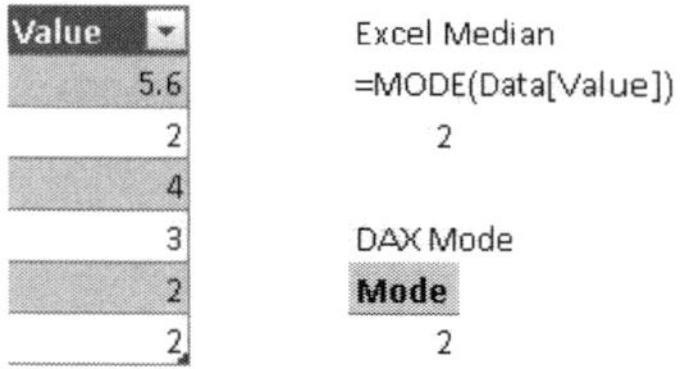

FIGURE 6-2 Example of mode calculation in Excel and DAX.

Percentile

The percentile is the value below which a given percentage of values in a group falls. The formula ignores blank values, which are not considered part of the population. The calculation in DAX requires several steps, described in the Complete Pattern section, which shows how to obtain the same results of the Excel functions PERCENTILE, PERCENTILE.INC, and PERCENTILE.EXC.

Quartile

The quartiles are three points that divide a set of values into four equal groups, each group comprising a quarter of the data. You can calculate the quartiles using the Percentile pattern, following these correspondences:

- First quartile = lower quartile = 25th percentile

- Second quartile = median = 50th percentile
- Third quartile = upper quartile = 75th percentile

Complete Pattern

A few statistical calculations have a longer description of the complete pattern, because you might have different implementations depending on data models and other requirements.

Moving Average

Usually you evaluate the moving average by referencing the day granularity level. The general template of the following formula has these markers:

- <number_of_days> is the number of days for the moving average.
- <date_column> is the date column of the date table if you have one, or the date column of the table containing values if there is no separate date table.
- <measure> is the measure to compute as the moving average.

The simplest pattern uses the AVERAGEX function in DAX, which automatically considers only the days for which there is a value.

```
Moving AverageX <number_of_days> Days:=
AVERAGEX (
    FILTER (
        ALL ( <date_column> ),
        <date_column> > ( MAX ( <date_column> ) - <number_of_days> )
            && <date_column> <= MAX ( <date_column> )
    ),
    <measure>
)
```

As an alternative, you can use the following template in data models without a date table and with a measure that can be aggregated (such as SUM) over the entire period considered.

```
Moving Average <number_of_days> Days:=
CALCULATE (
    IF (
        COUNT ( <date_column> ) >= <number_of_days>,
        <measure> / COUNT ( <date_column> )
    ),
    FILTER (
        ALL ( <date_column> ),
        <date_column> > ( MAX ( <date_column> ) - <number_of_days> )
            && <date_column> <= MAX ( <date_column> )
    )
)
```

The previous formula considers a day with no corresponding data as a measure that has 0 value. This can happen only when you have a separate date table, which might contain days for which there are no corresponding transactions. You can fix the denominator for the average using only the number of days for which there are transactions using the following pattern, where:

- <fact_table> is the table related to the date table and containing values computed by the measure.

```
Moving Average <number_of_days> Days No Zero:=
CALCULATE (
    IF (
        COUNT ( <date_column> ) >= <number_of_days>,
        <measure> / CALCULATE ( COUNT ( <date_column> ), <fact_table> )
    ),
    FILTER (
        ALL ( <date_column> ),
        <date_column> > ( MAX ( <date_column> ) - <number_of_days> )
            && <date_column> <= MAX ( <date_column> )
    )
)
```

You might use the DATESBETWEEN or DATESINPERIOD functions instead of FILTER, but these work only in a regular date table, whereas you can apply the pattern described above also to non-regular date tables and to models that do not have a date table.

For example, consider the different results produced by the following two measures.

```
Moving Average 7 Days :=
CALCULATE (
    IF (
        COUNT ( 'Date'[Date] ) >= 7,
        SUM ( Sales[Amount] ) / COUNT ( 'Date'[Date] )
    ),
    FILTER (
        ALL ( 'Date'[Date] ),
        'Date'[Date] > ( MAX ( 'Date'[Date] ) - 7 )
            && 'Date'[Date] <= MAX ( 'Date'[Date] )
    )
)

Moving Average 7 Days No Zero :=
CALCULATE (
    IF (
        COUNT ( 'Date'[Date] ) >= 7,
        SUM ( Sales[Amount] ) / CALCULATE ( COUNT ( 'Date'[Date] ), Sales )
    ),
    FILTER (
        ALL ( 'Date'[Date] ),
        'Date'[Date] > ( MAX ( 'Date'[Date] ) - 7 )
            && 'Date'[Date] <= MAX ( 'Date'[Date] )
    )
)
```

In Figure 6-03, you can see that there are no sales on September 11, 2005. However, this date is included in the Date table; thus, there are 7 days (from September 11 to September 17) that have only 6 days with data.

Row Labels	Total Amount	Moving Average 7 Days	Moving Average 7 Days No Zero	Moving AverageX 7 Days
9/1/2005	14,313.08	16,950.57	16,950.57	16,950.57
9/2/2005	35,782.70	18,535.05	18,535.05	18,535.05
9/3/2005	11,433.91	19,146.10	19,146.10	19,146.10
9/4/2005	21,113.06	21,139.89	21,139.89	21,139.89
9/5/2005	10,734.81	19,846.95	19,846.95	19,846.95
9/6/2005	22,168.72	19,486.58	19,486.58	19,486.58
9/7/2005	15,012.18	18,651.21	18,651.21	18,651.21
9/8/2005	10,734.81	18,140.03	18,140.03	18,140.03
9/9/2005	24,463.05	16,522.93	16,522.93	16,522.93
9/10/2005	10,734.81	16,423.06	16,423.06	16,423.06
9/11/2005		13,406.91	15,641.40	15,641.40
9/12/2005	6,978.26	12,870.26	15,015.30	15,015.30
9/13/2005	8,351.46	10,896.37	12,712.43	12,712.43
9/14/2005	17,891.35	11,307.68	13,192.29	13,192.29
9/15/2005	14,313.08	11,818.86	13,788.67	13,788.67
9/16/2005	15,012.18	10,468.73	12,213.52	12,213.52
9/17/2005	13,956.52	10,928.98	12,750.47	12,750.47
9/18/2005	17,891.35	13,484.88	13,484.88	13,484.88
9/19/2005	25,568.71	16,140.66	16,140.66	16,140.66
[illegible]	[illegible]	[illegible]	[illegible]	[illegible]

FIGURE 6-03 Example of a Moving Average calculation considering and ignoring dates with no sales.

The measure Moving Average 7 Days has a lower number between September 11 and September 17, because it considers September 11 as a day with 0 sales. If you want to ignore days with no sales, then use the measure Moving Average 7 Days No Zero. This could be the right approach when you have a complete date table but you want to ignore days with no transactions. Using the Moving Average 7 Days formula, the result is correct because AVERAGEX automatically considers only non-blank values.

Keep in mind that you might improve the performance of a moving average by persisting the value in a calculated column of a table with the desired granularity, such as date, or date and product. However, the dynamic calculation approach with a measure offers the ability to use a parameter for the number of days of the moving average (e.g., replace <number_of_days> with a measure implementing the Parameters Table pattern in the next chapter).

Median

The median corresponds to the 50th percentile, which you can calculate using the Percentile pattern. However, the Median pattern allows you to optimize and simplify the median calculation using a single measure, instead of the several measures required by the Percentile pattern. You can use this approach when you calculate the median for values included in <value_column>, as shown below:

```
Median :=
(
    MINX (
        FILTER (
            <value_column>,
            CALCULATE (
                COUNT ( <value_column> ),
                <value_column>
                    <= EARLIER ( <value_column> )
            )
                > COUNT ( <value_column> ) / 2
        ),
        <value_column>
    )
        + MINX (
            FILTER (
                VALUES ( <value_column> ),
                CALCULATE (
                    COUNT ( <value_column> ),
                    <value_column>
                        <= EARLIER ( <value_column> )
                )
                    > ( COUNT ( <value_column> ) - 1 ) / 2
            ),
            <value_column>
        )
) / 2
```

To improve performance, you might want to persist the value of a measure in a calculated column, if you want to obtain the median for the results of a measure in the data model. However, before doing this optimization, you should implement the MedianX calculation based on the following template, using these markers:

- <granularity_table> is the table that defines the granularity of the calculation. For example, it could be the Date table if you want to calculate the median of a measure calculated at the day level, or it could be VALUES ('Date'[YearMonth]) if you want to calculate the median of a measure calculated at the month level.
- <measure> is the measure to compute for each row of <granularity_table> for the median calculation.
- <measure_table> is the table containing data used by <measure>. For example, if the <granularity_table> is a dimension such as 'Date', then the <measure_table> will be 'Internet Sales' containing the Internet Sales Amount column summed by the Internet Total Sales measure.

```
MedianX :=
(
    MINX (
        TOPN (
            COUNTROWS ( CALCULATETABLE ( <granularity_table>, <measure_table> ) ) / 2,
            CALCULATETABLE ( <granularity_table>, <measure_table> ),
            <measure>
            0
        ),
        <measure>
    )
        + MINX (
            TOPN (
                ( COUNTROWS ( CALCULATETABLE ( <granularity_table>, <measure_table> ) ) + 1
                ) / 2,
                CALCULATETABLE ( <granularity_table>, <measure_table> ),
                <measure>,
                0
            ),
            <measure>
        )
) / 2
```

For example, you can write the median of Internet Total Sales for all the Customers in Adventure Works as follows:

```
MedianX :=
(
    MINX (
        TOPN (
            COUNTROWS ( CALCULATETABLE ( Customer, 'Internet Sales' ) ) / 2,
            CALCULATETABLE ( Customer, 'Internet Sales' ),
            [Internet Total Sales],
            0
        ),
        [Internet Total Sales]
    )
        + MINX (
            TOPN (
                ( COUNTROWS ( CALCULATETABLE ( Customer, 'Internet Sales' ) ) + 1 ) / 2,
                CALCULATETABLE ( Customer, 'Internet Sales' ),
                [Internet Total Sales],
                0
            ),
            [Internet Total Sales]
        )
) / 2
```

TIP The following pattern:

```
CALCULATETABLE ( <granularity_table>, <measure_table> )
```

is used to remove rows from <granularity_table> that have no corresponding data in the current selection. It is a faster way than using the following expression:

```
FILTER ( <granularity_table>, NOT ( ISBLANK ( <measure> ) ) )
```

However, you might replace the entire CALCULATETABLE expression with just <granularity_table> if you want to consider blank values of the <measure> as 0.

The performance of the MedianX formula depends on the number of rows in the table iterated and on the complexity of the measure. If performance is bad, you might persist the <measure> result in a calculated column of the <table>, but this will remove the ability of applying filters to the median calculation at query time.

Percentile

Excel has two different implementations of percentile calculation with three functions: PERCENTILE, PERCENTILE.INC, and PERCENTILE.EXC. They all return the K-th percentile of values, where K is in the range 0 to 1. The difference is that PERCENTILE and PERCENTILE.INC consider K as an inclusive range, while PERCENTILE.EXC considers the K range 0 to 1 as exclusive.

All of these functions and their DAX implementations receive a percentile value as parameter, which we call K.

- <K> percentile value is in the range 0 to 1.

The two DAX implementations of percentile require a few measures that are similar, but different enough to require two different set of formulas. The measures defined in each pattern are:

- **K_Perc:** The percentile value – it corresponds to <K>.
- **PercPos:** The position of the percentile in the sorted set of values.
- **ValueLow:** The value below the percentile position.
- **ValueHigh:** The value above the percentile position.
- **Percentile:** The final calculation of the percentile.

You need the ValueLow and ValueHigh measures in case the PercPos contains a decimal part, because then you have to interpolate between ValueLow and ValueHigh in order to return the correct percentile value.

Figure 6-04 shows an example of the calculations made with Excel and DAX formulas, using both algorithms of percentile (inclusive and exclusive).

Value
2
3
3
5
6
7
8
9

DAX Percentile

Row Labels	Percentile_Inc	Percentile_Exc
0 %	2.00	
25 %	3.00	3.00
50 %	5.50	5.50
75 %	7.25	7.75
100 %	9.00	

Excel	PERCENTILE	
K	.INC	.EXC
0.00	2.00	
0.25	3.00	3.00
0.50	5.50	5.50
0.75	7.25	7.75
1.00	9.00	

FIGURE 6-04 Percentile calculations using Excel formulas and the equivalent DAX calculation.

In the following sections, the Percentile formulas execute the calculation on values stored in a table column, Data[Value], whereas the PercentileX formulas execute the calculation on values returned by a measure calculated at a given granularity.

Percentile Inclusive

The Percentile Inclusive implementation is the following.

```
K_Perc := <K>

PercPos_Inc :=
(
    CALCULATE (
        COUNT ( Data[Value] ),
        ALLSELECTED ( Data[Value] )
    ) - 1
) * [K_Perc]

ValueLow_Inc :=
MINX (
    FILTER (
```

```
        VALUES ( Data[Value] ),
        CALCULATE (
            COUNT ( Data[Value] ),
            Data[Value]
                <= EARLIER ( Data[Value] )
        )
            >= ROUNDDOWN ( [PercPos_Inc], 0 ) + 1
    ),
    Data[Value]
)

ValueHigh_Inc :=
MINX (
    FILTER (
        VALUES ( Data[Value] ),
        CALCULATE (
            COUNT ( Data[Value] ),
            Data[Value]
                <= EARLIER ( Data[Value] )
        )
            > ROUNDDOWN ( [PercPos_Inc], 0 ) + 1
    ),
    Data[Value]
)

Percentile_Inc :=
IF (
    [K_Perc] >= 0 && [K_Perc] <= 1,
    [ValueLow_Inc]
        + ( [ValueHigh_Inc] - [ValueLow_Inc] )
            * ( [PercPos_Inc] - ROUNDDOWN ( [PercPos_Inc], 0 ) )
)
```

Percentile Exclusive

The Percentile Exclusive implementation is the following.

```
K_Perc := <K>

PercPos_Exc :=
(
    CALCULATE (
        COUNT ( Data[Value] ),
        ALLSELECTED ( Data[Value] )
    ) + 1
) * [K_Perc]

ValueLow_Exc :=
MINX (
    FILTER (
        VALUES ( Data[Value] ),
        CALCULATE (
            COUNT ( Data[Value] ),
            Data[Value]
                <= EARLIER ( Data[Value] )
        )
            >= ROUNDDOWN ( [PercPos_Exc], 0 )
    ),
    Data[Value]
)

ValueHigh_Exc :=
MINX (
    FILTER (
        VALUES ( Data[Value] ),
        CALCULATE (
            COUNT ( Data[Value] ),
            Data[Value]
                <= EARLIER ( Data[Value] )
        )
            > ROUNDDOWN ( [PercPos_Exc], 0 )
    ),
```

```
    Data[Value]
)

Percentile_Exc :=
IF (
    [K_Perc] > 0 && [K_Perc] < 1,
    [ValueLow_Exc]
        + ( [ValueHigh_Exc] - [ValueLow_Exc] )
            * ( [PercPos_Exc] - ROUNDDOWN ( [PercPos_Exc], 0 ) )
)
```

PercentileX Inclusive

The PercentileX Inclusive implementation is based on the following template, using these markers:

- <granularity_table> is the table that defines the granularity of the calculation. For example, it could be the Date table if you want to calculate the percentile of a measure at the day level, or it could be VALUES ('Date'[YearMonth]) if you want to calculate the percentile of a measure at the month level.
- <measure> is the measure to compute for each row of <granularity_table> for percentile calculation.
- <measure_table> is the table containing data used by <measure>. For example, if the <granularity_table> is a dimension such as 'Date', then the <measure_table> will be 'Sales' containing the Amount column summed by the Total Amount measure.

```
K_Perc := <K>

PercPosX_Inc :=
(
    CALCULATE (
        COUNTROWS ( CALCULATETABLE ( <granularity_table>, <measure_table> ) ),
        ALLSELECTED ( <granularity_table> )
```

```
    ) - 1
) * [K_Perc]

ValueLowX_Inc :=
MAXX (
    TOPN (
        ROUNDDOWN ( [PercPosX_Inc], 0 ) + 1,
        CALCULATETABLE ( <granularity_table>, <measure_table> ),
        <measure>,
        1
    ),
    <measure>
)

ValueHighX_Inc :=
MAXX (
    TOPN (
        ROUNDUP ( [PercPosX_Inc], 0 ) + 1,
        CALCULATETABLE ( <granularity_table>, <measure_table> ),
        <measure>,
        1
    ),
    <measure>
)

PercentileX_Inc :=
IF (
    [K_Perc] >= 0 && [K_Perc] <= 1,
    [ValueLowX_Inc]
        + ( [ValueHighX_Inc] - [ValueLowX_Inc] )
            * ( [PercPosX_Inc] - ROUNDDOWN ( [PercPosX_Inc], 0 ) )
)
```

For example, you can write the PercentileX_Inc of Total Amount of Sales for all the dates in the Date table as follows:

```
K_Perc := <K>

PercPosX_Inc :=
(
    CALCULATE (
        COUNTROWS ( CALCULATETABLE ( 'Date', Sales ) ),
        ALLSELECTED ( 'Date' )
    ) - 1
) * [K_Perc]

ValueLowX_Inc :=
MAXX (
    TOPN (
        ROUNDDOWN ( [PercPosX_Inc], 0 ) + 1,
        CALCULATETABLE ( 'Date', Sales ),
        [Total Amount],
        1
    ),
    [Total Amount]
)

ValueHighX_Inc :=
MAXX (
    TOPN (
        ROUNDUP ( [PercPosX_Inc], 0 ) + 1,
        CALCULATETABLE ( 'Date', Sales ),
        [Total Amount],
        1
    ),
    [Total Amount]
)

PercentileX_Inc :=
IF (
    [K_Perc] >= 0 && [K_Perc] <= 1,
    [ValueLowX_Inc]
```

```
        + ( [ValueHighX_Inc] - [ValueLowX_Inc] )
            * ( [PercPosX_Inc] - ROUNDDOWN ( [PercPosX_Inc], 0 ) )
)
```

PercentileX Exclusive

The PercentileX Exclusive implementation is based on the following template, using the same markers used in PercentileX Inclusive:

```
K_Perc := <K>

PercPosX_Exc :=
(
    CALCULATE (
        COUNTROWS ( CALCULATETABLE ( <granularity_table>, <measure_table> ) ),
        ALLSELECTED ( <granularity_table> )
    ) + 1
) * [K_Perc]

ValueLowX_Exc :=
MAXX (
    TOPN (
        ROUNDDOWN ( [PercPosX_Exc], 0 ),
        CALCULATETABLE ( <granularity_table>, <measure_table> ),
        <measure>,
        1
    ),
    <measure>
)

ValueHighX_Exc :=
MAXX (
    TOPN (
        ROUNDUP ( [PercPosX_Exc], 0 ),
        CALCULATETABLE ( <granularity_table>, <measure_table> ),
```

```
        <measure>,
        1
    ),
    <measure>
)

PercentileX_Exc :=
IF (
    [K_Perc] > 0 && [K_Perc] < 1,
    [ValueLowX_Exc]
        + ( [ValueHighX_Exc] - [ValueLowX_Exc] )
            * ( [PercPosX_Exc] - ROUNDDOWN ( [PercPosX_Exc], 0 ) )
)
```

For example, you can write the PercentileX_Exc of Total Amount of Sales for all the dates in the Date table as follows:

```
K_Perc := <K>

PercPosX_Exc :=
(
    CALCULATE (
        COUNTROWS ( CALCULATETABLE ( 'Date', Sales ) ),
        ALLSELECTED ( 'Date' )
    ) + 1
) * [K_Perc]

ValueLowX_Exc :=
MAXX (
    TOPN (
        ROUNDDOWN ( [PercPosX_Exc], 0 ),
        CALCULATETABLE ( 'Date', Sales ),
        [Total Amount],
        1
    ),
```

```
    [Total Amount]
)

ValueHighX_Exc :=
MAXX (
    TOPN (
        ROUNDUP ( [PercPosX_Exc], 0 ),
        CALCULATETABLE ( 'Date', Sales ),
        [Total Amount],
        1
    ),
    [Total Amount]
)

PercentileX_Exc :=
IF (
    [K_Perc] > 0 && [K_Perc] < 1,
    [ValueLowX_Exc]
        + ( [ValueHighX_Exc] - [ValueLowX_Exc] )
            * ( [PercPosX_Exc] - ROUNDDOWN ( [PercPosX_Exc], 0 ) )
)
```

Download sample workbooks for both Excel 2010 and 2013 on
http://www.daxpatterns.com/statistical-patterns

Note that you can easily create a corresponding SQL Server Analysis Services Tabular project starting from the Excel 2013 file

CHAPTER 7

Parameter Table

The Parameter Table pattern is useful when you want to add a slicer to a PivotTable and make it modify the result of some calculation, injecting parameters into DAX expressions. To use it, you must define a table that has no relationships with any other table. Its only scope is to offer a list of possible choices to the end user in order to alter the calculations performed by one or more existing measures.

The DAX expression in measures checks the value selected and calculates the result accordingly. In most cases, users can select only one value, and multiple selections cannot perform a meaningful calculation. For example, the Parameter Table can choose the number of customers to show in a PivotTable sorted by sales amount, similar to a dynamic "top N customers" calculation, where a slicer selects the Nth value.

Basic Pattern Example

Suppose you want to provide the user with a slicer that can select the scale of measures to display, allowing the user to select a value in millions, thousands, or units. To do that, you must first create a Scale table that does not have any relationship with other tables in the data model, as shown in Figure 7-1.

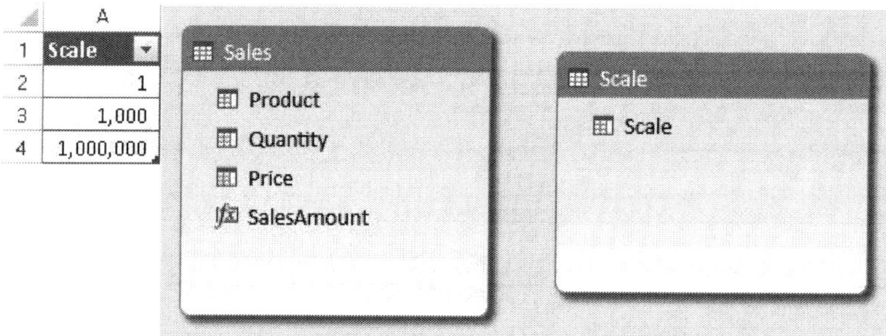

FIGURE 7-1 The Scale table does not have relationships with other tables.

Every measure in the data model has to divide the value by the scale selected, obtaining the value from a filter context containing a single selection, as shown in Figures 7-2 and 7-3.

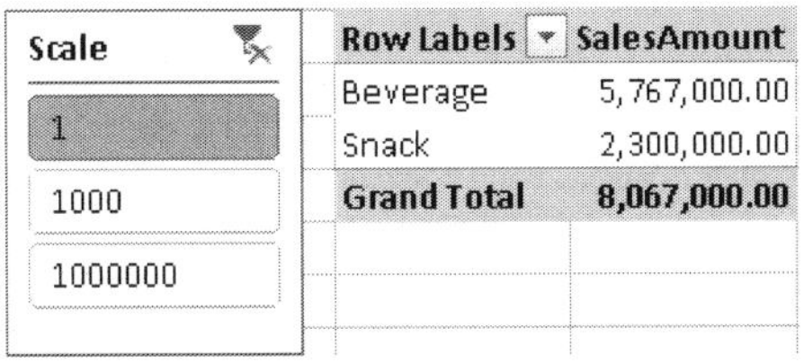

Scale

1

1000

1000000

Row Labels	SalesAmount
Beverage	5,767,000.00
Snack	2,300,000.00
Grand Total	**8,067,000.00**

FIGURE 7-2 The Scale slicer selection can change the visualization of the SalesAmount measure in the PivotTable. With "1" selected, there are no changes to original measures.

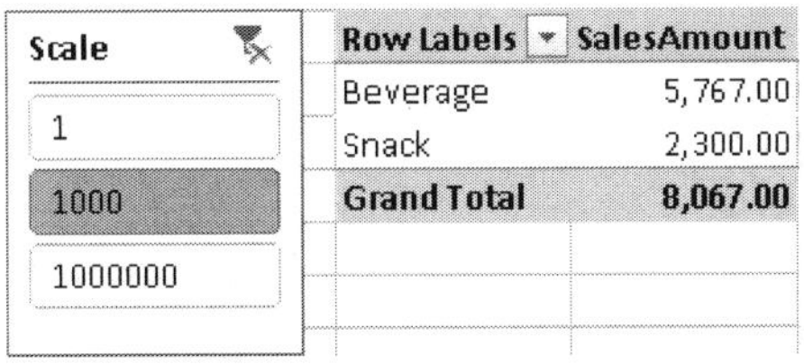

Scale

1

1000

1000000

Row Labels	SalesAmount
Beverage	5,767.00
Snack	2,300.00
Grand Total	**8,067.00**

FIGURE 7-3 Setting the Scale slicer selection to "1000" divides the original calculation by 1000 and shows the SalesAmount measure in thousands.

You define the Sales Amount measure as follows:

```
[Sales Amount] :=
IF (
    HASONEVALUE ( Scale[Scale] ),
    SUM ( Sales[SalesAmount] ) / VALUES ( Scale[Scale] ),
    SUM ( Sales[SalesAmount] )
)
```

This pattern is typically used when you want to inject a parameter inside a DAX measure. This example uses a scale, but you can use the same technique in many other scenarios.

It is interesting to note that the parameter works not only with a slicer, but on rows and columns as well. For example, in Figure 7-4, the Scale parameter displays different values in different columns.

SalesAmount	Column Labels		
Row Labels	1	1000	1000000
Beverage	5,767,000.00	5,767.00	5.77
Snack	2,300,000.00	2,300.00	2.30
Grand Total	8,067,000.00	8,067.00	8.07

FIGURE 7-4 The Scale parameter changes the presentation of the Sales Amount measure in every column.

Use Cases

You can use the Parameter Table pattern in a wide range of scenarios. Some interesting examples are shown below.

Algorithm Parameter and Simulation

You can pass one or more parameters to an algorithm by using a table for each parameter. For example, when you have a model with measures that can receive a parameter for the calculation, this pattern enables the user to change the parameters of the algorithm. This can be useful to simulate different scenarios based on different values of parameters in a simulation (e.g., discount based on volume sales level, percentage growth of revenues, drop rate in customer retention, and so on).

Algorithm Selection

You might decide to apply a different algorithm to the same measure. This means using a SWITCH statement that, according to the value selected, returns a different expression for the same measure. You will see an example later by looking at the Period Table pattern.

Ranking

You can parameterize the number of elements shown in a PivotTable according to a particular ranking. Even if you cannot define a dynamic set in DAX, you can define a measure that returns BLANK for items that you do not want to show according to the filter selected by the user. This scenario is demonstrated later in the "Limit Top N Elements in a Ranking" example.

Complete Pattern

Add a Parameter table to the data model. That table has no relationships with other tables, and usually has only one column, containing the parameter values. You might use up to three columns in case you want to add a textual description to the parameter value and to specify a particular display order by using the Sort by Column property. If many parameters will be used in your data model, you can add all of them to the same table in order to reduce the number of tables in the model. You obtain such a table by performing a Cartesian product between all the possible values of each parameter (also called a cross join of parameters values). In that case, all of the columns for each parameter have to participate in the cross join.

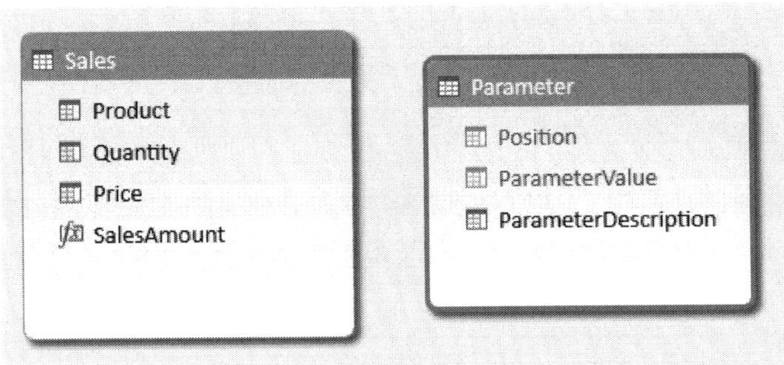

FIGURE 7-5 The Parameter table does not have relationships with other tables.

To get the selected value, use the VALUES function in the measure that uses the parameter. Usually you check the selection of one value only. If the selection is of all the parameters, it is like there is no selection at all and, in this case, you can return a default value. If the selection has more than one but not all parameters, you might consider this case as a multiple selection, which in most cases may be an invalid selection. The following code represents the complete pattern that you see applied later in more pattern examples.

```
ParameterSelection :=
IF (
    HASONEVALUE ( Parameter[ParameterValue] ),
    "Selection: " & VALUES ( Parameter[ParameterValue] ),
    IF (
        NOT ( ISFILTERED ( Parameter[ParameterDescription] ) ),
        "No Selection",
        "Multiple Selection"
    )
)
```

It is important that you use the ISFILTERED function on the visible column, which is the one directly used by the user (ParameterDescription in the essential pattern). You have to use the VALUES function on the value column (ParameterValue in the example).

You can replace the Selection, No Selection, and Invalid Selection expressions with specific formulas that perform a meaningful calculation in each case. For example, you might return BLANK in case of multiple selection (which is an invalid one) and apply a default parameter in case of no selection, applying the selected parameter to your formula if the selection has only one value.

More Pattern Examples

In this section, you see a few examples of the Parameters Table pattern.

Using a Single Parameter Table

You use a Single Parameter Table pattern to apply a discount to an existing Sales Amount measure, by creating a table in your model with the values that the user will select. For example, you can add the following table to your data model, without creating any relationship between this table and other tables in the same model. The Discounts table in Figure 7-6 shows the possible discount percentages applicable to the sales amount.

DiscountValue	Discount
0.05	5%
0.10	10%
0.15	15%
0.20	20%
0.25	25%
0.30	30%

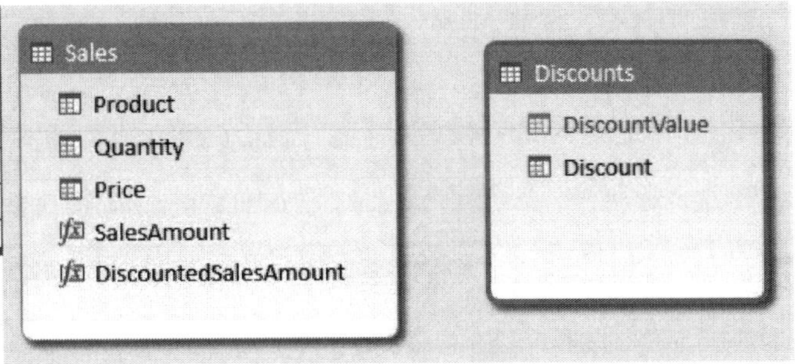

Sales
Product
Quantity
Price
SalesAmount
DiscountedSalesAmount

Discounts
DiscountValue
Discount

FIGURE 7-6 The Discounts table has two columns, one for the discount value and one for the displayed percentage.

The original Sales Amount formula simply multiplies Quantity by Price for each row in the Sales table and sums the total.

```
SalesAmount := SUMX ( Sales, Sales[Quantity] * Sales[Price] )
```

The Discounted Sales Amount has to apply the selected discount to the Sales Amount measure. In order to do that, you use the VALUES function and check that the selection has only one value before evaluating the expression. If the selection includes all the discounts, you do not apply any discount, whereas if the selection includes more than one (but not all) discounts, you return BLANK.

```
DiscountedSalesAmount :=
IF (
    HASONEVALUE ( Discounts[DiscountValue] ),
    [SalesAmount] * ( 1 - VALUES ( Discounts[DiscountValue] ) ),
    IF (
        NOT ( ISFILTERED ( Discounts[Discount] ) ),
```

```
            [SalesAmount],
            BLANK ()
        )
    )
```

The reason why the user can select all the values is that if there is no selection on the Discount slicer, or the user does not use the Discount attribute in the PivotTable, then all the values from Discount will appear as selected; in this scenario, it is important to provide a default value.

The HASONEVALUE function checks that the selection has only one discount. If this is not true, ISFILTERED checks whether the Discount column is part of the filter or not. If it is not in the filter, you evaluate the original SalesAmount measure; otherwise, you return BLANK because there is a selection of multiple discounts that is ambiguous.

In Figure 7-7, you see the PivotTable computed without selecting any discount: the two measures, SalesAmount and DiscountedSalesAmount, show the same value because the user did not apply any discount to the second measure.

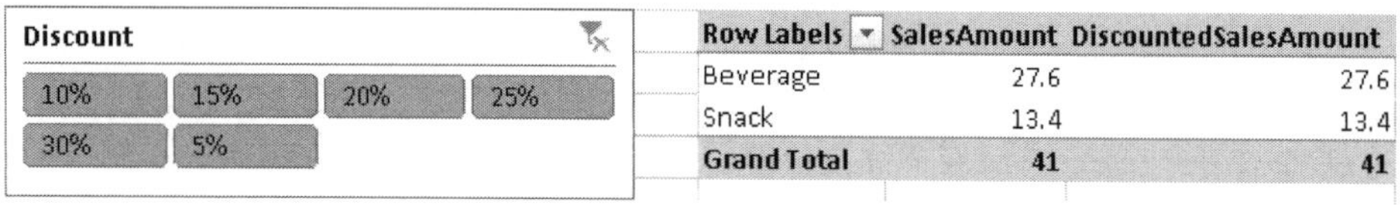

Discount

10% 15% 20% 25%
30% 5%

Row Labels	SalesAmount	DiscountedSalesAmount
Beverage	27.6	27.6
Snack	13.4	13.4
Grand Total	**41**	**41**

FIGURE 7-7 No discount is applied if the user selects all the discounts.

Figure 7-8 shows the PivotTable after selecting a 15% discount: the DiscountedSalesAmount now has a lower value than SalesAmount.

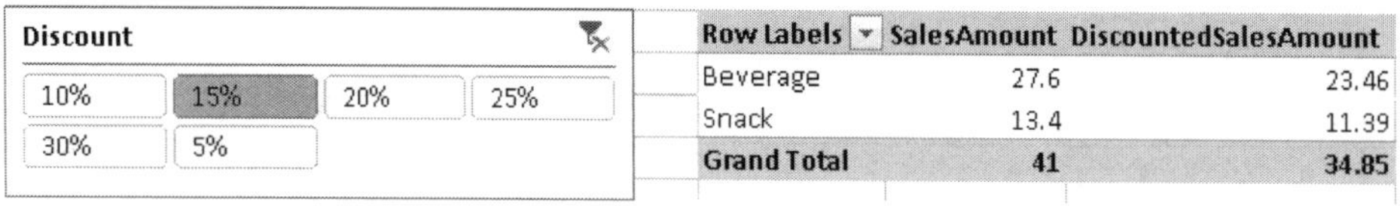

Discount

10% 15% 20% 25%
30% 5%

Row Labels	SalesAmount	DiscountedSalesAmount
Beverage	27.6	23.46
Snack	13.4	11.39
Grand Total	**41**	**34.85**

FIGURE 7-8 The user applies one discount to the DiscountedSalesAmount calculation.

Handling More Parameter Tables

You can apply the same pattern for a single parameter table multiple times. Applied in this way, however, parameters will be independent of each other—you can neither define cascading parameters nor create constraints between combinations of parameters that are not allowed. In such a case, consider using a single column that offers only valid combinations of multiple parameter values (see an example in the section Alternative to Cascading Parameters). Every parameter requires a separate table without any relationship with other tables.

For example, you can apply the discount percentage shown in the previous section only for those sales having a minimum quantity selected through another slicer. Thus, the minimum quantity valid for applying the discount is another parameter. Figure 7-9 shows the resulting PivotTable with the 15% discount applied only to sales rows with a quantity greater than or equal to 3.

Discount

10% 15% 20% 25%
30% 5%

MinQuantity

1 2 3 4 5

Row Labels	SalesAmount	DiscountedSalesAmount
Beverage	27.6	25.35
Snack	13.4	11.93
Grand Total	41	37.28

FIGURE 7-9 The parameters are used in two slicers—Discount and MinQuantity.

In this case, you need to create a table with one column (MinQuantity), with no relationships with other tables. The MinQuantity table contains all the numbers between 1 and 5.

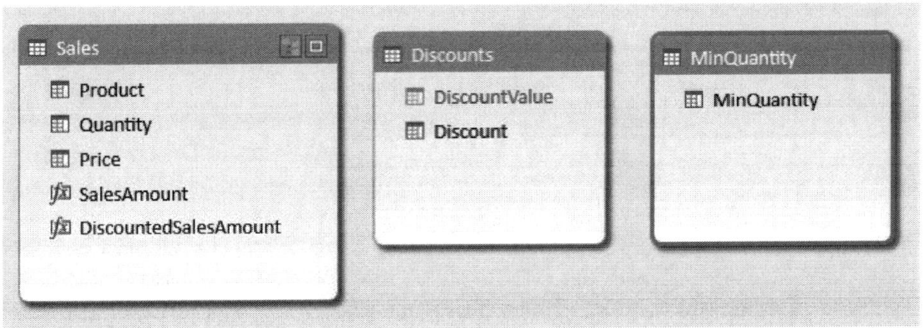

FIGURE 7-10 Each parameter has a different Parameter table in the data model.

In the Discounted Sales Amount measure you check the selection made on the Discounts and MinQuantity tables and, depending on that selection, you perform the right calculation. At first, it might seem necessary to use a SUMX with an IF statement in the formula, such as:

```
SUMX (
    Sales,
    [SalesAmount]
    * IF (
        Sales[Quantity] >= VALUES ( MinQuantity[MinQuantity] ),
        1 - VALUES ( Discounts[DiscountValue] ),
        1
      )
)
```

However, because the percentage will always be the same for all the discounted rows, you can also sum the result of two different CALCULATE functions:

```
CALCULATE (
    [SalesAmount] * ( 1 - VALUES ( Discounts[DiscountValue] ) ),
    Sales[Quantity] >= VALUES ( MinQuantity[MinQuantity] )
)

+ CALCULATE (
    [SalesAmount],
    Sales[Quantity] < VALUES ( MinQuantity[MinQuantity] )
)
```

The complete measure for Discounted Sales Amount is shown below. It includes the required checks for Discounts and MinQuantity selections, returning a BLANK if the user selected more than one but not all of the items in the Discounts and MinQuantity tables.

```
DiscountedSalesAmount :=
IF (
    HASONEVALUE ( Discounts[DiscountValue] ) && HASONEVALUE ( MinQuantity[MinQuantity] ),
    CALCULATE (
        [SalesAmount] * ( 1 - VALUES ( Discounts[DiscountValue] ) ),
        Sales[Quantity] >= VALUES ( MinQuantity[MinQuantity] )
    )
    + CALCULATE (
        [SalesAmount],
        Sales[Quantity] < VALUES ( MinQuantity[MinQuantity] )
    ),
    IF (
        NOT ( ISFILTERED ( Discounts[Discount] ) )
            && NOT ( ISFILTERED ( MinQuantity[MinQuantity] ) ),
        [SalesAmount],
        IF (
            HASONEVALUE ( Discounts[Discount] )
                && NOT ( ISFILTERED ( MinQuantity[MinQuantity] ) ) ,
            CALCULATE ( [SalesAmount] * ( 1 - VALUES ( Discounts[DiscountValue] ) ) ),
            BLANK ()
        )
    )
)
```

Alternative to Cascading Parameters

By using Excel slicers, you cannot show two parameters to the user in the form of cascading parameters, in which requesting the first parameter restricts the available options for the second parameter. You can partly work around this limitation by placing all cascading parameters in the same table, creating one row for each valid combination of parameters. Then, either you can display one slicer with a single description of the combination of the parameters, or you can display two or more slicers hiding the values not compatible with the current selection in other slicers.

Consider two flags, one that applies a discount simulation if customers have a fidelity card and the other that simulates a further discount if customers belong to a premier level of the fidelity card. The table in Figure 7-11 defines the two parameters, where the combination NO/YES is not valid.

Fidelity	Premier
YES	YES
YES	NO
NO	NO

FIGURE 7-11 This Parameters table shows only valid combinations.

If the user selects NO in the Fidelity slicer, the Premier slicer shows the YES option even if it is not a valid combination, as shown in Figure 7-12.

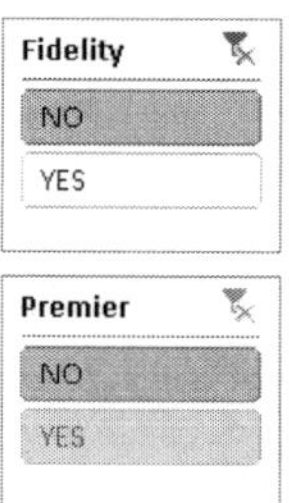

FIGURE 7-12 The Premier slicer shows YES even if it is not a valid combination.

To hide the YES option in the Premier slicer when the user selects the NO value in the Fidelity slicer, use the Slicer Settings dialog box, as shown in Figure 7-13. In the settings for the Premier slicer, check the Hide Items With No Data checkbox.

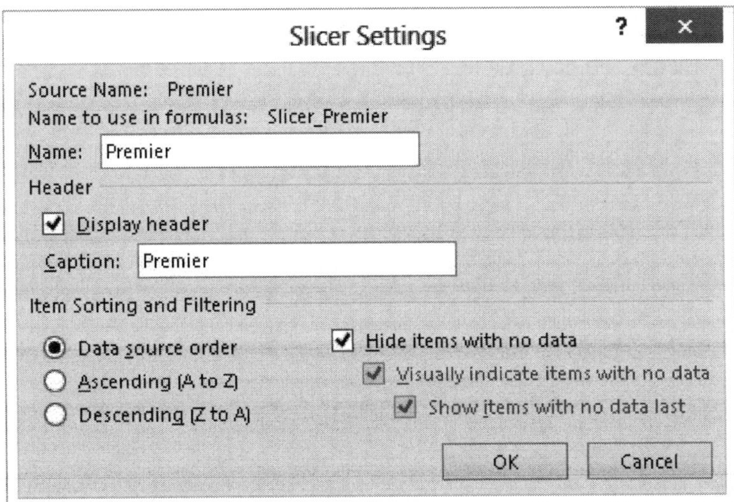

FIGURE 7-13 The Hide Items With No Data checkbox should be set in the Premier slicer settings.

With such a setting, the Premier slicer no longer displays the YES option when the user selects the NO value in the Fidelity slicer, as shown in Figure 7-14.

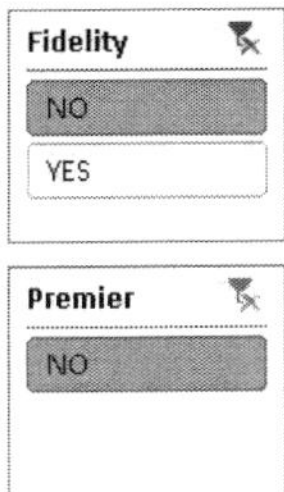

FIGURE 7-14 The Premier slicer no longer displays the YES option.

An alternative approach is to create a column that contains the description of each valid combination of parameters. By making this column visible and hiding the others, the user will be able to choose only a valid combination of parameters. As shown in Figure 7-15, you can use the Position column to define the sort order of the Parameter column.

Fidelity	Premier	Parameter	Position
YES	YES	Fidelity Premier	3
YES	NO	Fidelity Standard	2
NO	NO	Not Associated	1

FIGURE 7-15 The Parameter column contains descriptions of valid combinations of parameters, and the Position column defines the sort order of the Parameter column.

The Parameter slicer shows only the valid selections in the proper sort order.

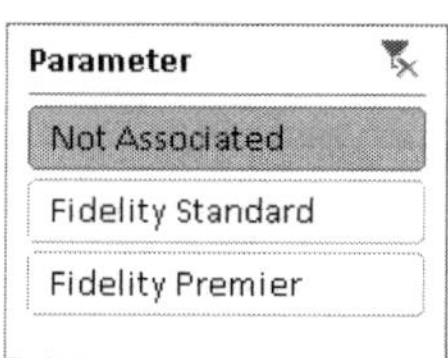

FIGURE 7-16 The Parameter slicer replaces distinct Fidelity and Premier slicers.

The drawback in this scenario is that a multiple selection of items in the same slicer is not meaningful. Unfortunately, it is not possible to force single selection for a slicer, so it is up to the measure expression to identify such a condition. The measures shown below return the selected value for Fidelity and Premier parameters, respectively. Before returning the value, they check the single selection of the Parameter column—if there is no selection or a multiple selection, they return a BLANK value.

```
FidelitySelection :=
IF (
    HASONEFILTER ( Parameters[Parameter] ),
    VALUES ( Parameters[Fidelity] ),
    BLANK ()
)

PremierSelection :=
IF (
    HASONEFILTER ( Parameters[Parameter] ),
    VALUES ( Parameters[Premier] ),
    BLANK ()
)
```

You can use the FidelitySelection and PremierSelection measures in other DAX expressions in order to execute algorithms according to the choice made by the user.

Period Table

As you read in other patterns, DAX provides several time intelligence functions useful for calculating information such as year-to-date, year-over-year, and so on. One drawback is that you have to define one measure for each of these calculations, and the list of measures in your model might grow too much.

A possible solution to this issue is to create a parameter table that contains one line for each calculation that you might want to apply to a measure. In this way, the end user has a shorter list of measures and possible operations on them, instead of having the Cartesian product of these two sets. This solution has its own drawbacks, however, and it may be better to create just the measures you really want to use in your data model, trying to expose only the combinations of measures and calculations that are meaningful for the expected analysis of your data.

If you decide to create a parameter table of calculations, the first step is to add a Period table in the Tabular model containing the list of possible calculations for a measure, as shown in Figure 7-17.

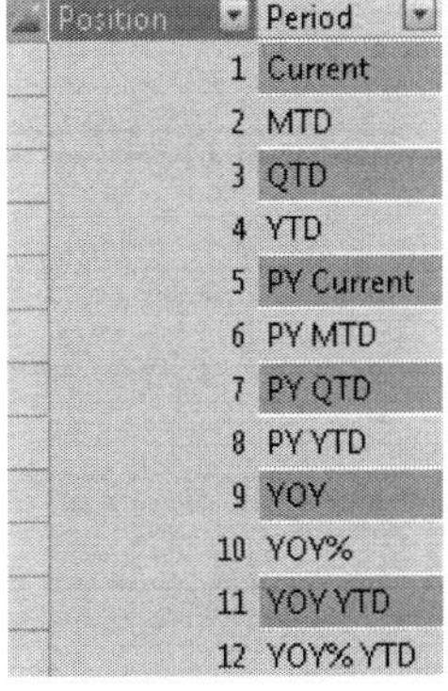

Position	Period
1	Current
2	MTD
3	QTD
4	YTD
5	PY Current
6	PY MTD
7	PY QTD
8	PY YTD
9	YOY
10	YOY%
11	YOY YTD
12	YOY% YTD

FIGURE 7-17 The Period table in the Tabular model contains the list of possible calculations.

In the Period table, the Position column is hidden and the Period column has the Sort By Column set to Position. As for any parameters table, you do not have to define any relationship between this table and other tables in your data model, because you use the selected item of the Period table to change the behavior of a measure through its DAX definition.

At this point, you define a single measure that checks the selected value of the Period table and uses a DAX expression to return the corresponding calculation. Because the Period table has no relationships, when the table is used as a filter the selected value in the Period table is always the one chosen by the user. Similarly, when the Period table is used in row or column labels in a PivotTable, the selected value is the corresponding value in a row or a column. In general, you follow this generic pattern:

```
IF (
    HASONEVALUE ( Period[Period] ),
    SWITCH (
        VALUES ( Period[Period] ),
        "Current", <expression>,
        "MTD", <expression>,
        …
```

The first condition checks that there are no multiple values active in the filter context. Then, in the next step, a SWITCH statement checks each value and evaluates the correct expression corresponding to the Period value. Assuming you already defined the necessary measures for time intelligence operations, you need to replace the expression tag with the corresponding specific measure. For example, you can define a generic Sales measure, which applies one of the operations described in the Period table to the Internet Total Sales measure:

```
Sales :=
    IF (
        HASONEVALUE ( Period[Period] ),
        SWITCH (
            VALUES ( Period[Period] ),
            "Current", [Internet Total Sales],
            "MTD", [MTD Sales],
            "QTD", [QTD Sales],
```

```
            "YTD", [YTD Sales],
            "PY Current", [PY Sales],
            "PY MTD", [PY MTD Sales],
            "PY QTD", [PY QTD Sales],
            "PY YTD", [PY YTD Sales],
            "YOY", [YOY Sales],
            "YOY%", [YOY Sales%],
            "YOY YTD", [YOY YTD Sales],
            "YOY% YTD", [YOY YTD Sales%],
            BLANK ()
        ),
        [Internet Total Sales]
    )
```

IMPORTANT The RTM version of Analysis Services 2012 has an issue in SWITCH implementation, which internally generates a series of nested IF calls. Because of a performance issue, if there are too many nested IF statements (or too many values to check in a SWITCH statement), there could be a slow response and abnormal memory consumption. Service Pack 1 of SQL Server 2012 and PowerPivot 2012 fixed this issue. This is not an issue in Excel 2013.

You have to repeat such a definition for each of the measures to which you want to apply the Period calculations. You can avoid defining all the internal measures by replacing each measure's reference with its corresponding DAX definition. This would make the Sales definition longer and hard to maintain, but it is a design choice you might follow.

TIP Remember that you can hide a measure by using the Hide From Client Tool command. If you do not want to expose internal calculations, you should hide all the measures previously defined and make only the Sales measure visible.

At this point, you can browse data by using the Period values crossed with the Sales measure. In Figure 7-18, the user displayed only the Sales measure; the Period values are in the columns, and a selection of years and quarters is in the rows.

Sales	Column Labels											
Row Labels	Current	MTD	QTD	YTD	PY Current	PY MTD	PY QTD	PY YTD	YOY	YOY%	YOY YTD	YOY% YTD
2002	**6,530,343.53**	**577,314.00**	**1,327,799.32**	**6,530,343.53**	**3,266,373.66**	**755,527.89**	**1,812,850.77**	**3,266,373.66**	**3,263,969.87**	**1.00**	**3,263,969.87**	**1.00**
1	1,791,698.45	644,135.20	1,791,698.45	1,791,698.45					1,791,698.45		1,791,698.45	
2	2,014,012.13	676,763.65	2,014,012.13	3,805,710.59					2,014,012.13		3,805,710.59	
3	1,396,833.62	350,466.99	1,396,833.62	5,202,544.20	1,453,522.89	473,943.03	1,453,522.89	1,453,522.89	-56,689.27	-0.04	3,749,021.32	2.58
4	1,327,799.32	577,314.00	1,327,799.32	6,530,343.53	1,812,850.77	755,527.89	1,812,850.77	3,266,373.66	-485,051.45	-0.27	3,263,969.87	1.00
2003	**9,791,060.30**	**1,731,787.77**	**4,009,218.46**	**9,791,060.30**	**6,530,343.53**	**577,314.00**	**1,327,799.32**	**6,530,343.53**	**3,260,716.77**	**0.50**	**3,260,716.77**	**0.50**
1	1,413,530.30	485,574.79	1,413,530.30	1,413,530.30	1,791,698.45	644,135.20	1,791,698.45	1,791,698.45	-378,168.15	-0.21	-378,168.15	-0.21
2	1,623,971.06	554,799.23	1,623,971.06	3,037,501.36	2,014,012.13	676,763.65	2,014,012.13	3,805,710.59	-390,041.08	-0.19	-768,209.23	-0.20
3	2,744,340.48	1,010,258.13	2,744,340.48	5,781,841.84	1,396,833.62	350,466.99	1,396,833.62	5,202,544.20	1,347,506.86	0.96	579,297.63	0.11
4	4,009,218.46	1,731,787.77	4,009,218.46	9,791,060.30	1,327,799.32	577,314.00	1,327,799.32	6,530,343.53	2,681,419.14	2.02	3,260,716.77	0.50

FIGURE 7-18 The Period calculations applied to the Sales measure.

As anticipated, this solution has several drawbacks:

- After you put Period in rows or columns, you cannot easily change the order of its items. You can change the order by using some Excel features, but it is not as immediate and intuitive as changing the Position value in the Period view used to populate the Period table.
- The number format of the measure cannot change for particular calculations requested through some Period values. For example, in Figure 7-18, you can see that the YOY% and YOY% YTD calculations do not display the Sales value as a percentage, because you can define a single number format for a measure in SSAS Tabular and you cannot dynamically change it by using an expression (as you can do in SSAS Multidimensional with MDX). A possible workaround is changing the number format directly in the client tool (Excel cells in this case), but you will lose the formatting as soon as you navigate into the PivotTable. Another workaround is returning the value as a formatted string, but the drawback in this case is that the client can no longer customize the formatting and the value is no longer a number, so it is harder to use it in further calculations in Excel.
- If you use more than one measure in the PivotTable, you must create a set by using the Manage Sets command in Excel based on column items, choosing only the combination of measures and Period values that you really want to see in the PivotTable.
- You have to create a specific DAX expression for each combination of Period calculations and measures that you want to support. This is not flexible and scalable as a more generic solution could be.

You have to evaluate case by case whether or not these drawbacks make the implementation of a Period table a good option.

Limit Top N Elements in a Ranking

You can easily choose the number of rows to display in a PivotTable by leveraging the TOPN function. By default, the PivotTable hides rows containing BLANK values for all the columns, so you can return BLANK for a measure that belongs to an item that is over the limit you define in the parameter. For example, if you want to display only the top 10 products by Sales Amount, you can write the Sales Amount measure in this way:

```
Top10SalesAmount :=
IF (
    HASONEVALUE ( Sales[Product] ),
    IF (
        RANKX (
            ALL ( Sales[Product] ),
            [SalesAmount]
        ) <= 10,
        [SalesAmount],
        BLANK ()
    )
)
```

You can replace the value shown in bold (10) with the selection of a parameter table, as in the previous example. Of course, you always have to check for the single selection made by the user in the filter or slicer for the parameter value.

Consider the data model in Figure 7-19, in which the Top table contains a single column with the possible selection for the TOP N elements in the ranking.

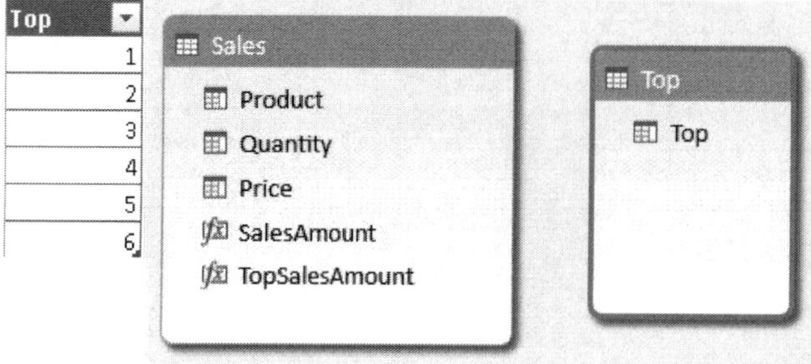

FIGURE 7-19 The Top table contains the value for the TOP N selection in the ranking.

In order to show the TOP N products, the TopSalesAmount measure compares the value returned by the RANKX function with the selected parameter and returns BLANK for the products that are outside the TOP N range.

```
TopSalesAmount :=
IF (
    HASONEVALUE ( 'Top'[Top] ),
    IF (
        RANKX (
            ALL ( Sales[Product] ),
            [SalesAmount]
        ) <= VALUES ( 'Top'[Top] ),
        [SalesAmount],
        BLANK ()
    )
)
```

Thanks to the default PivotTable behavior, a user browsing the data model in Excel will see only the first N products after selecting a value in the Top slicer. In the example in Figure 7-20, there is no relationship between the sort order of the displayed products and the filter (in this case, you see the Products sorted alphabetically).

Top

- 1
- 2
- 3
- 4
- 5
- 6

Row Labels	TopSalesAmount
Chicken	67.43
Fish	79.92
Meat	74.22
Grand Total	**262.57**

FIGURE 7-20 Selecting 3 in the Top slicer displays only the first 3 products by Sales Amount.

Note that this pattern assumes that a BLANK value for the measure hides a product in the report. This assumption could be false—if you select other measures in the same PivotTable or if you use other client tools to browse the data model, a product with BLANK values could be visible anyway.

Download sample workbooks for both Excel 2010 and 2013 on
http://www.daxpatterns.com/parameter-table

Note that you can easily create a corresponding SQL Server Analysis Services Tabular project starting from the Excel 2013 file

CHAPTER 8

Static Segmentation

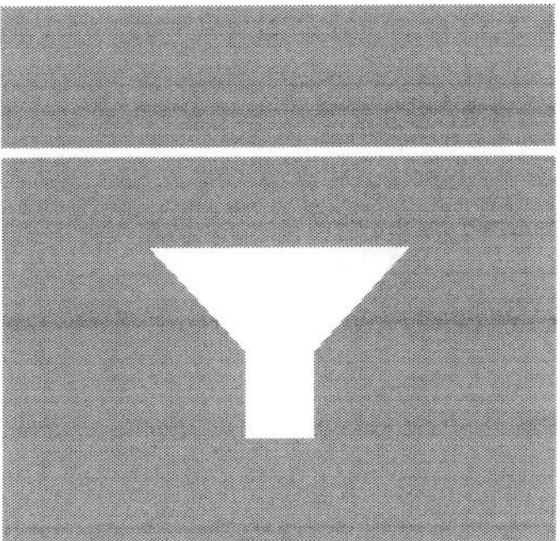

The Static Segmentation pattern groups a continuous numeric value in a finite number of clusters by using a configuration defined in a parameter table (see pattern in Chapter 7). The static segmentation happens in a calculated column that is useful when you want to filter and group data according to the range of values. The parameter table is invisible and used only to control the segmentation algorithm.

You can use a similar approach to control a classification algorithm driven by a separate parameter table. Because the result of the segmentation process is not dynamic (it is stored in a calculated column), this parameter table also is invisible and is used only to avoid storing fixed parameters in DAX expressions. In Chapter 9 you will see the Dynamic Segmentation pattern, which uses measures, not calculated columns, to perform its calculation.

Basic Pattern Example

Suppose you want to slice data by price, grouping price values in ranges that you can customize by changing a configuration table. To do that, you must first create a Ranges table that does not have any relationship with other tables in the data model, as shown in Figure 8-1.

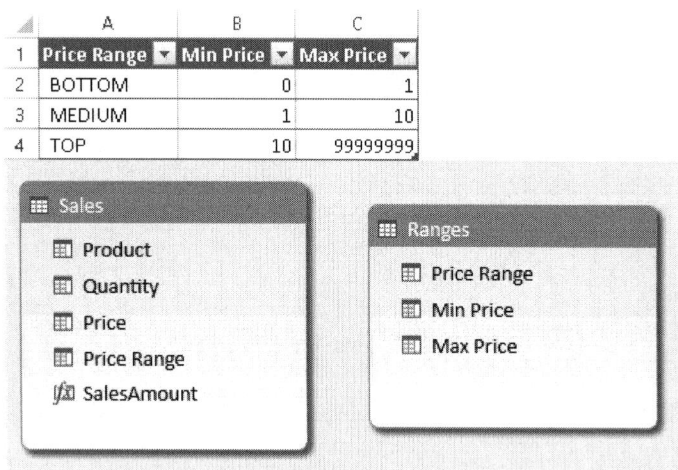

	A	B	C
1	Price Range	Min Price	Max Price
2	BOTTOM	0	1
3	MEDIUM	1	10
4	TOP	10	99999999

FIGURE 8-1 The Ranges table does not have relationships with other tables.

You create a calculated column in the table containing the price you want to segment, as shown in Figure 8-2.

Product	Quantity	Price	Price Range
Snack	300000	1.2	MEDIUM
Snack	800000	0.8	BOTTOM
Beverage	200000	2.5	MEDIUM
Beverage	10000	14.9	TOP
Beverage	590000	3.8	MEDIUM
Snack	500000	1	MEDIUM
Snack	400000	1.2	MEDIUM
Beverage	890000	2.5	MEDIUM

FIGURE 8-2 The Sales table contains a calculated column with the Price Range for every row.

The DAX expression of the Price Range calculated column returns the description of the range to which the current price belongs.

```
[Price Range] =
CALCULATE (
    VALUES ( Ranges[Price Range] ),
    FILTER(
        Ranges,
        Sales[Price] >= Ranges[Min Price]
        && Sales[Price] < Ranges[Max Price]
    )
)
```

You can use calculated column like this as a filter in a PivotTable, as shown in Figure 8-3.

SalesAmount	Column Labels	
Row Labels	Beverage	Snack
BOTTOM		640,000
MEDIUM	4,967,000	1,340,000
TOP	149,000	
Grand Total	**5,116,000**	**1,980,000**

FIGURE 8-3 The range descriptions from the calculated column appear in the rows of the PivotTable.

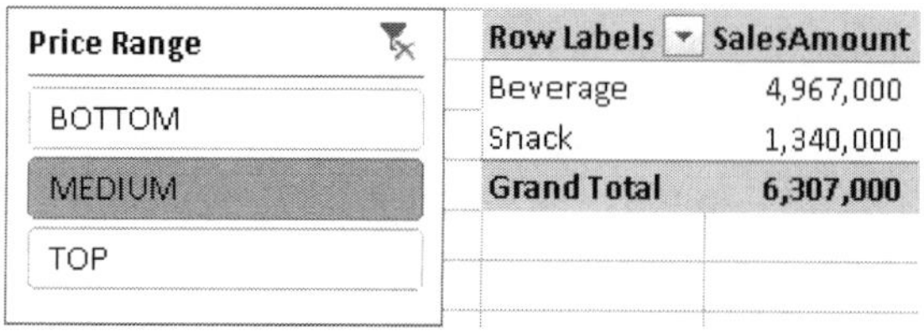

Price Range
BOTTOM
MEDIUM
TOP

Row Labels	SalesAmount
Beverage	4,967,000
Snack	1,340,000
Grand Total	**6,307,000**

FIGURE 8-4 The range descriptions can also be used in a slicer.

The static segmentation pattern is not dynamic because it uses calculated columns. If you want a dynamic behavior based on measures other than columns, use the dynamic pattern described in Chapter 9.

Use Cases

You can use the Static Segmentation pattern any time you need to reduce the number of values in a column in order to group data by a smaller number of elements, using a configuration table to define the number and the boundaries of the groups. Some interesting use cases are shown below.

Classify Items by Attribute Value

You can apply the Static Segmentation pattern to a table that represents an entity, such as Products, Customers, and so on. In a star schema, such a table is called a **dimension table**. A few practical examples are:

- Group Products by Price
- Group Customers by Age
- Group Countries by Population

Group Transactions by Value

You can group transactions according to the value of a column—for example, grouping sales by price. In a star schema, such a table is called a **fact table**. This approach is recommended whenever the values of the columns might be different for every row, regardless of other attributes. For example, if a product can have different prices in different transactions, you will create a calculated column in the Sales table instead of the Products table, because you want to use the transaction price instead of the product list price. A few practical examples are:

- Group Orders by Price
- Group Sales by Gross Margin
- Group Purchases by Discount

Complete Pattern

Add a Segments table to the data model, as shown in Figure 8-5. That table has no relationships with other tables, and usually has at least three columns: the range description and the minimum and maximum values for the range. You might use another column to specify a particular display order by using the Sort By Column property. You should hide the Segments table by using the Hide From Client Tools command on the table (available in either Grid or Diagram view).

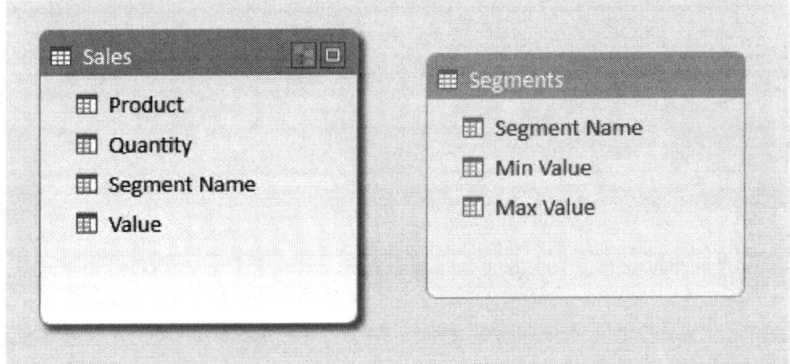

FIGURE 8-5 The Segments table does not have relationships with other tables and is hidden from client tools.

You create a calculated column (Segment Name in the Sales table in Figure 8-5) that evaluates the corresponding segment for each row of the table containing the value to segment (the Value column in this case). You use the VALUES function in the DAX expression of the calculated column that looks for the corresponding range of values in the Segments table.

```
[Segment Name] =
CALCULATE (
    VALUES ( Segments[Segment Name] ),
    FILTER (
        Segments,
        Sales[Value] >= Segments[Min Value]
        && Sales[Value] < Segments[Max Value]
    )
)
```

If you have a misconfigured table with many segments that include the value of one row in the Sales table, you will get a calculation error in the calculated column. The error will propagate to all the rows of the Sales table, regardless of the rows that generate an invalid value. To avoid this runtime error, you can use the IFERROR statement. In the following example, the string returned in case of an error starts with an angle bracket, so that it will display at the beginning of a sorted list, highlighting the presence of an incorrect configuration in the Segments table.

```
[Segment Name] =
IFERROR (
    CALCULATE (
        VALUES ( Segments[Segment Name] ),
        FILTER (
            Segments,
            Sales[Value] >= Segments[Min Value]
            && Sales[Value] < Segments[Max Value]
        )
    ),
    "<config error>"
)
```

If you want to display the segments in a particular sort order, you can create a Segment Position column in the Segments and Sales tables, as shown in Figure 8-6.

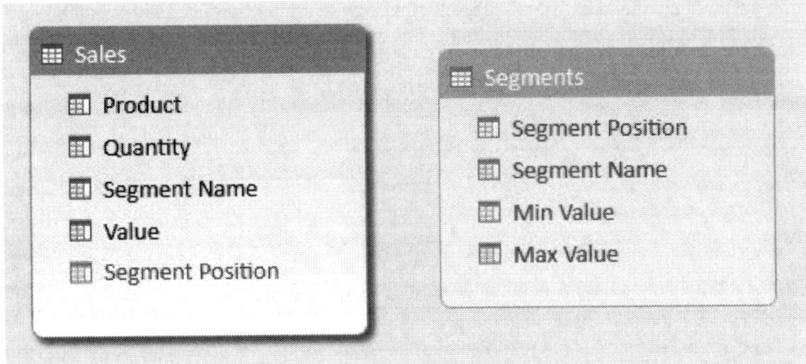

FIGURE 8-6 The Segments table and the Segment Position column in the Sales table are hidden from client tools.

The Segment Position column in the Segments table must have the same cardinality as the Segment Name column.

	A	B	C	D
1	Segment Position	Segment Name	Min Value	Max Value
2	1	LOW	0	1
3	2	MEDIUM	1	10
4	3	HIGH	10	99999999

FIGURE 8-7 The Segment Position value identifies each Segment Name.

You can copy the Segment Position column in the Sales table by using a statement similar to the one you used for Segment Name:

```
[Segment Position] =
IFERROR(
    CALCULATE (
        VALUES ( Segments[Segment Position] ),
        FILTER (
            Segments,
            Sales[Value] >= Segments[Min Value]
            && Sales[Value] < Segments[Max Value]
        )
    ),
    -1
)
```

In case of an error, you return -1, so that the error message will display at the beginning of a sorted list. You might consider using the Segment Position column to create a relationship between the two tables, making the Segment Name visible in the Segments table. However, such a relationship might be expensive in terms of memory usage, so consider this option only if the Segments table has a high number of values (in the order of thousands). Perform some memory size and performance tests before using the relationship.

Download sample workbooks for both Excel 2010 and 2013 on
http://www.daxpatterns.com/static-segmentation

Note that you can easily create a corresponding SQL Server Analysis Services Tabular project starting from the Excel 2013 file

CHAPTER 9

Dynamic Segmentation

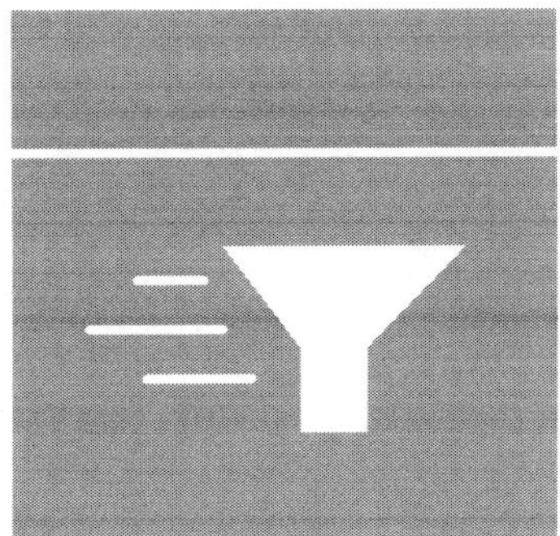

The Dynamic Segmentation pattern alters the calculation of one or more measures by grouping data according to specific conditions, typically range boundaries for a numeric value, defined in a parameter table (see the Parameter Table pattern in Chapter 7). Dynamic segmentation uses the columns of the parameter table to define the clusters. The grouping is dynamically evaluated at query time, considering some or all of the filters applied to other columns in the data model. Thus, the parameter table and its segment name column are visible to the client tools.

If you need to store the result of a segmentation in a calculated column, refer to the Static Segmentation pattern described in Chapter 8.

Basic Pattern Example

Suppose you want to slice data by price, grouping price values in ranges that you can customize by changing a configuration table. Every price can belong to one or more groups. With dynamic segmentation, if the user selects more than one group, you still count each price only once. Thus, the resulting measure is non-additive.

To do that, you first create a Ranges table that does not have any relationship with other tables in the data model. The example in Figure 9-1 shows an overlap between the MEDIUM and TOP price ranges, defined by prices within 10 and 100.

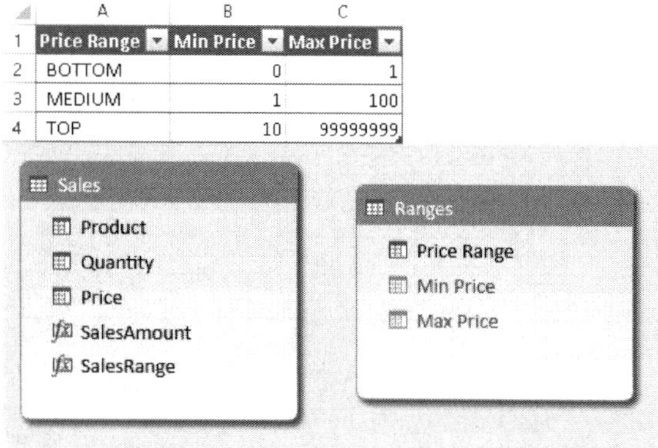

	A	B	C
1	Price Range	Min Price	Max Price
2	BOTTOM	0	1
3	MEDIUM	1	100
4	TOP	10	99999999

FIGURE 9-1 The Ranges table does not have relationships with other tables.

The measures you want to segment have to evaluate only the rows with a price within the selected segments. Thus, assuming that SalesAmount is the original measure, you define the corresponding SalesRange measure that handles segmentation as follows:

```
[SalesRange] :=
CALCULATE (
    [SalesAmount],
    FILTER (
        VALUES ( Sales[Price] ),
        COUNTROWS (
            FILTER(
                Ranges,
                Sales[Price] >= Ranges[Min Price]
                && Sales[Price] < Ranges[Max Price]
            )
        ) > 0
    )
)
```

The SalesRange measure defined in this way handles multiple selection within the Ranges table. However, this calculation may have some performance penalty. You can find a faster calculation that handles only single selections later, in the Complete Pattern section.

You can use such a measure in a PivotTable. For example, Figure 9-2 shows a PivotTable where the TOP segment contains sales in a price (14.90 per unit) that belongs to both MEDIUM and TOP ranges. In the calculation for Grand Total, such sales are considered only once, so the Grand Total corresponds to MEDIUM range.

SalesRange	Column Labels	
Row Labels	Beverage	Snack
BOTTOM		640,000
MEDIUM	5,116,000	1,340,000
TOP	149,000	
Grand Total	5,116,000	1,980,000

FIGURE 9-2 You can use the SalesRange measure in a Pivot Table.

The Dynamic Segmentation pattern can be used in a more complex way by filtering data in an entity table (such as Products or Customers) instead of directly filtering data in the fact table.

Use Cases

You can use the Dynamic Segmentation pattern any time you need to evaluate a measure and group its results dynamically into discrete clusters, using a configuration table to define the number and the boundaries of the groups. With dynamic segmentation, each entity can belong to more than one cluster (this is not possible in static segmentation).

Classify Items by Measure

You can apply the Dynamic Segmentation pattern to a table that represents an entity, such as Products or Customers. In a star schema, usually the entity is stored in a dimension table. But if the entity you want to group (for example, an invoice identifier) is stored in a fact table containing transactions, you can apply the measure to that table. You can use any measure to define the segment ownership of an entity. A few practical examples are:

- Group Products by Sales Amount, by Margin, by Price
- Group Customers by Sales Amount, by Margin, by Age
- Group Countries by Sales Amount, by Margin, by Population
- Group Sales by Invoice Amount

Complete Pattern

Add a Segments table to the data model, as shown in Figure 9-3. That table has no relationships with other tables, and usually has at least three columns: the range description and the minimum and maximum values for the range. You might use another column to specify a particular display order by using the Sort By Column property (in the example, the Segment Name is sorted by Segment Position).

You should hide the Min Value and Max Value columns by using the Hide From Client Tools command on these columns (available in either Grid or Diagram view).

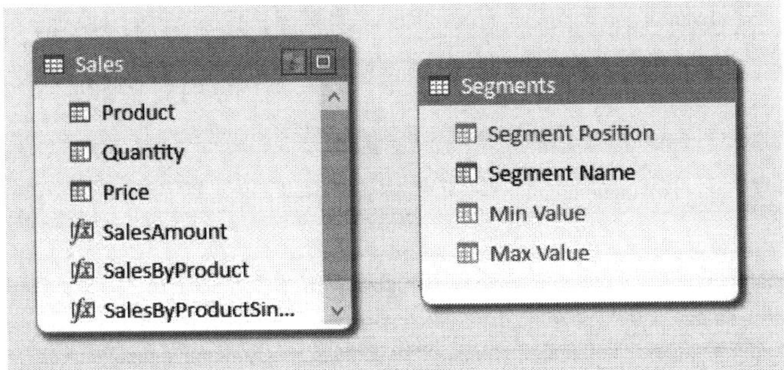

FIGURE 9-3 The Segments table does not have relationships with other tables.

You create a measure (SalesByProduct in the Sales table in Figure 9-3) that evaluates the corresponding segment for each row of the table containing the entity to segment (in this case, you group products by SalesAmount).

```
SalesByProduct :=
IF (
    ISFILTERED ( Segments[Segment Name] ),
    CALCULATE (
        [SalesAmount],
        FILTER (
            VALUES ( Sales[Product] ),
            COUNTROWS (
                FILTER (
                    Segments,
                    [SalesAmount] >= Segments[Min Value]
                    && [SalesAmount] < Segments[Max Value]
                )
            ) > 0
        )
    ),
    [SalesAmount]
)
```

Such a measure evaluates the expression in a CALCULATE function that filters the entities that have to be grouped in the selected segments. The outermost FILTER iterates the list of products, whereas the innermost FILTER iterates the selected segments, checking whether the product falls within the range of at least one segment. In this way, every product can belong to zero, one, or more segments. If a product has a SalesAmount that is not included in any segment, you do not get an error. The outermost IF function checks whether there is a selection active on Segment Name, so that no segmentation will occur if there is no selection over Segments. Thus, the Grand Total in a PivotTable will contain all the data even if there are products that do not belong to any segment.

Handling the multiple selection of segments might slow the calculation, so you might use a faster algorithm that works with only one segment selected and returns BLANK when two or more segments are selected.

```
SalesByProductSingle:=
IF (
    ISFILTERED ( Segments[Segment Name] ),
    IF (
        HASONEVALUE ( Segments[Segment Name] ),
        CALCULATE (
            [SalesAmount],
            FILTER (
                VALUES ( Sales[Product] ),
                [SalesAmount] >= VALUES ( Segments[Min Value]  )
                    && [SalesAmount] < VALUES ( Segments[Max Value]  )
            )
        ),
        BLANK ()
    ),
    [SalesAmount]
)
```

Figure 9-4 shows an example of a Segments table containing segments with non-overlapping ranges for SalesAmount, as specified by the Min Value and Max Value columns.

	A	B	C	D
1	Segment Position	Segment Name	Min Value	Max Value
2	1	LOW	0	500,000
3	2	MEDIUM	500,000	5,000,000
4	3	HIGH	5,000,000	99,999,999

FIGURE 9-4 The Segments table contains three non-overlapping ranges.

You see in Figure 9-5 that the SalesByProduct and SalesByProductSingle measures (as defined above) produce the same result if there is a single selection of segment.

Row Labels	SalesByProduct	SalesByProductSingle
⊟MEDIUM	**1,980,000**	**1,980,000**
Snack	1,980,000	1,980,000
⊟HIGH	**5,116,000**	**5,116,000**
Beverage	5,116,000	5,116,000
Grand Total	**7,096,000**	**7,096,000**

FIGURE 9-5 Each measure shows only products from the related range.

Figure 9-6 shows that with multiple selection of segments, the SalesByProductSingle measure always returns a blank value, whereas the SalesByProduct measure produces a correct result—one that considers the union of selected segments.

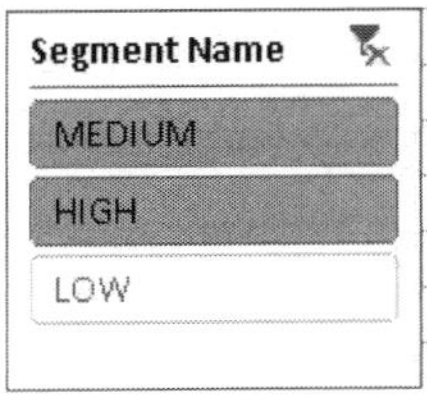

Segment Name

MEDIUM

HIGH

LOW

Row Labels	SalesByProduct	SalesByProductSingle
Beverage	5,116,000	
Snack	1,980,000	
Grand Total	**7,096,000**	

FIGURE 9-6 Multiple selection of segments produces blank results in the SalesByProductSingle measure.

More Pattern Examples

In this section, you will see a few examples of the Dynamic Segmentation pattern.

Dynamically Group Customers by Sales Amount

You can dynamically create groups of customers by using a measure such as SalesAmount. In each query, every customer belongs to just one group; the calculation will apply slicers and filters to measure evaluation but ignore entities put in rows and columns of a PivotTable. For example, Figure 9-7 shows three clusters (LOW, MEDIUM, and HIGH) of customers grouped by the amount of sales of red bikes. The clusters do not consider the product model (in columns), but filter the SalesAmount by using the ProductCategoryName selection in the slicer and the Color selection in the PivotTable filter.

ProductCategoryName: Accessories, Bikes, Clothing, Components, (blank)

Color	Red			
ClusteredSales	**Column Labels**			
Row Labels	**Road-150**	**Road-250**	**Road-650**	**Grand Total**
LOW			$318,257.47	$318,257.47
MEDIUM	$5,353,091.92	$1,640,884.05	$2,880.28	$6,996,856.25
HIGH	$196,804.85	$134,384.25		$331,189.10
Grand Total	**$5,549,896.77**	**$1,775,268.30**	**$321,137.75**	**$7,646,302.82**

FIGURE 9-7 Sales of red bikes segmented by price range.

The Clusters table in Figure 9-8 has no overlaps between ranges, but you can define a Clusters table with overlapping ranges.

Position	Cluster	Min Sales	Max Sales
1	LOW	1	1,000
2	MEDIUM	1,000	5,000
3	HIGH	5,000	99,999,999

FIGURE 9-8 The Clusters table defines three non-overlapping ranges.

The Clusters table has no relationship with other tables in the data model. Figure 9-9 shows the tables imported from Adventure Works, including Products, Customers, and Sales.

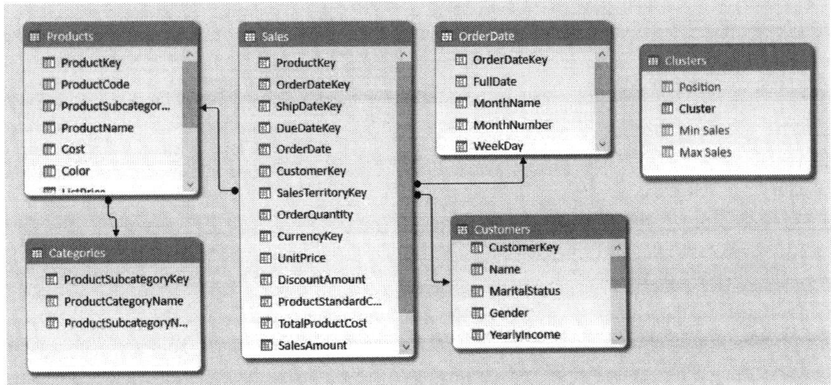

FIGURE 9-9 The Clusters table does not have relationships with other tables in the data model.

In this case, the entity used to define the clusters (Customers) is in a table related to the Sales table, which contains the columns used to compute the measure (SalesAmount). Thus, the ClusteredSales measure that computes the value using the selected clusters has to use a more complex FILTER function inside the CALCULATE function: for each customer, it has to evaluate the sum of SalesAmount applying existing filters and slicers, but removing all the filters defined in rows and columns. The ALLSELECTED function has exactly this purpose. The ClusteredSales measure is shown below.

```
ClusteredSales :=
CALCULATE (
    SUM ( Sales[SalesAmount] ),
    FILTER (
        ADDCOLUMNS (
            Customers,
            "CustomerSales",
            CALCULATE (
                SUM ( Sales[SalesAmount] ),
                CALCULATETABLE ( Customers ),
                ALLSELECTED ()
            )
        ),
        COUNTROWS (
            FILTER (
                'Clusters',
```

```
                [CustomerSales] >= 'Clusters'[Min Sales]
                && [CustomerSales] < 'Clusters'[Max Sales]
            )
        ) > 0
    )
)
```

There is another important note in the previous formula. You have to evaluate the sum of the SalesAmount measure for each customer in the iteration defined by the ADDCOLUMNS function. The CALCULATE statement (passed as an argument to ADDCOLUMNS) transforms the row context (on Customers) into a filter context. However, the presence of ALLSELECTED in the CALCULATE function would remove the filter context (from Customers) obtained by the row context. To restore it, a CALCULATETABLE statement (on Customers) is included in another argument, so that the "current" customer is added to the filter context again. Without this CALCULATETABLE function, the result in Figure 9-7 would have put all the customers in the same cluster (HIGH), considering the total of all the customers for each customer during the iteration made by the ADDCOLUMNS function.

You can see the list of customers belonging to each cluster by putting the customer names in rows under the cluster Name. If you have no overlapping segments, every customer will be included in only one cluster, as you see in Figure 9-10.

ClusteredSales	Column Labels			
Row Labels	Accessories	Bikes	Clothing	Grand Total
⊟LOW				
Aaron Adams	$63.97		$53.99	$117.96
Aaron Alexander			$69.99	$69.99
Aaron Bryant	$74.98		$58.98	$133.96
Zoe Sanders	$4.99			$4.99
Zoe Torres	$14.98			$14.98
Zoe Watson	$64.97		$24.49	$89.46
⊟MEDIUM				
Aaron Allen		$3,399.99		$3,399.99
Aaron Baker		$1,700.99	$49.99	$1,750.98
Aaron Campbell	$34.99	$1,120.49		$1,155.48
Aaron Evans	$48.97	$2,384.07		$2,433.04

FIGURE 9-10 The Clusters table in the example has no overlapping segments, so every customer belongs to only one cluster.

Please note that without the ALLSELECTED function called in the CALCULATE statement for the CustomerSales calculated field, the cluster evaluation would happen cell by cell, and the same customer might belong to several clusters. For example, without ALLSELECTED, the clusters in Figure 9-10 would be computed considering the sales of each product category, which appear on columns, instead of the sales of all the products for each customer, as shown.

Download sample workbooks for both Excel 2010 and 2013 on
http://www.daxpatterns.com/dynamic-segmentation

Note that you can easily create a corresponding SQL Server Analysis Services Tabular project starting from the Excel 2013 file

CHAPTER 10

ABC Classification

The ABC Classification pattern is a specialization of the Static Segmentation pattern (Chapter 8), that implements the ABC analysis in DAX, which is also known as ABC/Pareto analysis, because it is based on the Pareto principle. The resulting ABC class is calculated at process time, so it is static and uses calculated columns to store the result of classification. You can use this pattern to determine the core business of a company, typically in terms of best products or best customers. You can find more information on ABC analysis at http://en.wikipedia.org/wiki/ABC_analysis.

Basic Pattern Example

Suppose you want to analyze the importance of products for the revenues of your company using ABC analysis. You have to assign each product to a class (A, B, or C) for which the following is true:

- Products in class A account for 70 percent of the revenues.
- Products in class B account for 20 percent of the revenues.
- Products in class C account for the remaining 10 percent of the revenues.

In the Products table, you create a calculated column that contains the ABC class to use as a grouping attribute in reports. The Products table has a relationship with the Sales table.

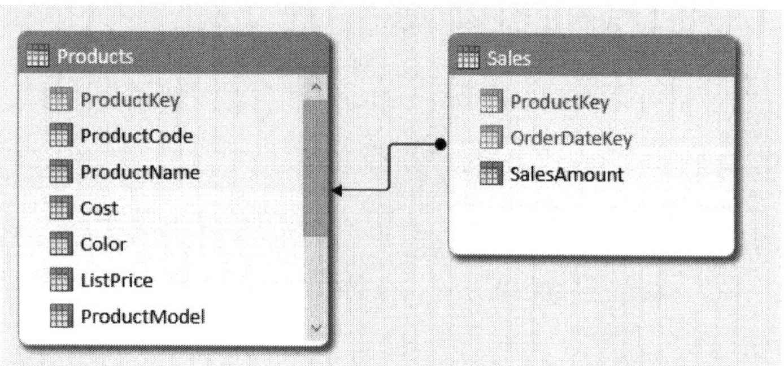

FIGURE 10-1 The Products table has a relationship with the Sales table.

To implement ABC classification, you then create a few more calculated columns in the Products table. All of these columns except ABC Class will be hidden from the client tools:

- **ProductSales:** the total of sales for the product (current row).
- **CumulatedSales:** the total of sales for all the products that sold more than or the same total sales of the product (current row).
- **CumulatedPercentage:** the RunningTotalSales value represented as a percentage of the grand total of sales.
- **ABC Class:** the class of the product, which could be A, B, or C.

You define the calculated columns using the following DAX formulas:

```
[ProductSales] =
CALCULATE ( SUM ( Sales[SalesAmount] ) )

[CumulatedSales] =
CALCULATE (
    SUM ( Products[ProductSales] ),
    ALL ( Products ),
    Products[ProductSales] >= EARLIER ( Products[ProductSales] )
)

[CumulatedPercentage] =
Products[CumulatedSales] / SUM ( Products[ProductSales] )

[ABC Class] =
SWITCH (
    TRUE (),
    Products[CumulatedPercentage] <= 0.7, "A",
    Products[CumulatedPercentage] <= 0.9, "B",
    "C"
)
```

ProductName	ProductSales	CumulatedSales	CumulatedPercentage	ABC Class
Mountain-200 Sil...	$347,998.49	$19,618,580.47	66.82 %	A
Road-250 Black, 44	$346,955.70	$19,965,536.17	68.01 %	A
Mountain-200 Bl...	$340,150.30	$20,305,686.47	69.16 %	A
Touring-1000 Yell...	$333,769.80	$20,639,456.27	70.30 %	B
Road-250 Red, 58	$327,408.90	$20,966,865.17	71.42 %	B
Road-250 Red, 52	$324,965.55	$21,291,830.72	72.52 %	B

FIGURE 10-2 Calculated columns in the Products table implement ABC classification.

You can use the new ABC Class column as a filter in a pivot tables, as shown in Figure 10-3 and Figure 10-4.

Sum of SalesAmount	Column Labels			
Row Labels	A	B	C	Grand Total
Mountain-200	$7,929,475.24			$7,929,475.24
Road-150	$5,549,896.77			$5,549,896.77
Road-250	$2,587,856.70	$1,863,403.43		$4,451,260.13
Touring-1000	$2,658,238.05	$333,769.80		$2,992,007.85
Road-350-W	$1,580,219.71			$1,580,219.71
Road-550-W		$1,157,466.17	$357,156.19	$1,514,622.36
Mountain-100		$1,341,121.04		$1,341,121.04
Road-750		$779,205.57		$779,205.57
Road-650			$645,379.50	$645,379.50
Touring-2000		$353,521.35	$98,402.85	$451,924.20
Mountain-400-W		$220,074.14	$197,758.93	$417,833.07
Touring-3000			$400,869.00	$400,869.00

FIGURE 10-3 Every product model might have sales in classes A, B, and C.

ABC Class

A B C

Row Labels	Sum of SalesAmount
Mountain-200 Black, 46	$1,373,469.55
Mountain-200 Black, 42	$1,363,142.09
Mountain-200 Silver, 38	$1,339,462.79
Mountain-200 Silver, 46	$1,301,100.10
Mountain-200 Black, 38	$1,294,866.14
Mountain-200 Silver, 42	$1,257,434.57
Road-150 Red, 48	$1,205,876.99
Road-150 Red, 62	$1,202,298.72
Road-150 Red, 52	$1,080,637.54
Road-150 Red, 56	$1,055,589.65
Road-150 Red, 44	$1,005,493.87

FIGURE 10-4 The slicer filters only products in class A.

You use the ABC classification to create a static segmentation of entities in a data model. If the entity you want to classify does not have the granularity of a table, you have to use slightly different formulas, as described in the Complete Pattern section.

Use Cases

You can use the ABC Classification pattern whenever you want to focus attention on a smaller number of elements in a set—for example, when you have to allocate limited resources in a more efficient way. The following is a small list of common use cases, but real world applications are countless.

Inventory Management

You can use ABC classification as an inventory categorization technique to help manage stock and reduce overall inventory cost. Items in class A are the most important for the business and you should analyze their value more often, whereas items in class C are less important and items in class B are in an intermediate state. For example, you might increase the stock availability and negotiate for better prices for products in class A, reducing time and resources for items in classes B and C.

The measure used as a target for ABC classification in inventory management might include multiple criteria that consider volume (sales amount), profitability (contribution margin on inventory investment), and velocity (number of times an item is ordered).

Customer Segmentation

You can use ABC classification of customers to calibrate resources allocated for sales and marketing, such as investment on customer retention policies, prioritization of technical support calls, assignment of dedicated account managers, and so on. The measures used as a target for classification are usually revenue and margin.

Marketing Segmentation

You might use ABC classification to segment products for allocating marketing budget used to promote and push product sales. The measures used as a target for classification are usually revenue and margin, whereas the item considered can be the SKU of the product or a group of features (e.g., category, model, color, and so on).

Complete Pattern

You calculate the ABC classification for an entity with the following template, using these markers:

- <granularity_table> is the table that defines the subdivision level of the entities you want to classify. For example, it could be the Products table if you want to classify products.
- <granularity_attribute> is an attribute you want to use as a classification target (something that groups entities into a smaller number of elements). For example, it could be Products[ProductModel], the ProductModel column of the Products table.
- <measure> is the value to compute for each entity <granularity_table> for ABC classification.

```
[EntityMeasure] =
CALCULATE ( <measure> )

[CumulatedPercentage] =
CALCULATE (
    <measure>,
    ALL ( <granularity_table> ),
    <granularity_table>[EntityMeasure]
        >= EARLIER ( <granularity_table>[EntityMeasure] )
)
    / CALCULATE ( <measure>, ALL ( <granularity_table> ) )

[ABC Class] =
SWITCH (
    TRUE (),
    <granularity_table>[CumulatedPercentage] <= 0.7, "A",
    <granularity_table>[CumulatedPercentage] <= 0.9, "B",
    "C"
)
```

For example, you would implement the ABC Product calculated column in a model with Products and Sales tables as follows:

```
[ProductSales] =
CALCULATE ( [Sales Amount] )

[ProductPercentage] =
CALCULATE (
    [Sales Amount],
    ALL ( Products ),
    Products[ProductSales] >= EARLIER ( Products[ProductSales] )
)
    / CALCULATE ( [Sales Amount], ALL ( Products ) )

[ABC Product] =
SWITCH (
    TRUE (),
    Products[ProductPercentage] <= 0.7, "A",
    Products[ProductPercentage] <= 0.9, "B",
    "C"
)
```

ProductName	ProductModel	ProductSales	ProductPercentage	ABC Product
Mountain-200 Sil...	Mountain-200	$347,998.49	66.82 %	A
Road-250 Black, 44	Road-250	$346,955.70	68.01 %	A
Mountain-200 Bl...	Mountain-200	$340,150.30	69.16 %	A
Touring-1000 Yell...	Touring-1000	$333,769.80	70.30 %	B
Road-250 Red, 58	Road-250	$327,408.90	71.42 %	B
Road-250 Red, 52	Road-250	$324,965.55	72.52 %	B

FIGURE 10-5 The ABC Product column evaluates each row in the Products table.

If you want to calculate the ABC classification for an attribute of the entity, you use a slightly different template only for the EntityMeasure calculated column:

```
[EntityMeasure] =
CALCULATE (
    <measure>,
    ALL ( <granularity_table> ),
    <granularity_table>[<granularity_attribute>]
        = EARLIER( <granularity_table>[<granularity_attribute>] )
)
```

For example, you implement the ABC Model calculated column in the same model with Products and Sales tables as follows:

```
[ModelSales] =
CALCULATE (
    [Sales Amount],
    ALL ( Products ),
    Products[ProductModel] = EARLIER ( Products[ProductModel] )
)

[ModelPercentage] =
CALCULATE (
    [Sales Amount],
    ALL ( Products ),
    Products[ModelSales] >= EARLIER ( Products[ModelSales] )
)
    / CALCULATE ( [Sales Amount], ALL ( Products ) )

[ABC Model] =
SWITCH (
    TRUE (),
    Products[ModelPercentage] <= 0.7, "A",
    Products[ModelPercentage] <= 0.9, "B",
    "C"
)
```

All the products belonging to the same model share the same ABC Model classification.

ProductName	ProductModel	ModelSales	ModelPercentage	ABC Model
Road-250 Red, 52	Road-250	$4,451,260.13	61.07%	A
Road-250 Red, 48	Road-250	$4,451,260.13	61.07%	A
Road-250 Red, 44	Road-250	$4,451,260.13	61.07%	A
Touring-1000 Blu...	Touring-1000	$2,992,007.85	71.27%	B
Touring-1000 Blu...	Touring-1000	$2,992,007.85	71.27%	B
Touring-1000 Blu...	Touring-1000	$2,992,007.85	71.27%	B

FIGURE 10-6 The ABC Model column calculates the same value for all the products of the same model.

To use ABC classification on a single denormalized table, you must slightly change the EntityMeasure definition as follows:

```
[EntityMeasure] =
CALCULATE (
    <measure>,
    ALLEXCEPT ( <granularity_table>, <granularity_table>[<granularity_attribute>] )
)
```

For example, you would implement ABC Product and ABC Model calculated columns in a model with a single denormalized Sales table as follows:

```
[ProductSales] =
CALCULATE (
    [Sales Amount],
    ALLEXCEPT ( Sales, Sales[Product] )
)

[ProductPercentage] =
CALCULATE (
    [Sales Amount],
    ALL ( Sales ),
    Sales[ProductSales]
        >= EARLIER ( Sales[ProductSales] )
)
    / CALCULATE ( [Sales Amount], ALL ( Sales ) )

[ABC Product] =
SWITCH (
    TRUE,
    Sales[ProductPercentage] <= 0.7, "A",
    Sales[ProductPercentage] <= 0.9, "B",
    "C"
)
```

```
[ModelSales] =
CALCULATE (
    [Sales Amount],
    ALLEXCEPT ( Sales, Sales[Model] )
)

[ModelPercentage] =
CALCULATE (
    [Sales Amount],
    ALL ( Sales ),
    Sales[ModelSales]
        >= EARLIER ( Sales[ModelSales] )
)
    / CALCULATE ( [Sales Amount], ALL ( Sales ) )

[ABC Model] =
SWITCH (
    TRUE (),
    Products[ModelPercentage] <= 0.7, "A",
    Products[ModelPercentage] <= 0.9, "B",
    "C"
)
```

OrderDate	Product	Model	Amount	ProductSales	ProductPercentage	ABC Product
7/1/2001	Road-650 Red, 44	Road-650	2,097.29	912,943.77	64.42 %	A
7/1/2001	Road-650 Black, 58	Road-650	1,258.38	845,779.55	69.65 %	A
7/1/2001	Road-650 Black, 44	Road-650	838.92	485,223.99	78.74 %	B
7/1/2001	Road-150 Red, 56	Road-150	2,146.96	1,475,678.55	33.59 %	A
7/1/2001	Road-450 Red, 44	Road-450	874.79	302,678.72	85.80 %	B

FIGURE 10-7 The ABC Product column implemented in a single denormalized table.

OrderDate	Product	Model	Amount	ModelSales	ModelPercentage	ABC Model
7/1/2001	AWC Logo Cap	Cycling Cap	20.75	43,075.52	99.10 %	C
7/1/2001	Long-Sleeve Logo Jers...	Long-Sleev...	115.36	402,516.81	95.01 %	C
7/1/2001	HL Mountain Frame - ...	HL Mountai...	1,445.19	3,365,069.27	77.17%	B
7/1/2001	Mountain-100 Black, 38	Mountain-100	6,074.98	9,432,630.72	42.89 %	A
7/1/2001	Mountain-100 Black, 48	Mountain-100	4,049.99	9,432,630.72	42.89 %	A

FIGURE 10-8 The ABC Model column implemented in a single denormalized table.

Download sample workbooks for both Excel 2010 and 2013 on
http://www.daxpatterns.com/abc-classification

Note that you can easily create a corresponding SQL Server Analysis Services Tabular project starting from the Excel 2013 file

CHAPTER 11

Handling Different Granularities

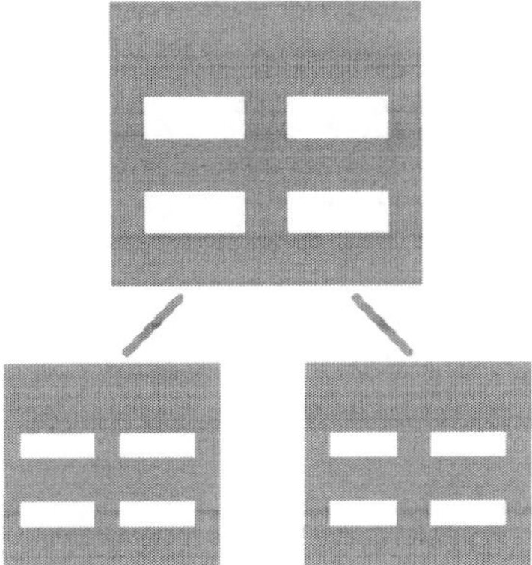

The Handling Different Granularities pattern is a technique to show and hide measures depending on the level of granularity of the underlying data. For example, you do not want to display a measure at the day level if it is a total for the month.

Basic Pattern Example

Suppose you have sales data at the day level and advertising expenses at the month level. The data source assigns the entire month's advertising cost to the first day of each month, as shown in Figure 11-1.

Date	SalesAmount
1/1/2014	100
1/15/2014	90
1/29/2014	85
2/12/2014	120
2/26/2014	110
3/12/2014	105
3/26/2014	106
4/9/2014	98
4/23/2014	114
5/7/2014	83
5/21/2014	102
6/4/2014	95
6/18/2014	100
7/2/2014	90

Date	AdvertisingAmount
1/1/2014	20
2/1/2014	20
3/1/2014	20
4/1/2014	20
5/1/2014	15
6/1/2014	15
7/1/2014	15
8/1/2014	15
9/1/2014	20
10/1/2014	20
11/1/2014	20
12/1/2014	20

FIGURE 11-1 The Sales table has a daily granularity; the Advertising table has a month granularity.

You have a common referenced Date table, based on the Date column. However, you do not want to display the sum of AdvertisingAmount at the day level, because this would produce the result in Figure 11-2. Such a display would suggest that the advertising happens only the first day of each month. You want to see the value of advertisements only at the month level, not at the day level.

Row Labels	Sum of SalesAmount	Sum of AdvertisingAmount
2014	**2,701**	**220**
January	**275**	**20**
1/1/2014	100	20
1/15/2014	90	
1/29/2014	85	
February	**230**	**20**
2/1/2014		20
2/12/2014	120	
2/26/2014	110	
March	**211**	**20**
April	**212**	**20**

FIGURE 11-2 When the Sum of AdvertisingAmount is displayed at the day level, it appears on the first day of each month.

You can create a measure that hides the value when there is a filter or selection at the day granularity level.

```
[Total Advertising] :=
IF (
    NOT ( ISFILTERED ( 'Date'[Date] ) ),
    SUM ( Advertising[AdvertisingAmount] )
)
```

The ISFILTERED function returns true if there is a filter active on the column specified in the argument. The Date table used in this example has only Year, Month, and Date columns. If you have other day columns, such as Day Number or Week Day Name, you should check whether a filter is active on these columns, too.

By using the Total Advertising measure, you do not show the value of advertising at the day level, as shown in Figure 11-3.

Row Labels	Total Sales	Total Advertising	Advertising %
2014	**2,701**	**220**	**8.15 %**
January	**275**	**20**	**7.27 %**
1/1/2014	100		
1/15/2014	90		
1/29/2014	85		
February	**230**	**20**	**8.70 %**
2/12/2014	120		
2/26/2014	110		
March	**211**	**20**	**9.48 %**
April	[illegible]	[illegible]	[illegible]

FIGURE 11-3 The Total Advertising measure is visible only at the month and year level.

You use this technique whenever you want to show a calculation only at a valid granularity level.

Use Cases

You can use the Handling Different Granularities pattern whenever you want to hide a measure or the result of an expression, based on the current selection. For example, if you defined the budget at the month level, and you do not have an algorithm that allocates the monthly budget at the day level, you can hide the difference between sales and budget at the day level.

Compare Budget and Revenues

When you have a budget to compare with data, and the budget table does not have the same granularity as the other measures, you must accommodate the different granularities. This is common for time periods: the sales budget may be defined at the month or quarter level, whereas revenues are available at the day level. It happens also for other attributes, such as the product: the budget may be defined at the product category level, but not at the unit (SKU) level. Moreover, you probably have other attributes, such as the customer or the payment type, for which you do not have a budget definition at all.

You should hide measures that compare budget and revenues if the granularity is not available for both measures. For example, you should not display a key performance indicator (KPI) that shows the revenues vs. the planned goal if the user browsing data selects a single product (or day) but the budget is available only at the product category (or month) level. The Handling Different Granularities pattern helps you to implement this control. If you want to allocate the budget for higher granularities, you should consider the Budget pattern.

Compare Sales and Purchases

When you compare sales and purchases in the same data model, you probably have a different set of attributes for these measures. When certain attributes are selected, you cannot calculate a measure that evaluates the differences between cost and revenues. For example, you probably know the customer for the sales and the vendor for the purchases. If a report contains a selection of one or more customers, you might not be able to evaluate how much of the purchases are related to those sales. Thus, you hide the measure that compares sales and purchases if a selection is active on a customer or on a vendor.

Complete Pattern

You have to handle data at different granularities when at least two tables contain different levels of stored information. For example, Figure 11-4 shows one table with SalesAmount recorded at the day level, whereas AdvertisingAmount is in another table with one value for each month.

Date	SalesAmount
1/1/2014	100
1/15/2014	90
1/29/2014	85
2/12/2014	120
2/26/2014	110
3/12/2014	105
3/26/2014	106
4/9/2014	98
4/23/2014	114
5/7/2014	83
5/21/2014	102
6/4/2014	95
6/18/2014	100

Year	Month	AdvertisingAmount
2014	1	20
2014	2	20
2014	3	20
2014	4	20
2014	5	15
2014	6	15
2014	7	15
2014	8	15
2014	9	20
2014	10	20
2014	11	20
2014	12	20

FIGURE 11-4 The Sales table has data at the day level; the Advertising table has data at the month level.

If you import these tables in a data model and try to link them to a common Date table, it will not work. In fact, as you see in Figure 11-5, the Advertising table does not have a Date column available to create the relationship with the Date table.

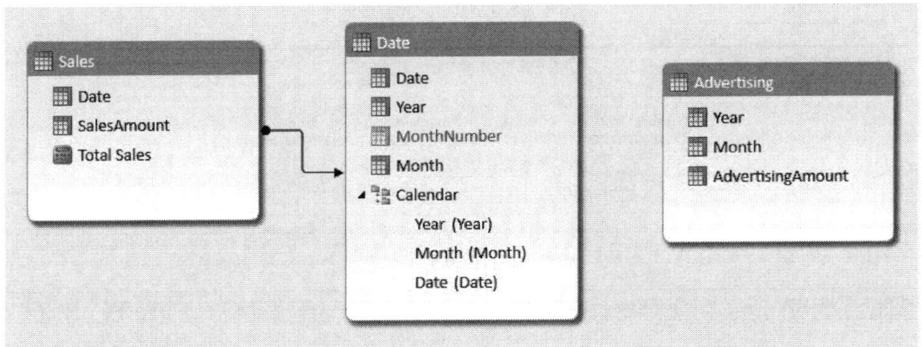

FIGURE 11-5 The Advertising table does not have a Date column to create a relationship with the Date table.

You can solve the problem by creating a fictitious date that allows you to define the missing relationship. Such a date could be the first day of the corresponding month. You define the calculated column Date in the Advertising table with the following formula. You can see the result in Figure 11-6.

```
[Date] =
DATE ( Advertising[Year], Advertising[Month], 1 )
```

AdvertisingAmount	Year	Month	Date
20	2014	1	1/1/2014
20	2014	2	2/1/2014
20	2014	3	3/1/2014
20	2014	4	4/1/2014
15	2014	5	5/1/2014
15	2014	6	6/1/2014

FIGURE 11-6 The Date column in the Advertising table corresponds to the first day of the month.

Once you have the Date column, you can create the relationship between Advertising and Date, as you see in Figure 11-7.

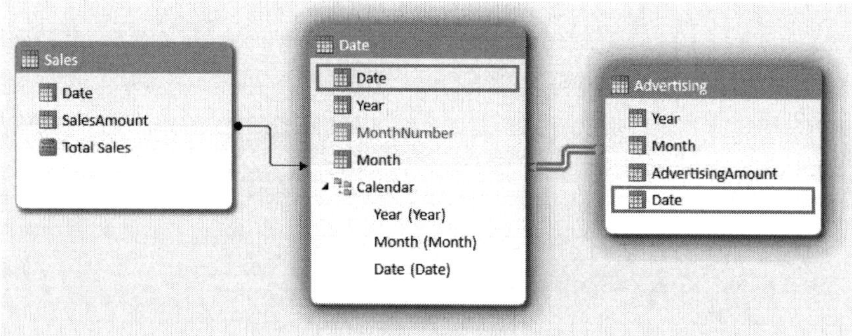

FIGURE 11-7 The relationship between Advertising and Date tables uses the Date calculated column.

Since the Date you created is not a real one, when browsing data you should hide any measure derived from the Advertising table if the evaluation happens at the day level. The only valid levels are Month and Year. Thus, you have to define the Total Advertising measure by checking whether the Date column is filtered in the Date table or not:

```
[Total Advertising] :=
IF (
    NOT ( ISFILTERED ( 'Date'[Date] ) ),
    SUM ( Advertising[AdvertisingAmount] )
)
```

In case there was a WeekDay column or a MonthDayNumber in the Date table, you should include these columns in the test, as in the following example:

```
[Total Advertising] :=
IF (
    NOT (
        ISFILTERED ( 'Date'[Date] )
        || ISFILTERED ( 'Date'[WeekDay] )
        || ISFILTERED ( 'Date'[MonthDayNumber] )
    ),
    SUM ( Advertising[AdvertisingAmount] )
)
```

As a general pattern, you apply the following template to return a blank value when the current selection is not valid for the granularity of a measure, using these markers:

- <unchecked measure> is the original measure, which ignores the granularity of the query.
- <invalid_granularity_column_N> is a column that has more detail (higher granularity) than the one available for the <unchecked measure>.

```
[Checked Measure] :=
IF (
    NOT (
        ISFILTERED ( <invalid_granularity_column_1> )
        || ISFILTERED ( <invalid_granularity_column_2> )
        ...
        || ISFILTERED ( <invalid_granularity_column_N> )
    ),
    <unchecked measure>
)
```

Once you have created a checked measure, other calculations based on that measure might avoid duplicating the test on granularity, as soon as the blank propagates into the result in the DAX expression used. For example, the Advertising% measure can be defined in this way, and returns blank when the Total Advertising is blank, as you see in Figure 11-8.

```
Advertising % := DIVIDE ( [Total Advertising], [Total Sales] )
```

Row Labels	Total Sales	Total Advertising	Advertising %
⊟2014	2,701	220	8.15 %
⊟January	275	20	7.27 %
1/1/2014	100		
1/15/2014	90		
1/29/2014	85		
⊟February	230	20	8.70 %
2/12/2014	120		
2/26/2014	110		
⊞March	211	20	9.48 %
⊞April	212	20	9.43 %
⊞May	185	15	8.11 %
⊞June	195	15	7.69 %
⊞July	295	15	5.08 %
⊞August	215	15	6.98 %
⊞September	204	20	9.80 %
⊞October	197	20	10.15 %
⊞November	197	20	10.15 %
⊞December	285	20	7.02 %
Grand Total	2,701	220	8.15 %

FIGURE 11-8 The Advertising% and Total Advertising measures display blank at the day granularity level.

More Pattern Examples

This section demonstrates how to handle different granularities without a relationship between tables.

Simulate a Relationship at Different Granularities

You can use DAX to filter data as if a relationship exists between two tables, even if there is no relationship between them in the data model. This is useful whenever a logical relationship does not correspond to a physical one.

The data model you use in DAX allows you to create relationships using only one column, which needs to be the key of the lookup table. When you have data at different granularities, you also have a logical relationship that would involve a hierarchical level not corresponding to the key of the lookup table. For instance, in the previous example of the pattern, you assign a specific date for a measure that has a month granularity (e.g., Advertising), and in order to display data in the correct way, you hide the measure when the user browses data at a day level instead of a month level. An alternative approach is to write a DAX measure that "simulates" a relationship between Advertising and Date tables at the month level.

The scenario is the same as was in Figure 11-5: the Advertising table cannot have a relationship with the Date table. This time, you do not create a fictitious Date column to create the relationship. Instead, you create a YearMonth column in both Date and Advertising table, so that you have a column representing the granularity of the logical relationship between the tables. You use a single column to simplify the required DAX code and improve performance.

You define the YearMonth calculated column in the Advertising and Date tables as follows. The resulting Advertising table is shown in Figure 11-9.

```
Advertising[YearMonth] = Advertising[Year] * 100 + Advertising[Month]

'Date'[YearMonth] = 'Date'[Year] * 100 + 'Date'[MonthNumber]
```

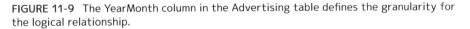

AdvertisingAmount	Year	Month	YearMonth
20	2014	1	201401
20	2014	2	201402
20	2014	3	201403
20	2014	4	201404
15	2014	5	201405
15	2014	6	201406

FIGURE 11-9 The YearMonth column in the Advertising table defines the granularity for the logical relationship.

The YearMonth column exists in the Date and Advertising tables, but a physical relationship is not possible because you might have many rows with the same value in both tables. You might create a third table having YearMonth granularity, but this could be confusing for the user and would not help the calculation much. The resulting data model is the one shown in Figure 11-10.

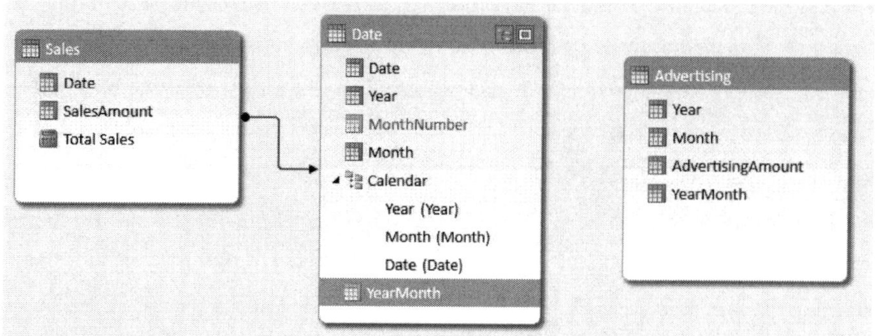

FIGURE 11-10 The logical relationship between Date and Advertising using YearMonth cannot be a physical one.

The Total Advertising measure has to filter the sum of AdvertisingAmount using a CALCULATE function. You pass a filter argument with the list of YearMonth values that have to be included in the calculation, and you implement this using a FILTER that iterates all the YearMonth values in the Advertising table, keeping only those with at least a corresponding value in Date[YearMonth] that is active in the current filter context.

```
[Total Advertising] :=
IF (
    NOT ( ISFILTERED ( 'Date'[Date] ) ),
    CALCULATE (
        SUM ( Advertising[AdvertisingAmount] ),
        FILTER (
            ALL ( Advertising[YearMonth] ),
            CONTAINS  (
                VALUES ( 'Date'[YearMonth] ),
                'Date'[YearMonth],
                Advertising[YearMonth]
            )
        )
    )
)
```

When you browse the data, the result is the same as shown in Figure 11-8.

In general, you apply the following template to return a measure filtered by applying a logical relationship through columns that are not keys in any of the tables involved, using these markers:

- <target_measure> is the measure defined in the target table.
- <target_granularity_column> is the column that defines the logical relationship in the table that contains rows that should be filtered by the relationship.
- <lookup_granularity_column> is the column that defines the logical relationship in the lookup table, which should propagate the filter to the target table.

```
[Filtered Measure] :=
CALCULATE (
    <target_measure>,
    FILTER (
        ALL ( <target_granularity_column> ),
            CONTAINS (
                VALUES ( <lookup_granularity_column> ),
                <lookup_granularity_column>,
                <target_granularity_column>
            )
        )
    )
)
```

If you have many logical relationships, you pass one FILTER argument to CALCULATE for each relationship.

```
[Filtered Measure] :=
CALCULATE (
    <target_measure>,
    FILTER (
        ALL ( <target_granularity_column_1> ),
            CONTAINS (
                VALUES ( <lookup_granularity_column_1> ),
                <lookup_granularity_column_1>,
                <target_granularity_column_1>
```

```
            )
        )
    ),
    ...


  FILTER (
          ALL ( <target_granularity_column_N> ),
              CONTAINS  (
                  VALUES ( <lookup_granularity_column_N > ),
                  <lookup_granularity_column_N >,
                  <target_granularity_column_N >
              )
          )
      )
  )
```

In the Total Advertising measure, you keep the initial IF statement that checks whether to display the data at the current selected granularity or not. If you omit this control, the value would be propagated to other granularities (e.g., you would see the monthly Advertising value repeated for all the days in the month).

Download sample workbooks for both Excel 2010 and 2013 on
http://www.daxpatterns.com/handling-different-granularities

Note that you can easily create a corresponding SQL Server Analysis Services Tabular project starting from the Excel 2013 file

CHAPTER 12

Budget Patterns

The budget patterns are techniques you use to compare budget information with other data. They are an extension of the handling of different granularities and, as such, use allocation algorithms to display the budget at granularities for which it is not available.

Basic Pattern Example

Suppose you have sales data at the day and product level, and the budget for each product at the year level, as shown in Figure 12-1.

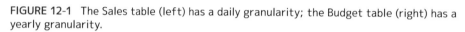

Date	Product	SalesAmount
1/1/2014	Bike	100
1/1/2014	Shirt	11
1/15/2014	Bike	90
1/15/2014	Shirt	8
1/29/2014	Bike	85
1/29/2014	Shirt	6
2/12/2014	Bike	120
2/12/2014	Shirt	5

Year	Product	BudgetAmount
2014	Bike	2,500
2014	Shirt	270

FIGURE 12-1 The Sales table (left) has a daily granularity; the Budget table (right) has a yearly granularity.

In the data model, both Sales and Budget tables reference the Products table through a relationship, because the product granularity is common to both Sales and Budget. Only the Sales table, however, references the Date table, because the Budget table cannot have a relationship using the Year column. Even if a "logical" relationship exists between Budget and Date at the year level, such a relationship does not exist as a physical one in the data model, as you see in Figure 12-2. The Date table also contains a WorkingDay flag, which is TRUE only for working days.

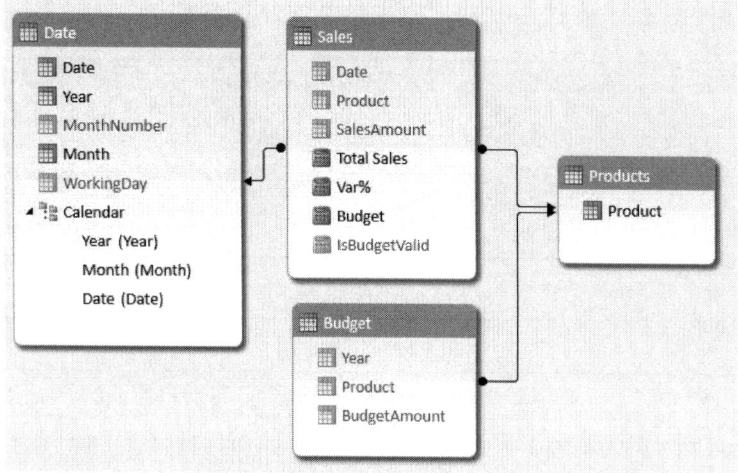

FIGURE 12-2 The Budget table does not have a physical relationship with the Date table.

The Total Sales measure is a simple sum of the SalesAmount column in the Sales table.

```
[Total Sales] :=
SUM ( Sales[SalesAmount] )
```

You define the measures related to the budget in the Sales table, hiding the Budget table from the client tools. In this way, you will not have a warning about a missing relationship in the data model while browsing data.

Using the DAX function ISFILTERED, you check whether the current filter on Date has the same year granularity of the budget or if it has a higher granularity. When the granularity is different, the measure IsBudgetValid returns FALSE, and you need to allocate the budget on months or days.

```
[IsBudgetValid] :=
NOT (
    ISFILTERED ( 'Date'[Date] )
        || ISFILTERED ( 'Date'[Month] )
        || ISFILTERED ( 'Date'[MonthNumber] )
)
```

The Budget measure returns the sum of BudgetAmount if the budget granularity is compatible with the budget definition. If the granularity is different, then you must compute the budget using an allocation algorithm, which depends on business requirements. In this example, you allocate the same budget for each working day in the year. For each year, you calculate the ratio between the working days in the current filter and the total working days in the year. The SUMX function iterates over the years selected, and for each year retrieves the corresponding budget using a FILTER that simulates the relationship at the year granularity.

```
[Budget] :=
IF (
    [IsBudgetValid],
    SUM ( Budget[BudgetAmount] ),
    SUMX (
        VALUES ( 'Date'[Year] ),
        CALCULATE (
```

```
                COUNTROWS ( 'Date' ),
                'Date'[WorkingDay] = TRUE
            )
                / CALCULATE (
                    COUNTROWS ( 'Date' ),
                    ALLEXCEPT ( 'Date', 'Date'[Year] ),
                    'Date'[WorkingDay] = TRUE
                )
                * CALCULATE (
                    SUM ( Budget[BudgetAmount] ),
                    FILTER ( ALL ( Budget[Year] ), Budget[Year] = 'Date'[Year] )
                )
        )
    )
```

The variance between Total Sales and Budget is a trivial measure. Using DIVIDE, you avoid the division by zero error in case the budget is not available.

```
[Var%] :=
DIVIDE ( [Total Sales] - [Budget], [Budget] )
```

You can see the results of the Total Sales, Budget, and Var% measures in Figure 12-3. You split the budget by month according to the number of working days in each month.

	Column Labels					
	Bike			Shirt		
Row Labels	Total Sales	Budget	Var%	Total Sales	Budget	Var%
2014	2,701	2,500.00	8.04 %	249	270.00	-7.78 %
January	275	220.31	24.83 %	25	23.79	5.07 %
February	230	191.57	20.06 %	17	20.69	-17.83 %
March	211	201.15	4.90 %	11	21.72	-49.37 %
April	212	210.73	0.60 %	23	22.76	1.06 %
May	185	210.73	-12.21 %	5	22.76	-78.03 %
June	195	201.15	-3.06 %	20	21.72	-7.94 %
July	295	220.31	33.90 %	27	23.79	13.48 %
August	215	201.15	6.89 %	15	21.72	-30.95 %
September	204	210.73	-3.19 %	23	22.76	1.06 %
October	197	220.31	-10.58 %	29	23.79	21.88 %
November	197	191.57	2.83 %	24	20.69	16.00 %
December	285	220.31	29.37 %	30	23.79	26.09 %
Grand Total	2,701	2,500.00	8.04 %	249	270.00	-7.78 %

FIGURE 12-3 The yearly advertising budget has been distributed by month.

You use this technique whenever you want to allocate a budget to a different granularity. If more tables are involved in the allocation, you will need to use a more complex pattern, as you will see in the Complete Pattern section.

Use Cases

You can use the budget patterns whenever you have a table with data of one granularity and you want to allocate numbers to a different granularity, based on an allocation algorithm that meets your business requirements.

Fixed Allocation of Budget over Time

If you want to evenly split a yearly budget into a monthly budget, you use a fixed allocation. For example, you divide the year value by 12 in order to obtain the monthly value, or you divide the year value by 365 (or 366 for leap years) and then multiply the result by the number of days in each month. In either case, you have an allocation that is deterministic and depends only on the calendar.

Budget Allocation Based on Historical Data

You might want to use historical data to allocate the budget over attributes that are not available as levels of the budget. For example, if you have a budget defined by product category, you can allocate the budget by product according to the ratio of sales between each product and the corresponding product category for the previous year. You can allocate the budget for multiple attributes at the same time—for example, also for the date, to obtain a seasonal allocation based on previous sales.

Complete Pattern

The Budget table and the measure it is being compared to may define data at different granularity levels. For example, the budget shown in Figure 12-4 is defined by product category and month/year, whereas the sales quantity is available by day, product, and territory. The budget does not include the territory at all.

Category	Year	Month	Budget
Accessories	2014	1	175
Accessories	2014	2	150
Accessories	2014	3	185
Accessories	2014	4	180
Accessories	2014	5	190
Accessories	2014	6	195
Accessories	2014	7	160
Accessories	2014	8	160
Accessories	2014	9	125
Accessories	2014	10	125
Accessories	2014	11	150
Accessories	2014	12	175
Bikes	2014	1	25
Bikes	2014	2	25
Bikes	2014	3	25
Bikes	2014	4	25
Bikes	2014	5	25
Bikes	2014	6	30
Bikes	2014	7	30
Bikes	2014	8	30
Bikes	2014	9	30
Bikes	2014	10	30
Bikes	2014	11	30
Bikes	2014	12	30

FIGURE 12-4 The Budget table has a granularity of product category and month/year.

The data model contains a Sales table with relationships to Date, Territory, and Product tables. As you see in Figure 12-5, the Budget table does not have any physical relationships, even though it has a logical relationship with Date (at the Month level) and Product (at the Category level).

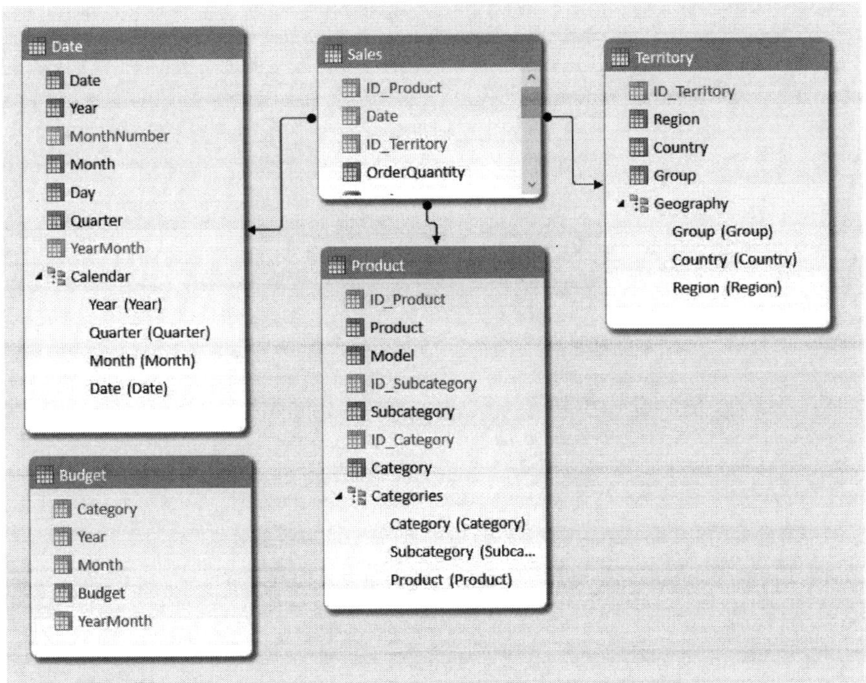

FIGURE 12-5 The Budget table does not have relationships with other tables.

You need a single column in the Budget table for each logical relationship it has in the data model. For example, you need a single column to simplify calculation of the logical relationship between the Budget and Date tables. If you define a YearMonth calculated column in the Date table using Year and MonthNumber with the following formula, you will have a unique value for each year and month, as shown in Figure 12-6.

```
'Date'[YearMonth] =
'Date'[Year] * 100 + 'Date'[MonthNumber]
```

Date	Year	MonthNumber	Month	Day	Quarter	YearMonth
1/30/2013	2013	1	January	30	Q1	201301
1/31/2013	2013	1	January	31	Q1	201301
2/1/2013	2013	2	February	1	Q1	201302
2/2/2013	2013	2	February	2	Q1	201302
2/3/2013	2013	2	February	3	Q1	201302
2/4/2013	2013	2	February	4	Q1	201302

FIGURE 12-6 The YearMonth column in the Date table defines a logical relationship with the same granularity as the Budget table.

If you also define the same YearMonth column in the Budget table with the following formula, you see the result in Figure 12-7.

```
Budget[YearMonth] =
Budget[Year] * 100 + Budget[Month]
```

Category	Year	Month	Budget	YearMonth
Accessories	2014	1	175	201401
Accessories	2014	2	150	201402
Accessories	2014	3	185	201403
Accessories	2014	4	180	201404
Accessories	2014	5	190	201405
Accessories	2014	6	195	201406
Accessories	2014	7	160	201407

FIGURE 12-7 The YearMonth column in the Budget table defines the time granularity of the budget.

The Budget measure is calculated differently, depending on the granularity of the existing filter. You only need to apply budget allocation (AllocatedBudget) if the query requests a higher granularity than the one available in the budget definition; otherwise you can use a simpler (and faster) formula (BudgetCalc). You split the Budget calculation using other hidden measures, whereas Quantity and Var% are visible and simpler to define.

```
[Quantity] :=
SUM ( Sales[OrderQuantity] )

[Budget] :=
IF (
    [IsBudgetValid],
    [BudgetCalc],
    [AllocatedBudget]
)

[Var%] :=
DIVIDE ( [Quantity] - [Budget], [Budget] )
```

You can check whether the current filter has a granularity corresponding to the one available in the Budget table by counting the number of rows in the Sales table in two conditions: with the current filter context and by removing the filters on granularities that are not available in the budget itself. If the two numbers are different, than the budget is not valid at the granularity of the current filter context. You implement the IsBudgetValid measure with the following template, using these markers:

- <fact_table> is the table that contains the data used to calculate the measure that you will compare with the budget.
- <lookup_granularity_column> is a column in the lookup table that defines a logical relationship between the budget and an entity in the data model. For example, if you define the budget at the month level using two columns (Year and Month), then you use a YearMonth calculated column to define the logical relationship between Date and Budget tables.

```
[IsBudgetValid] :=
(
    COUNTROWS ( <fact_table> )
        = CALCULATE (
            COUNTROWS ( <fact_table> ),
            ALL ( <fact_table> ),
            VALUES ( <lookup_granularity_column_1> ),
            ...
            VALUES ( <lookup_granularity_column_N> )
        )
)
```

You have to include a filter argument in the CALCULATE function for each logical relationship you have between Budget and other tables. You implement the IsBudgetValid measure in the example by using YearMonth and Category columns, without specifying any filter argument for the columns in the Territory table, since it is not included in the budget definition.

```
[IsBudgetValid] :=
(
    COUNTROWS ( Sales )
        = CALCULATE (
```

```
            COUNTROWS ( Sales ),
            ALL ( Sales ),
            VALUES ( 'Date'[YearMonth] ),
            VALUES ( Product[Category] )
        )
)
```

If the filter context is compatible with the budget granularity, you calculate the budget by applying the filters defined by the existing logical relationships. This is the pattern described in the Simulate a Relationship at Different Granularities section of Chapter 11, Handling Different Granularities. You define the BudgetCalc measure as follows:

```
[BudgetCalc] :=
CALCULATE (
    SUM ( Budget[Budget] ),
    FILTER (
        ALL ( Budget[YearMonth] ),
        COUNTROWS (
            FILTER (
                VALUES ( 'Date'[YearMonth] ),
                'Date'[YearMonth] = Budget[YearMonth]
            )
        ) > 0
    ),
    FILTER (
        ALL ( Budget[Category] ),
        COUNTROWS (
            FILTER (
                VALUES ( Product[category] ),
                Product[Category] = Budget[Category]
            )
        ) > 0
    )
)
```

When you need to allocate the budget to different granularities, you iterate over the granularity of the budget, applying an allocation factor to each value of the budget. You perform the iteration over the result of a CROSSJOIN of the logical relationships available in the Budget table. You can apply the following template, using this marker:

- <lookup_granularity_column> is the column that defines the logical relationship in the lookup table (a corresponding column exists in the Budget table).

```
[AllocatedBudget] :=
SUMX (
    CROSSJOIN (
        VALUES ( <lookup_granularity_column_1> ),
        ...
        VALUES ( <lookup_granularity_column_N> ),
    ),
    [AllocationFactor] * [BudgetCalc]
)
```

For example, you implement the AllocatedBudget measure in this scenario using the following definition:

```
[AllocatedBudget] :=
SUMX (
    CROSSJOIN (
        VALUES ( 'Date'[YearMonth] ),
        VALUES ( Product[Category] )
    ),
    [AllocationFactor] * [BudgetCalc]
)
```

The calculation of the allocation factor is the core of the allocation algorithm. You evaluate the ratio of a reference measure between its value calculated in the current filter context and its value calculated in the available granularity of the budget. The denominator of the ratio uses a CALCULATE function that applies a filter argument for each table that has a direct relationship with the data that are used to calculate the reference measure. You can apply the following template, using these markers:

- <reference_measure> is the measure used as a reference to calculate the allocation of the budget.
- <filter_budget_granularity_N> is a set of filter arguments in the CALCULATE function that remove the part of the filter context defining a granularity higher than the one available for the budget.

```
[AllocationFactor] :=
<reference_measure>
    / CALCULATE (
        <reference_measure>,
        <filter_budget_granularity_1>,
        ...
        <filter_budget_granularity_N>
    )
```

The reference measure might correspond to the actual value that the budget is compared with, but calculated in a different period (e.g., budget sales allocated according to the sales of the previous year), or it could be another measure calculated in the same period (e.g., budget costs allocated according to the revenues of the same period).

Each filter argument you pass to the CALCULATE statement in the denominator of the AllocationFactor measure has to remove the parts of the filter context that are not available in the granularity of the budget. For example, if you have the budget by month and product category, you have to remove the filters for day, product name, and product subcategory, so that the remaining filters match the budget granularity. You apply a different technique for each table that has a direct relationship with the table containing data used by the measure. In the data model of this example, the Quantity measure sums the QuantitySold column from the Sales table, so you consider only the tables having a relationship with Sales: Date, Product, and Territory.

Three different filter-removal templates are available, depending on the logical relationship of each table with the budget:

- **ALLEXCEPT** removes the filters from the columns that have a higher granularity than the one available in the budget, for the tables that have a logical relationship with the budget.

```
ALLEXCEPT ( <table>, <lookup_granularity_column> )
```

- Use the **ALL / VALUES** technique in place of ALLEXCEPT when you need to remove filters from a table marked as a date table.

```
ALL ( <table> ), VALUES ( <lookup_granularity_column> ) )
```

- Use the **ALL** technique for all the tables that do not have a logical relationship with the budget.

```
ALL ( <table> )
```

The markers used in the previous templates are the following:

- <table> is the table considered for filter removal; it has a direct relationship with the table containing data used by the measure implementing the allocation algorithm.
- <lookup_granularity_column> is a column of the table that has a granularity corresponding to the granularity of the budget (e.g., YearMonth in the Date table in the previous example). You keep these columns in the filter context, removing all the other columns of the same table.

You apply an ALLEXCEPT or ALL / VALUES template for each lookup granularity column you have in the CROSSJOIN arguments of the AllocatedBudget measure, and you apply the ALL template to all the other tables involved.

In this example, you allocate the budget based on the quantity sold in the previous year, which is the QuantityPY reference measure. You remove the filter from all the Product columns except for Category and ID_Category (these columns have the same granularity). You also remove the filters from all the Date columns except for YearMonth, using the ALL / VALUES template instead of ALLEXCEPT because the table is marked as Date table. The special behavior of DAX for Date tables requires a different approach than ALLEXCEPT, which would not produce correct results in this particular case. Finally, you apply the ALL template to the Territory table, which has a relationship with Sales, but is not part of the budget granularity.

You implement the AllocationFactor and QuantityPY measures using the following definitions:

```
[AllocationFactor] :=
[QuantityPY]
    / CALCULATE (
        [QuantityPY],
        ALLEXCEPT (
            Product,
            Product[Category],
            Product[ID_Category]
        ),
        ALL ( 'Date' ), VALUES ( 'Date'[YearMonth] ),
        ALL ( Territory )
    )

[QuantityPY] :=
CALCULATE (
    [Quantity],
    SAMEPERIODLASTYEAR ( 'Date'[Date] )
)
```

You test the budget calculation for all the columns involved in allocation. The budget defined by year and month aggregates value at the year and quarter level, whereas it allocates the month value at the day level. For example, the budget in March 2014 allocates by day using the quantity sold in March 2013, as you see in Figure 12-8.

Row Labels	Quantity	Budget	Var%
⊟2013	2,443.00		
⊞Q1	643.00		
⊞Q2	673.00		
⊞Q3	516.00		
⊞Q4	611.00		
⊟2014	2,419.00	2,305.00	4.95%
⊟Q1	594.00	585.00	1.54%
⊞January	201.00	200.00	0.50%
⊞February	198.00	175.00	13.14%
⊟March	195.00	210.00	-7.14%
3/1/2014	4.00	11.20	-64.29%
3/2/2014	7.00	4.84	44.54%
3/3/2014	5.00	4.63	7.95%
3/4/2014	7.00	6.36	10.10%
3/5/2014	10.00	7.75	29.05%
3/6/2014	7.00	7.12	-1.63%
3/7/2014	16.00	4.63	245.43%
3/8/2014	5.00	4.84	3.24%
3/9/2014	5.00	9.05	-44.77%
3/10/2014	5.00	4.63	7.95%

Row Labels	Quantity
⊟2013	2,443.00
⊟Q1	643.00
⊞January	234.00
⊞February	185.00
⊟March	224.00
3/1/2013	12.00
3/2/2013	5.00
3/3/2013	5.00
3/4/2013	7.00
3/5/2013	8.00
3/6/2013	8.00
3/7/2013	5.00
3/8/2013	5.00
3/9/2013	10.00
3/10/2013	5.00

FIGURE 12-8 The Budget measure allocates the month value by day using the quantity sold in the same period in the previous year.

The budget allocation per Subcategory and Product in 2014 uses the quantity sold in 2013, as you see in Figure 12-9.

	Column Labels					
	⊞2013			⊞2014		
Row Labels	Quantity	Budget	Var%	Quantity	Budget	Var%
⊟Accessories	2,069.00			2,069.00	1,970.00	5.03%
⊞Bottles and Cages	1,023.00			997.00	975.67	2.19%
⊞Fenders	1,046.00			1,072.00	994.33	7.81%
⊟Bikes	374.00			350.00	335.00	4.48%
⊟Mountain Bikes	61.00			46.00	55.92	-17.74%
Mountain-100 Silver, 38	31.00			27.00	28.29	-4.54%
Mountain-100 Silver, 44	30.00			19.00	27.64	-31.25%
⊟Road Bikes	313.00			304.00	279.08	8.93%
Road-150 Red, 44	143.00			138.00	126.36	9.21%
Road-150 Red, 62	170.00			166.00	152.72	8.70%
Grand Total	2,443.00			2,419.00	2,305.00	4.95%

FIGURE 12-9 The Budget measure allocates the category value by subcategory and product using the quantity sold in 2013.

The budget allocation per Territory in 2014 uses the quantity sold in 2013, as you see in Figure 12-10.

	Column Labels					
	2013			2014		
Row Labels	**Quantity**	**Budget**	**Var%**	**Quantity**	**Budget**	**Var%**
Europe	**548.00**			**584.00**	**514.80**	**13.44%**
North America	**1,476.00**			**1,409.00**	**1,394.92**	**1.01%**
Canada	**430.00**			**390.00**	**410.49**	**-4.99%**
United States	**1,046.00**			**1,019.00**	**984.43**	**3.51%**
Central				1.00		
Northeast	2.00			1.00	1.83	-45.38%
Northwest	417.00			451.00	393.55	14.60%
Southeast	3.00			2.00	3.03	-34.08%
Southwest	624.00			564.00	586.01	-3.76%
Pacific	**419.00**			**426.00**	**395.28**	**7.77%**
Grand Total	**2,443.00**			**2,419.00**	**2,305.00**	**4.95%**

FIGURE 12-10 The Budget measure allocates value by group, country, and region using the quantity sold in 2013.

Download sample workbooks for both Excel 2010 and 2013 on
http://www.daxpatterns.com/budget-patterns

Note that you can easily create a corresponding SQL Server Analysis Services Tabular project starting from the Excel 2013 file

CHAPTER 13

Survey

The Survey pattern uses a data model and a DAX expression to analyze correlation between different transactions related to the same entity, such as a customer's answers to survey questions.

Basic Pattern Example

Suppose you have an Answers table containing the answers provided to a survey by customers defined in a Customers table. In the Answers table, every row contains an answer to a question. The first rows of the two tables are shown in Figure 13-1.

CustomerKey	Customer
1	Regina Mc Gee
2	Dewayne Forbes
3	Jolene Nunez
4	Tricia Ingram
5	Shane Anderson
6	Marjorie Perez
7	Olivia Stokes
8	Alisa Santos
9	Felix Lawson
10	Wendi Ross

CustomerKey	AnswerKey
1	1
1	2
1	14
1	15
2	3
2	12
2	14
2	17
3	4
3	7

FIGURE 13-1 Every row in the Customers table (left) has many related rows in the Answers table (right).

The Questions table in Figure 13-2 contains all the questions and possible answers, providing a unique key for each row. You can have questions with multiple-choice answers.

AnswerKey	Question	Answer
1	Sport Practiced	Baseball
2	Sport Practiced	Football
3	Sport Practiced	Tennis
4	Sport Practiced	Karate
5	Job	IT Pro
6	Job	Teacher
7	Job	Consultant
8	Yearly Net Income	< 10,000

FIGURE 13-2 The Questions table defines all the possible answers to each question.

You import the Questions table twice, naming it Filter1 and Filter2. You rename the columns Question and Answer with a suffix identifying the filter they belong to. Every Filter table will become a possible slicer or filter in the pivot table used to query the survey data model. As you see in Figure 13-3, the relationships between the Answers table and Filter1 and Filter2 are inactive.

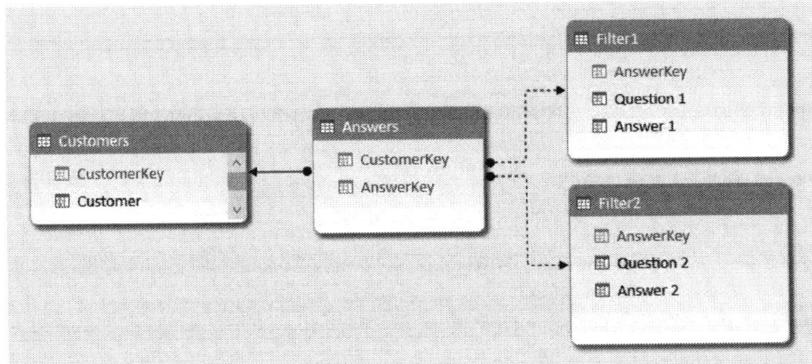

FIGURE 13-3 The Survey data model includes inactive relationships between the Filter and Answers tables.

You need two filter tables to define a logical AND condition between two questions. For example, to count how many customers have a job as a teacher and play tennis, you need to apply a calculation such as the one described in the CustomersQ1andQ2 measure below.

```
[CustomersQ1andQ2] :=
CALCULATE (
    COUNTROWS ( Customers ),
    CALCULATETABLE (
        Answers,
        USERELATIONSHIP ( Answers[AnswerKey], Filter2[AnswerKey] )
    ),
    CALCULATETABLE (
        Answers,
        USERELATIONSHIP ( Answers[AnswerKey], Filter1[AnswerKey] )
    )
)
```

Once you have this measure, you can use a pivot table to put answers from one question in rows, and put answers from another question in columns. The table in Figure 13-4 has sports in columns and jobs in rows, and you can see there are 16 customers who are tennis-playing teachers. The last column (Sport Practiced Total) shows how many customers practice at least one sport. For example, 33 teachers practice at least one sport.

CustomersQ1andQ2	Column L				
	Sport Practiced				Sport Practiced Total
Row Labels	Baseball	Football	Karate	Tennis	
Job	27	31	23	28	75
Consultant	10	17	10	9	30
IT Pro	16	14	11	13	41
Teacher	9	13	11	16	33

FIGURE 13-4 The pivot table crosses questions and answers from Filter1 and Filter2 tables.

If you want to compute the answers to just one question, you cannot use CustomersQ1andQ2, because it requires a selection from two different filters. Instead, use the CustomersQ1 measure, which computes the number of customers that answered the question selected in Filter1, regardless of what is selected in Filter2.

```
[CustomersQ1] :=
=
CALCULATE (
    COUNTROWS ( Customers ),
    CALCULATETABLE (
        Answers,
        USERELATIONSHIP ( Answers[AnswerKey], Filter1[AnswerKey] )
    )
)
```

In the DAX expression for CustomersQ1, you have to include the USERELATIONSHIP statement because the relationship with the Filter1 table in the data model is inactive, which is a required condition to perform the calculation defined in CustomersQ1andQ2. Figure 13-5 shows that there are 56 teachers, and you have seen in Figure 13-4 that only 33 of them practice at least one sport.

Row Labels	CustomersQ1
Job	117
Consultant	46
IT Pro	65
Teacher	56

FIGURE 13-5 The CustomersQ1 measure counts how many customers answered the questions selected in Filter1, regardless of the selection in Filter2.

Use Cases

You can use the Survey pattern when you want to analyze correlations between events happening to the same entity. The following is a list of some interesting use cases.

Answers to a Survey

A survey form usually has a set of questions with a predefined list of possible answers. You can have both single-choice and multiple-choice questions. You want to analyze correlations between different questions in the same survey, using a single data model that does not change depending on the structure of the survey. The data in the tables define the survey structure so you do not need to create a different structure for every survey.

Basket Analysis

You can analyze the products bought together in the same transaction, although the Survey pattern can only identify existing relationships. A more specific Basket Analysis pattern is available to detect products that the same customer buys in different transactions.

Evaluation of an Anamnesis (Medical History) Questionnaire

You can structure many questions of an anamnesis questionnaire in a data model that corresponds to the Survey pattern. You can easily analyze the distribution of answers in a set of questionnaires by using a pivot table, with a data model that does not change when new questions are added to the questionnaire. The Survey pattern also handles multiple-choice answers without requiring a column for each answer (which is a common pattern used to adapt this type of data for analysis with Excel).

Complete Pattern

Create a data model like the one shown in Figure 13-3. You might replace the Customers table with one that represents an entity collecting answers (e.g., a Form table). It is important to use inactive relationships between the Answers and Filters tables.

You can calculate the answers to a single question, regardless of selections made on other filter tables, with the following measures:

```
CustomersQ1 :=
IF (
    HASONEVALUE ( Filter1[Question 1] ),
    CALCULATE (
        COUNTROWS ( Customers ),
        CALCULATETABLE (
            Answers,
            USERELATIONSHIP ( Answers[AnswerKey], Filter1[AnswerKey] )
        )
    )
)

CustomersQ2 :=
IF (
    HASONEVALUE ( Filter2[Question 2] ),
    CALCULATE (
        COUNTROWS ( Customers ),
        CALCULATETABLE (
            Answers,
            USERELATIONSHIP ( Answers[AnswerKey], Filter2[AnswerKey] )
        )
    )
)
```

The HASONEVALUE function checks whether the user selected only one question. If more than one question is selected in a filter table, the interpretation could be ambiguous: should you consider an

AND or an OR condition between the two questions? The IF statement returns BLANK when multiple questions are selected within the same filter table.

Selecting multiple answers, however, is possible and it is always interpreted as an OR condition. For example, if the user selects both Baseball and Football answers for the Sport Practiced question, it means she wants to know **how many customers practice baseball, or football, or both**. This is the reason why the CALCULATE statement evaluates the number of rows in the Customers table, instead of counting the number of rows in the Answers table.

In case the user uses two filter tables, one question is possible for each filter. The answers to each question are considered in an OR condition, but the two questions are considered in an AND condition. For example, if the user selects Consultant and Teacher answers for the Job question in Filter1, and she selects Baseball and Football for the Sport Practiced question in Filter2, it means she wants to know how many customers who are consultants or teachers also practice baseball, or football, or both. You implement such a calculation with the following measure:

```
CustomersQ1andQ2 :=
SWITCH (
    TRUE,
    NOT ( ISCROSSFILTERED ( Filter2[AnswerKey] ) ), [CustomersQ1],
    NOT ( ISCROSSFILTERED ( Filter1[AnswerKey] ) ), [CustomersQ2],
    IF (
        HASONEVALUE ( Filter1[Question 1] )
            && HASONEVALUE ( Filter2[Question 2] ),
        IF (
            VALUES ( Filter2[Question 2] )
                <> VALUES ( Filter1[Question 1] ),
            CALCULATE (
                COUNTROWS ( Customers ),
                CALCULATETABLE (
                    Answers,
                    USERELATIONSHIP ( Answers[AnswerKey], Filter2[AnswerKey] )
                ),
                CALCULATETABLE (
                    Answers,
                    USERELATIONSHIP ( Answers[AnswerKey], Filter1[AnswerKey] )
```

```
                    )
                )
            )
        )
    )
```

There are a few more checks in this formula in order to handle special conditions. If there are no filters active on the Filter2 table, then you can use the calculation for a single question, using the CustomersQ1 measure. In a similar way, if there are no filters active on the Filter1 table, you can use the CustomersQ2 measure. The ISCROSSFILTERED function just checks a column of the filter table to do that.

If a filter is active on both the Filter1 and Filter2 tables, then you want to calculate the number of customers satisfying the filters only if the user selected a single but different question in both Filter1 and Filter2; otherwise, you return a BLANK. For example, even if there are no filters on questions and answers in the pivot table rows in Figure 13-6, there are no duplicated rows with the answers to the Gender question, because we do not want to show an intersection between the same questions.

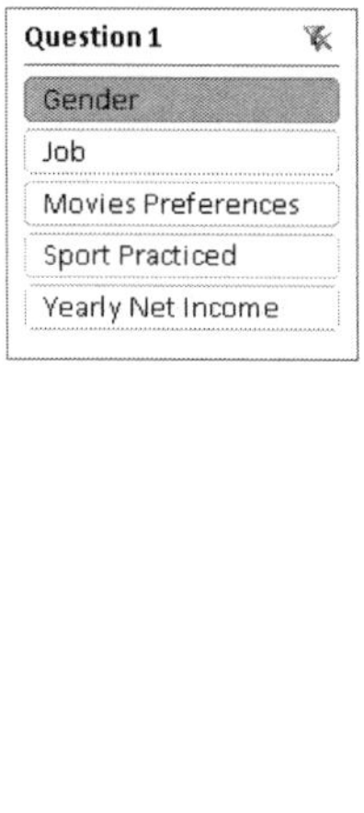

Question 1

- Gender
- Job
- Movies Preferences
- Sport Practiced
- Yearly Net Income

CustomersQ1andQ2	Column Labels		
Row Labels	**Female**	**Male**	**Grand Total**
Job	**26**	**28**	**54**
Consultant	9	15	24
IT Pro	15	19	34
Teacher	11	12	23
Movies Preferences	**25**	**27**	**52**
Cartoons	9	16	25
Comedy	9	10	19
Horror	13	15	28
Sport Practiced	**31**	**27**	**58**
Baseball	15	12	27
Football	13	12	25
Karate	7	8	15
Tennis	10	7	17
Yearly Net Income	**31**	**31**	**62**
< 10,000	11	10	21
> 80,000	11	16	27
10,000 - 20,000	6	12	18
20,000 - 40,000	10	11	21
40,000 - 80,000	8	9	17
Grand Total	**43**	**41**	**84**

FIGURE 13-6 Questions and answers from Filter1 are in rows, questions from Filter2 are in the slicer, and answers from Filter2 are in columns. The slicer only selects the Gender question in Filter2, so the Gender question and its answers do not appear in rows, because the CustomersQ1andQ2 measure returns BLANK when the same question appears in both Filter1 and Filter2.

When you look at the result for a question without selecting an answer, the number you see is the number of unique customers who gave at least one answer to that question. However, it is important to consider that the data model always supports multiple-choice questions, even when the nature of the question is single-choice. For example, the Gender question is a single-choice one and the sum of Male and Female answers should correspond to the number of unique customers who answered the Gender question. However, you might have conflicting answers to the Gender question for the same customer. The data model does not provide any constraint that prevents such a conflict: you have to check data quality before importing data.

IMPORTANT Using a drillthrough action on measures used in the Survey pattern will produce unexpected results. The drillthrough only returns data filtered by active relationships in the data model, ignoring any further calculation or filter made through DAX expressions. If you want to obtain the list of customers that gave a particular combination of answers, you have to put the customer name in the pivot table rows and use slicers of pivot table filters to select the desired combination of questions and answers.

Slicer Differences in Excel 2010 and Excel 2013

When you use slicers to display a selection of questions and answers, remember that there is slightly different behavior between Excel 2010 and Excel 2013. If you have a slicer with questions and another with answers for the same filter, you would like the slicer for the answers to display only the possible choices for the selected question. In Excel 2010, you can only change the position of the answers, so that possible choices for the selected question are displayed first in the slicer: to do that, set the Show Items With No Data Last checkbox (in the Slicer Settings dialog box shown in Figure 13-7).

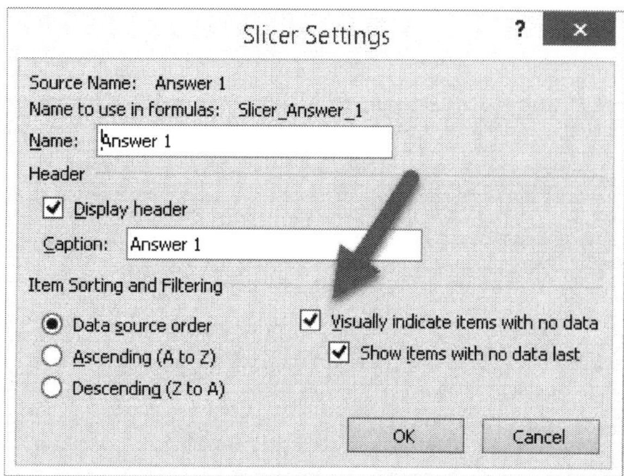

FIGURE 13-7 The Slicer Settings dialog box in Excel 2010.

Using this setting, the Female and Male answers for the selected Gender question are displayed first in the Answer1 slicer, as you see in Figure 13-8.

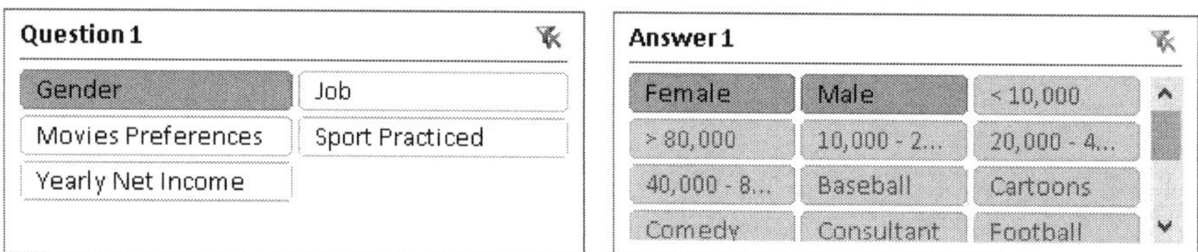

FIGURE 13-8 In Excel 2010, the slicer for answers displays possible choices for the selected question first in the list.

With Excel 2013, you can hide the answers belonging to questions that are not selected, by setting the Hide Items With No Data checkbox shown in Figure 13-9.

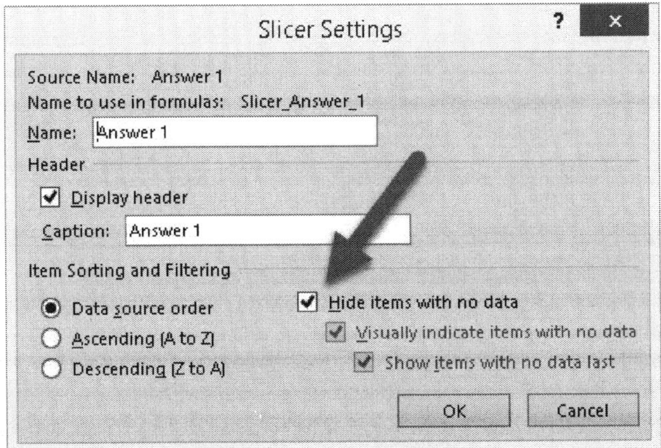

FIGURE 13-9 The Slicer Settings dialog box in Excel 2013.

In this way, the Answer1 slicer does not display answers unrelated to the selection made in the Question1 slicer, as you see in Figure 13-10.

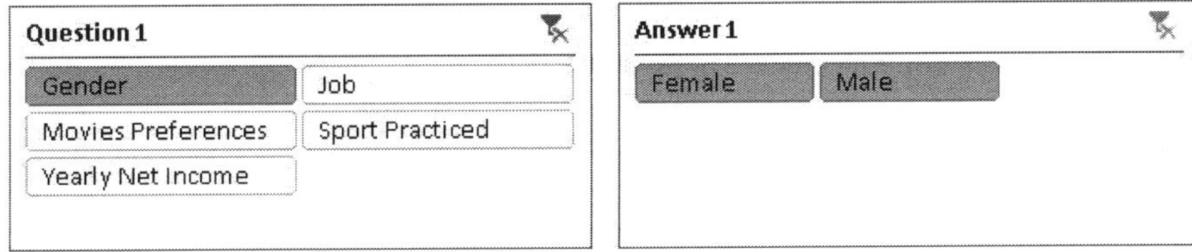

FIGURE 13-10 In Excel 2013, the slicer for answers does not display questions unrelated to the selected question.

Download sample workbooks for both Excel 2010 and 2013 on
http://www.daxpatterns.com/survey

Note that you can easily create a corresponding SQL Server Analysis Services Tabular project starting from the Excel 2013 file

CHAPTER 14

Basket Analysis

The Basket Analysis pattern enables analysis of co-occurrence relationships among transactions related to a certain entity, such as products bought in the same order, or by the same customer in different purchases. This pattern is a specialization of the Survey pattern presented in the previous chapter.

Basic Pattern Example

Suppose you have a Sales table containing one row for each row detail in an order. The SalesOrderNumber column identifies rows that are part of the same order, as you see in Figure 14-1.

OrderDateKey	ProductCode	SalesOrderNumber	SalesOrderLineNumber	OrderQuantity	SalesAmount
20071221	BK-M68B-46	SO60495	1	1	$2,294.99
20071221	FE-6654	SO60495	2	1	$21.98
20071221	HL-U509	SO60495	3	1	$34.99
20071221	BK-M68S-42	SO60496	1	1	$2,319.99
20071221	BC-M005	SO60496	2	1	$9.99
20071221	WB-H098	SO60496	3	1	$4.99
20071221	HY-1023-70	SO60496	4	1	$54.99
20071221	BK-M68S-46	SO60497	1	1	$2,319.99
20071221	BC-M005	SO60497	2	1	$9.99
20071221	WB-H098	SO60497	3	1	$4.99

FIGURE 14-1 In the Sales table, rows with the same SalesOrderNumber value are details of the same order.

The OrderDateKey and ProductCode columns reference the Date and Product tables, respectively. The Product table contains the attributes that are the target of the analysis, such as the product name or category. You create a copy of the Product table, called Filter Product, which contains the same data and has the prefix "Filter" before all table and column names. The relationship between the Sales table and the Filter Product table is inactive, as shown in Figure 14-2.

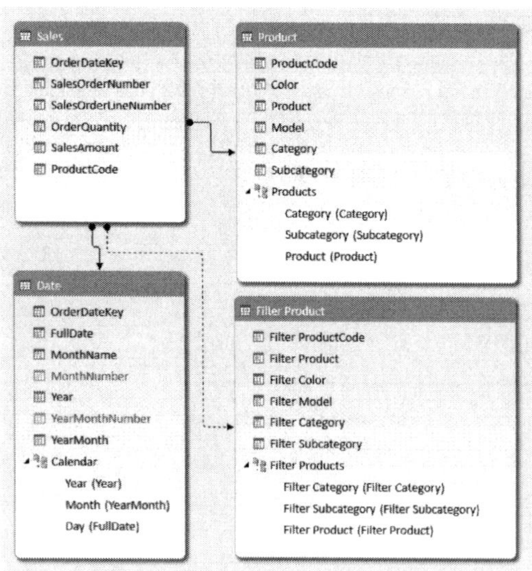

FIGURE 14-2 The Product table has a copy, Filter Product, which has an inactive relationship with the Sales table.

The Filter Product table enables users to specify a second product (or related attribute) as a filter in a pivot table for a measure that considers only orders that contain both products. For example, the pivot table in Figure 14-3 shows the number of orders of each bike accessory and, in the same row, the number of orders with that accessory plus the product filtered by the Filter Product slicer (in this case, Patch Kit/8 Patches).

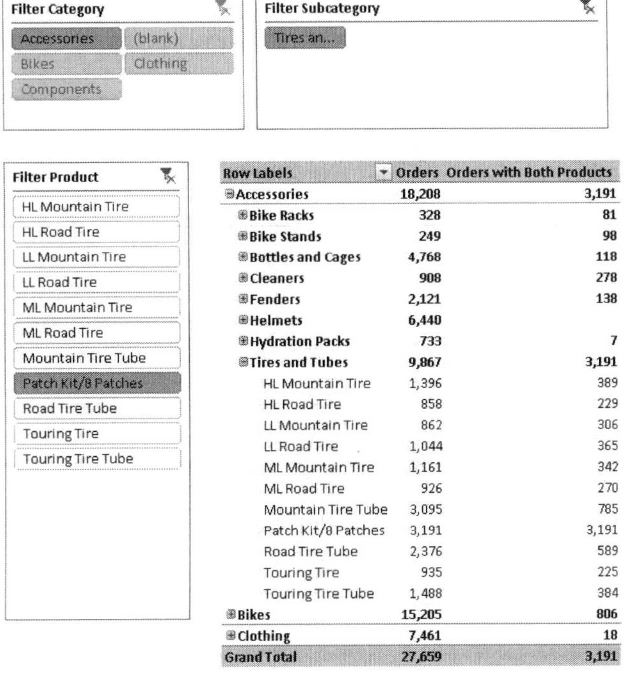

Row Labels	Orders	Orders with Both Products
⊟Accessories	18,208	3,191
⊞Bike Racks	328	81
⊞Bike Stands	249	98
⊞Bottles and Cages	4,768	118
⊞Cleaners	908	278
⊞Fenders	2,121	138
⊞Helmets	6,440	
⊞Hydration Packs	733	7
⊟Tires and Tubes	9,867	3,191
HL Mountain Tire	1,396	389
HL Road Tire	858	229
LL Mountain Tire	862	306
LL Road Tire	1,044	365
ML Mountain Tire	1,161	342
ML Road Tire	926	270
Mountain Tire Tube	3,095	785
Patch Kit/8 Patches	3,191	3,191
Road Tire Tube	2,376	589
Touring Tire	935	225
Touring Tire Tube	1,488	384
⊞Bikes	15,205	806
⊞Clothing	7,461	18
Grand Total	27,659	3,191

FIGURE 14-3 The Orders with Both Products measure shows how many orders include both the product listed in the row (from the Product table) and the one selected in the Filter Product slicer.

The Orders measure is a simple distinct count of the SalesOrderNumber column.

```
[Orders] := DISTINCTCOUNT ( Sales[SalesOrderNumber] )
```

The Orders with Both Products measure implements a similar calculation, applying a filter that considers only the orders that also contain the product selected in the Filter Product table:

```
[Orders with Both Products] :=
CALCULATE (
    DISTINCTCOUNT ( Sales[SalesOrderNumber] ),
```

```
    CALCULATETABLE (
        SUMMARIZE ( Sales, Sales[SalesOrderNumber] ),
        ALL ( Product ),
        USERELATIONSHIP ( Sales[ProductCode], 'Filter Product'[Filter ProductCode] )
    )
)
```

This is a generic approach to basket analysis, which is useful for many different calculations, as you will see in the complete pattern.

Use Cases

You can use the Basket Analysis pattern in scenarios when you want to analyze relationships between different rows in the same table that are connected by attributes located in the same table or in lookup tables. The following is a list of some interesting use cases.

Cross-Selling

With basket analysis, you can determine which products to offer to a customer, increasing revenues and improving your relationship with the customer. For example, you can analyze the products bought together by other customers, and then offer to your customer the products bought by others with a similar purchase history.

Upselling

During the definition of an order, you can offer an upgrade, an add-on, or a more expensive item. Basket analysis helps you to identify which product mix is more successful, based on order history.

Sales Promotion

You can use purchase history to define special promotions that combine or discount certain products. Basket analysis helps you to identify a successful product mix and to evaluate the success rate of a promotion encouraging customers to buy more products in the same order.

Complete Pattern

Create a data model like the one shown in Figure 14-4. The Filter Product table is a copy of the Product table and has the prefix "Filter" for each name (table, columns, hierarchies, and hierarchy levels). The relationship between the Sales and Filter Product tables is inactive. When doing basket analysis, users will use the Filter Product table to apply a second filter to product attributes.

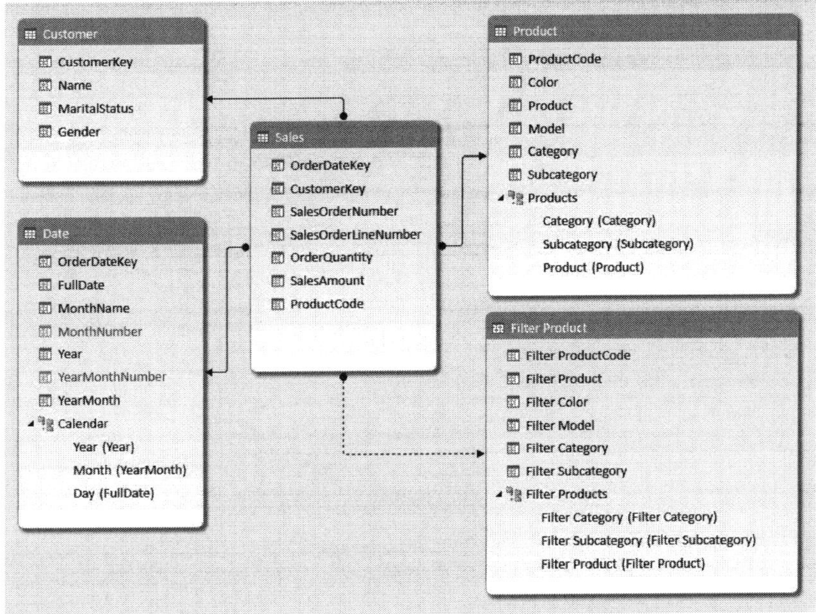

FIGURE 14-4 The data model has an inactive relationship between the Sales and Filter Product tables.

The pivot table in Figure 14-5 shows the number of orders with different conditions depending on the selection of products made in rows and slicers.

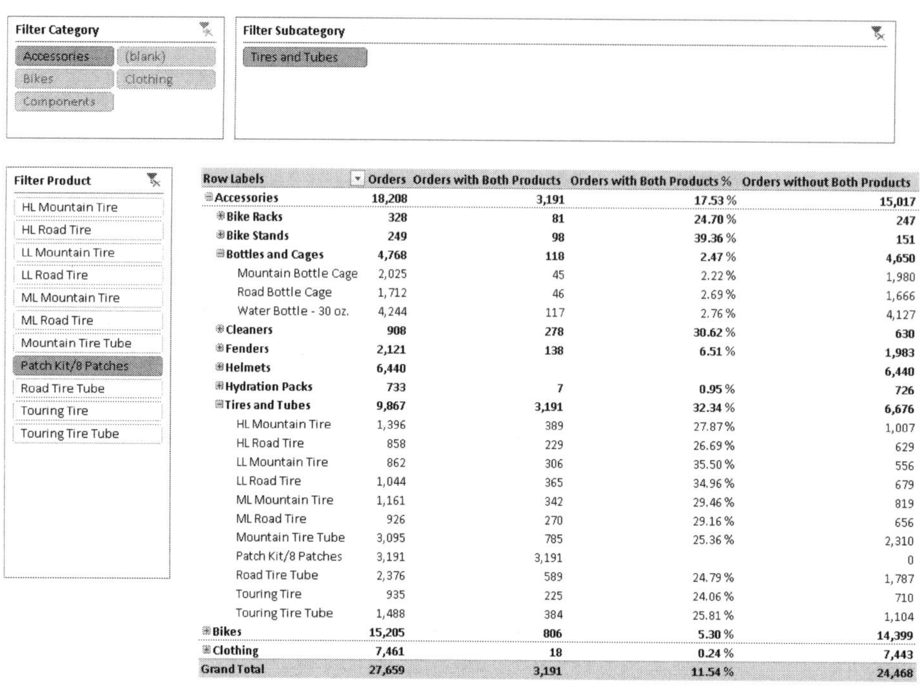

Row Labels	Orders	Orders with Both Products	Orders with Both Products %	Orders without Both Products
Accessories	**18,208**	**3,191**	**17.53 %**	**15,017**
Bike Racks	**328**	**81**	**24.70 %**	**247**
Bike Stands	**249**	**98**	**39.36 %**	**151**
Bottles and Cages	**4,768**	**118**	**2.47 %**	**4,650**
Mountain Bottle Cage	2,025	45	2.22 %	1,980
Road Bottle Cage	1,712	46	2.69 %	1,666
Water Bottle - 30 oz.	4,244	117	2.76 %	4,127
Cleaners	**908**	**278**	**30.62 %**	**630**
Fenders	**2,121**	**138**	**6.51 %**	**1,983**
Helmets	**6,440**			**6,440**
Hydration Packs	**733**	**7**	**0.95 %**	**726**
Tires and Tubes	**9,867**	**3,191**	**32.34 %**	**6,676**
HL Mountain Tire	1,396	389	27.87 %	1,007
HL Road Tire	858	229	26.69 %	629
LL Mountain Tire	862	306	35.50 %	556
LL Road Tire	1,044	365	34.96 %	679
ML Mountain Tire	1,161	342	29.46 %	819
ML Road Tire	926	270	29.16 %	656
Mountain Tire Tube	3,095	785	25.36 %	2,310
Patch Kit/8 Patches	3,191	3,191		0
Road Tire Tube	2,376	589	24.79 %	1,787
Touring Tire	935	225	24.06 %	710
Touring Tire Tube	1,488	384	25.81 %	1,104
Bikes	**15,205**	**806**	**5.30 %**	**14,399**
Clothing	**7,461**	**18**	**0.24 %**	**7,443**
Grand Total	**27,659**	**3,191**	**11.54 %**	**24,468**

FIGURE 14-5 Measures for orders containing one or both of the products selected in rows and slicers.

The products hierarchy in the pivot table rows filters all the orders, and the Orders measure displays how many orders include at least one of the products selected (this is the number of orders that contain at least one of the products of the category/subcategory selected in the bold rows).

```
[Orders] := DISTINCTCOUNT ( Sales[SalesOrderNumber] )
```

The slicers around the pivot table show the selection of attributes from the Filter Product table (Filter Category, Filter Subcategory, and Filter Product). In this example, only one product is selected (Patch Kit/8 Patches). The Orders with Both Products measure shows how many orders contain at least one of the products selected in the pivot table rows and also the filtered product (Patch Kit/8 Patches) selected in the Filter Product slicer.

```
[Orders with Both Products] :=
CALCULATE (
    DISTINCTCOUNT ( Sales[SalesOrderNumber] ),
    CALCULATETABLE (
        SUMMARIZE ( Sales, Sales[SalesOrderNumber] ),
        ALL ( Product ),
        USERELATIONSHIP ( Sales[ProductCode], 'Filter Product'[Filter ProductCode] )
    )
)
```

The Orders with Both Products % measure shows the percentage of orders having both products; it is obtained by comparing the Orders with Both Products measure with the Orders measure. However, if the product selected is the same in both the Product and Filter Product tables, you hide the result returning BLANK, because it is not useful to see 100% in these cases.

```
[SameProductSelection] :=
IF (
    HASONEVALUE ( Product[ProductCode] )
        && HASONEVALUE ( 'Filter Product'[Filter ProductCode] ),
    IF (
        VALUES ( Product[ProductCode] )
            = VALUES ( 'Filter Product'[Filter ProductCode] ),
        TRUE
    )
)

[Orders with Both Products %] :=
IF (
    NOT ( [SameProductSelection] ),
    DIVIDE ( [Orders with Both Products], [Orders] )
)
```

The Orders without Both Products measure is simply the difference between Orders and Orders with Both Products measures. This number represents the number of orders containing the product selected in the pivot table, but not the product selected in the Filter Product slicer.

```
[Orders without Both Products] :=
[Orders] - [Orders with Both Products]
```

You can also create measures analyzing purchases made by each customer in different orders. The pivot table in Figure 14-6 shows the number of customers with different conditions depending on the selection of products in rows and slicers.

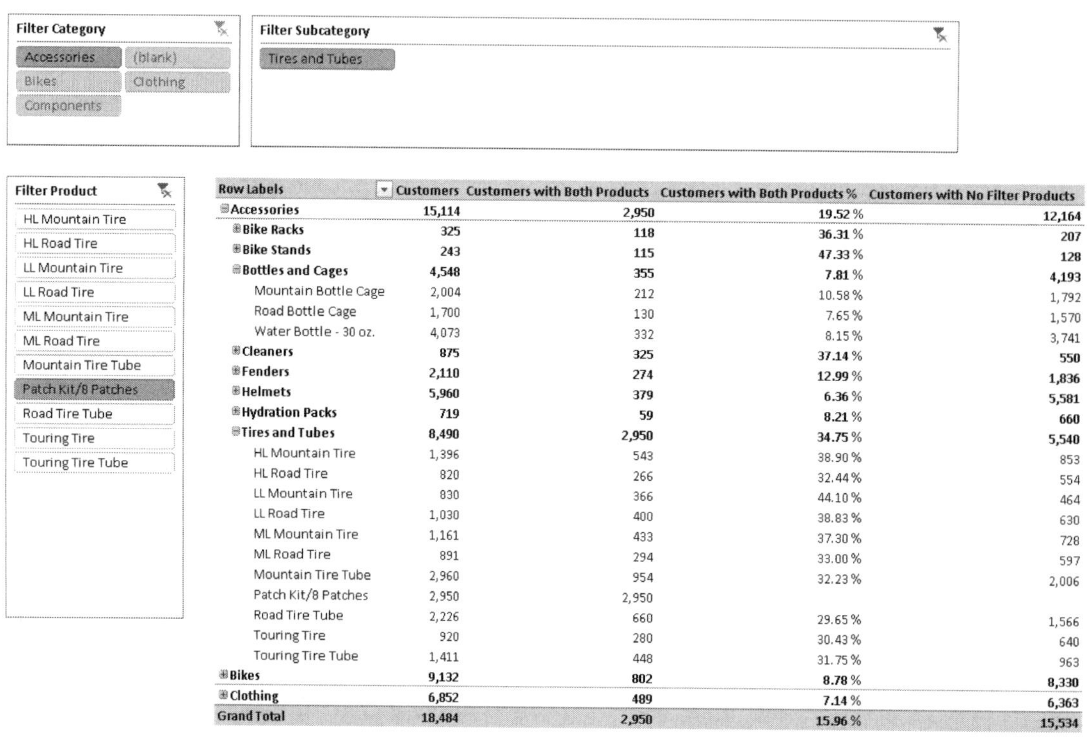

Row Labels	Customers	Customers with Both Products	Customers with Both Products %	Customers with No Filter Products
Accessories	15,114	2,950	19.52 %	12,164
Bike Racks	325	118	36.31 %	207
Bike Stands	243	115	47.33 %	128
Bottles and Cages	4,548	355	7.81 %	4,193
Mountain Bottle Cage	2,004	212	10.58 %	1,792
Road Bottle Cage	1,700	130	7.65 %	1,570
Water Bottle - 30 oz.	4,073	332	8.15 %	3,741
Cleaners	875	325	37.14 %	550
Fenders	2,110	274	12.99 %	1,836
Helmets	5,960	379	6.36 %	5,581
Hydration Packs	719	59	8.21 %	660
Tires and Tubes	8,490	2,950	34.75 %	5,540
HL Mountain Tire	1,396	543	38.90 %	853
HL Road Tire	820	266	32.44 %	554
LL Mountain Tire	830	366	44.10 %	464
LL Road Tire	1,030	400	38.83 %	630
ML Mountain Tire	1,161	433	37.30 %	728
ML Road Tire	891	294	33.00 %	597
Mountain Tire Tube	2,960	954	32.23 %	2,006
Patch Kit/8 Patches	2,950	2,950		
Road Tire Tube	2,226	660	29.65 %	1,566
Touring Tire	920	280	30.43 %	640
Touring Tire Tube	1,411	448	31.75 %	963
Bikes	9,132	802	8.78 %	8,330
Clothing	6,852	489	7.14 %	6,363
Grand Total	18,484	2,950	15.96 %	15,534

FIGURE 14-6 Measures for customers who bought one or both of the products selected in rows and slicers.

The selection in the pivot table is identical to the one used for counting orders. The measures are also similar—you just replace the distinct count calculation in the formulas, using the CustomerKey column on the Sales table.

```
[Customers] := DISTINCTCOUNT ( Sales[CustomerKey] )

[Customers with Both Products] :=
CALCULATE (
```

```
    DISTINCTCOUNT ( Sales[CustomerKey] ),
    CALCULATETABLE (
        SUMMARIZE ( Sales, Sales[CustomerKey] ),
        ALL ( Product ),
        USERELATIONSHIP ( Sales[ProductCode], 'Filter Product'[Filter ProductCode] )
    )
)

[Customers with Both Products %] :=
IF (
    NOT ( [SameProductSelection] ),
    DIVIDE ( [Customers with Both Products], [Customers] )
)
```

To count or list the number of customers who never bought the product that you want to filter for, there is a more efficient technique. Use the Customers with No Filter Products measure, as defined below.

```
[Customers with No Filter Products] :=
COUNTROWS (
    FILTER (
        CALCULATETABLE ( Customer, Sales ),
        ISEMPTY (
            CALCULATETABLE (
                Sales,
                ALL ( Product ),
                USERELATIONSHIP ( Sales[ProductCode], 'Filter Product'[Filter ProductCode] )
            )
        )
    )
)
```

You can use the result of the FILTER statement as a filter argument for a CALCULATE statement—for example, to evaluate the sales amount of the filtered selection of customers. If the ISEMPTY function is not available in your version of DAX, then use the following implementation:

```
[Customers with No Filter Products Classic] :=
COUNTROWS (
    FILTER (
        CALCULATETABLE ( Customer, Sales ),
        CALCULATE (
            COUNTROWS ( Sales ),
            ALL ( Product ),
            USERELATIONSHIP ( Sales[ProductCode], 'Filter Product'[Filter ProductCode] )
        ) = 0
    )
)
```

IMPORTANT The ISEMPTY function is available only in Microsoft SQL Server 2012 Service Pack 1 Cumulative Update 4 or later versions. For this reason, ISEMPTY is available only in Power Pivot for Excel 2010 build 11.00.3368 (or later version) and SQL Server Analysis Services 2012 build 11.00.3368 (or later version). At the moment of writing, ISEMPTY is not available in any version of Excel 2013, updates of which depend on the Microsoft Office release cycle and not on SQL Server service packs.

More Pattern Examples

In this section, you will see a few examples of the Basket Analysis pattern.

Products More Likely Bought with Another Product

If you want to determine which products are most likely to be bought with another product, you can use a pivot table that sorts products by one of the percentage measures you have seen in the complete pattern. For example, you can use a slicer for Filter Product and place the product names in pivot table rows. You use either the Orders with Both Products % measure or the Customers with Both Products % measure to sort the products by rows, so that the first rows in the pivot table show the products that are most likely to be sold with the product selected in the slicer. The example shown in Figure 14-7 sorts products by the Customers with Both Products % measure in a descending way, so that you see which products are most commonly sold to customers who bought the product selected in the Filter Product slicer.

Filter Product

LL Road Tire	Long-Sleeve Logo Jersey, L	Long-Sleeve Logo Jersey, M
Long-Sleeve Logo Jersey, S	Long-Sleeve Logo Jersey, XL	ML Mountain Tire
ML Road Tire	Mountain Bottle Cage	Mountain Tire Tube
Mountain-100 Black, 38	Mountain-100 Black, 42	Mountain-100 Black, 44

Row Labels	Orders with Both Products %	Customers with Both Products %
HL Mountain Tire	68.55 %	71.70 %
ML Mountain Tire	66.84 %	70.20 %
LL Mountain Tire	55.45 %	60.60 %
All-Purpose Bike Stand	21.69 %	34.98 %
Hitch Rack - 4-Bike	17.99 %	32.62 %
Patch Kit/8 Patches	24.60 %	32.34 %
Bike Wash - Dissolver	17.95 %	29.37 %
Sport-100 Helmet, Black	21.73 %	26.88 %

FIGURE 14-7 Products that are most commonly sold to customers who bought the Mountain Tire Tube product.

Customers Who Bought Product A and Not Product B

Once you know that certain products have a high chance to be bought together, you can obtain a list of customers who bought product A and never bought product B. You use two slicers, Product and Filter Product, selecting one or more products in each one. The pivot table has the customer names in rows. For customers who bought at least one product selected in the Product slicer but never bought any of the products selected in the Filter Product slicer, the Customers with No Filter Products measure should return 1.

The example shown in Figure 14-8 shows the list of customers who bought an HL Mountain Tire or an ML Mountain Tire, but never bought a Mountain Tire Tube. You may want to contact these customers and offer a Mountain Tire Tube.

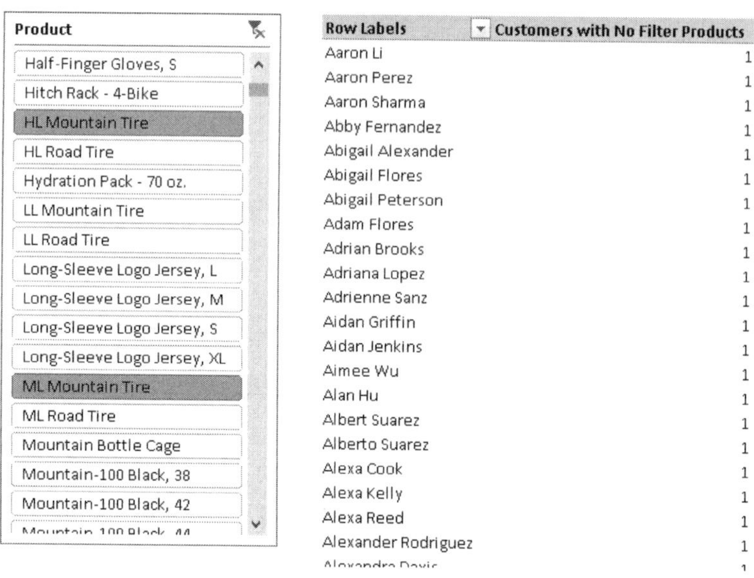

FIGURE 14-8 Customers who bought one product (HL Mountain Tire or ML Mountain Tire) but not the item in the Filter Product table (Mountain Tire Tube).

Download sample workbooks for both Excel 2010 and 2013 on
http://www.daxpatterns.com/basket-analysis

Note that you can easily create a corresponding SQL Server Analysis Services Tabular project starting from the Excel 2013 file

CHAPTER 15

New and Returning Customers

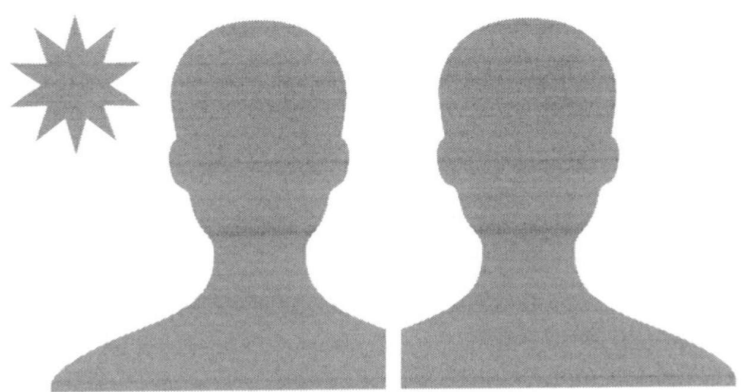

The New and Returning Customers pattern dynamically calculates the number of customers with certain behaviors based on their purchase history. This calculation can be computing-intensive and, thus, a critical part of the pattern is an efficient implementation.

Basic Pattern Example

Suppose you have a Sales table containing one row for each row detail in an order, as shown in Figure 15-1.

OrderDateKey	ProductCode	CustomerKey	SalesOrderNumber	SalesOrderLineNumber	OrderQuantity	SalesAmount
20070801	TT-M928	21407	SO51881	1	1	$4.99
20070801	TT-M928	14870	SO51900	1	1	$4.99
20070802	TT-M928	25811	SO51927	1	1	$4.99
20070802	TT-M928	15319	SO51948	1	1	$4.99
20070803	TT-M928	18174	SO51997	1	1	$4.99
20070803	TT-M928	17882	SO51998	1	1	$4.99
20070804	TT-M928	26132	SO52028	1	1	$4.99

FIGURE 15-1 The Sales table must contain at least date and customer columns.

The OrderDateKey and CustomerKey columns reference the Date and Customer tables, respectively. The pattern assumes that there is one row per customer. If the Customer table contains more than one row for the same customer (such as in a Slowly Changing Dimension, where there is one row for each version of the same customer), then the application key that uniquely identifies the customer should be copied (denormalized) in the Sales table.

You create the New Customers measure to count how many customers have never bought a product before, considering the past sales of only the current selection of products.

```
[New Customers] :=
COUNTROWS (
    FILTER (
        ADDCOLUMNS (
            VALUES ( Sales[CustomerKey] ),
            "PreviousSales", CALCULATE (
                COUNTROWS ( Sales ),
                FILTER (
                    ALL ( 'Date' ),
                    'Date'[FullDate] < MIN ( 'Date'[FullDate] )
                )
            )
        ),
```

```
        [PreviousSales] = 0
    )
)
```

In Figure 15-2 you can see the result of the New Customers measure: because the slicer is filtering only the Bikes category, the pivot table displays how many customers bought a bike for the first time in each month.

Category	
Accessories	Bikes
Clothing	
Components	

Row Labels	Customers	New Customers	Returning Customers
2007	**4,875**	**3,264**	**1,611**
January	244	244	
February	272	272	
March	272	272	
April	294	294	
May	335	335	
June	321	321	
July	511	202	309
August	495	196	299
September	579	206	373
October	616	244	372
November	686	282	404
December	1,042	396	646
2008	**5,451**	**2,178**	**3,273**
January	777	247	530
February	838	265	573
March	872	300	572
April	975	370	605
May	1,131	497	634
June	1,171	499	672
Grand Total	**8,773**	**5,442**	**3,331**

FIGURE 15-2 The pivot table shows new and returning customers considering only sales of bikes.

The Customers measure is simply a distinct count.

```
[Customers] := DISTINCTCOUNT ( Sales[CustomerKey] )
```

The Returning Customers measure counts how many customers made at least one purchase in the past and made another purchase in the current period.

```
[Returning Customers] :=
COUNTROWS (
    CALCULATETABLE (
        VALUES ( Sales[CustomerKey] ),
        VALUES ( Sales[CustomerKey] ),
        FILTER (
            ALL ( 'Date' ),
            'Date'[FullDate] < MIN ( 'Date'[FullDate] )
        )
    )
)
```

You can also calculate the number of new customers by using the difference between the Customers and Returning Customers measures. This can be a good approach for simple formulas, but the technique used in this example is useful for implementing complex calculations, such as Lost Customers and Recovered Customers, as described in the complete pattern.

Use Cases

The New and Returning Customers pattern is useful in scenarios where you analyze customers' behavior and loyalty based on recurring purchasing behaviors. The following is a list of some interesting use cases.

Customer Retention

A company that uses customer retention strategies should analyze the results of its efforts by evaluating the behavior of its existing customer base. The New and Returning Customers pattern includes measures that enable such analysis, such as calculating the number of lost and returning customers. You can also analyze the results of actions targeted to lost customers by using the Recovered Customers measure.

Customer Attrition

If a company does not have a subscription model, identifying a lost customer requires the definition of a period of time within which the customer should make a purchase to be considered an active customer. Identifying lost customers is a key to analyzing customer attrition, customer churn, customer turnover, and customer defection.

Churning

To evaluate the churn rate of a customer base, you can use the New and Returning Customers pattern to obtain the number of new, lost, returning, and recovered customers.

Customer Loyalty

You can analyze customer loyalty by using several measures of the New and Returning Customers pattern, such as Returning Customers and Lost Customers. Usually you evaluate these measures against the total number of customers, comparing the resulting ratio over time.

Complete Pattern

The complete pattern includes many different measures. Examples of implementation of all the measures are shown after the definitions and the data model below.

Definition of Measures

The measures used in the pattern are defined as follows:

- **New Customers:** customers who have never purchased any of the selected products.
- **Returning Customers:** customers who bought at least one of the selected products in the past (no matter when).
- **Lost Customers:** customers who bought any of the selected products in the past but did not buy in the last period (defined as a number of days/months/years).
- **Recovered Customers:** customers who were considered lost before the defined period (like Lost Customers) but made a purchase in the period.

For each measure, there is also an "absolute" version that ignores the current product selection for past purchases:

- **Absolute New Customers:** customers who have never purchased before, regardless of the product selection.
- **Absolute Returning Customers:** customers who bought any product at any time in the past.
- **Absolute Lost Customers:** like Lost Customers, but considering any purchase made in the past, regardless of the current selection of products.
- **Absolute Recovered Customers:** customers who were considered lost before the defined period, regardless of the current selection of products (like Absolute Lost Customers), but made a purchase in the period.

Data Model

You need a data model similar to the one shown in Figure 15-3, with a Sales table that has a column containing a unique value for each customer (CustomerKey). If one customer has many keys (such as in a Slowly Changing Dimension Type 2, where every entity keeps the history of a changing attribute, storing one row for every version), you should denormalize the application key in the Sales table. The reason to do that is performance; you can avoid this denormalization by using a DAX calculation in the measure, but it would slow down query response time.

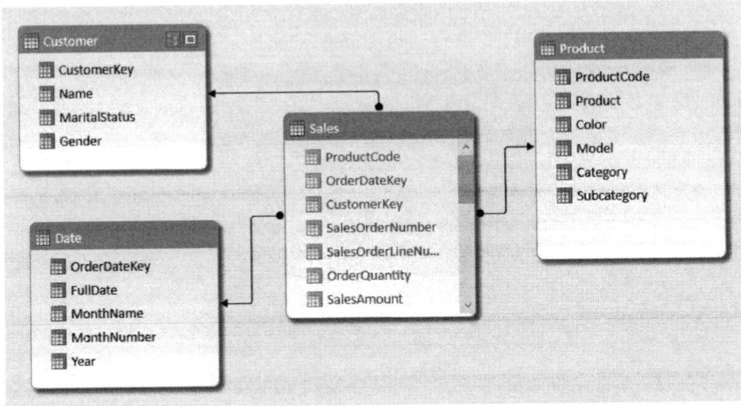

FIGURE 15-3 The data model includes a unique customer identifier in the Sales table.

The pivot table in Figure 15-4 shows the relative measures of this pattern in the columns and the different periods in the rows.

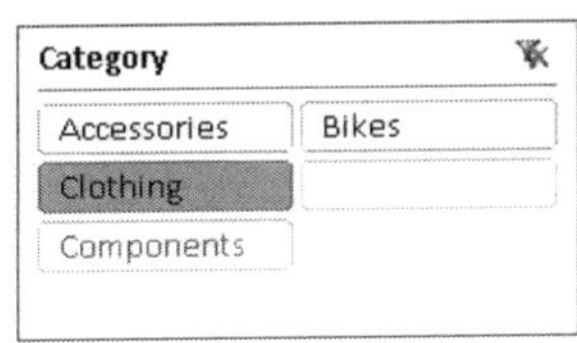

Row Labels	Customers	New Customers	Lost Customers	Returning Customers	Recovered Customers
2007	**2,867**	**2,867**			
July	153	153			
August	508	508	3		
September	536	516	150	20	
October	552	532	484	20	5
November	547	514	519	33	16
December	673	644	538	29	16
2008	**4,196**	**3,985**	**1,189**	**211**	**190**
January	632	572	555	60	46
February	633	581	612	52	32
March	642	599	616	43	28
April	683	628	636	55	41
May	699	633	631	66	51
June	771	687	663	84	62
July	346	285	683	61	45
Grand Total	**6,852**	**6,852**			

FIGURE 15-4 The columns show measures of the New and Returning Customers pattern.

The pivot table in Figure 15-5 shows the corresponding absolute measures of this pattern.

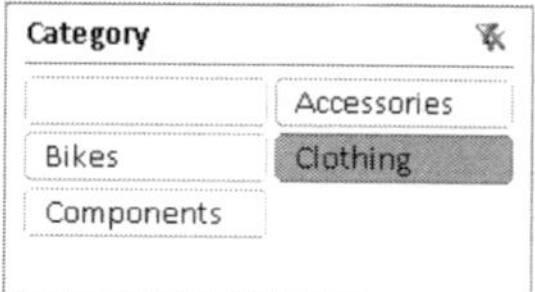

Row Labels	Customers	Absolute New Customers	Absolute Lost Customers	Absolute Returning Customers	Absolute Recovered Customers
2007	**2,867**	**2,359**	**523**	**508**	**736**
January			204		
February			305		
March			244		
April			286		
May			272		
June			294		
July	153	60	334	93	86
August	508	414	318	94	91
September	536	384	485	152	121
October	552	392	1,410	160	122
November	547	369	1,449	178	141
December	673	398	1,527	275	236
2008	**4,196**	**2,601**	**3,451**	**1,595**	**1,534**
January	632	377	1,591	255	212
February	633	356	1,795	277	232
March	642	369	1,683	273	236
April	683	392	1,734	291	246
May	699	371	1,749	328	284
June	771	403	1,871	368	317
July	346	206	2,039	140	99
Grand Total	**6,852**	**5,618**	**523**	**1,234**	**1,839**

FIGURE 15-5 The columns show absolute measures of the New and Returning Customers pattern.

Templates of Measures

In the templates below, you will find the following markers:

- <fact_table> is the table that contains the sales transactions.
- <product_table> is the table that contains the products.
- <customer_key_column> is a column in the fact table that contains a unique identifier for the customer (it is also called business key or application key).
- <date_column> is a column in the date table or (if you do not have a date table in the data model) the fact table that identifies the date of the sales transaction.

- <date_table> is the date table - if you do not have a date table in the data model, replace it with the column in the fact table that identifies the date of the sales transaction (<date_column>).
- <fact_date_column> is a column in the fact table that identifies the date of the sales transaction; its data type has to be datetime. If an external date table uses a different data type to establish the relationship with the fact table, the corresponding date has to be denormalized in the fact table to simplify this calculation.
- <days_lost_customer> is the number of days after the last purchase to consider a customer lost.

There are two groups of templates:

- Relative measures: consider past transactions of selected products only.
- Absolute measures: consider past transactions of all the products, regardless of the current selection.

Relative Measures for New/Lost/Recovered/Returning Customers

Relative template measures define the state of a customer (new/lost/recovered/returning) considering only the products in the current selection and ignoring any transaction by the same customer with other products.

You can calculate the number of new customers as a difference between the customers in the current period and the returning customers.

```
[New Customers] :=
DISTINCTCOUNT ( <customer_key_column> ) - [Returning Customers]
```

An alternative way to implement the same measure of new customers is by counting how many customers had no sales before the period selected.

```
[New Customers] :=
COUNTROWS (
```

```
        FILTER (
            ADDCOLUMNS (
                VALUES ( <customer_key_column> ),
                "PreviousSales",
                    CALCULATE (
                        COUNTROWS ( <fact_table> ),
                        FILTER (
                            ALL ( <date_table> ),
                            <date_column> < MIN ( <date_column> )
                        )
                    )
            ),
            ISBLANK ( [PreviousSales] )
        )
    )
```

The former version of New Customers (subtraction between distinct count of customers and returning customers) is usually faster. However, it is a good idea to test the performance of both approaches depending on the distribution of data in the data model and the type of queries used, and then to choose the implementation that is faster on a case-by-case basis.

You can evaluate the number of returning customers by using a technique that manipulates the filter context. The following measure combines two filters (the dates before the period selected, and the customers in the period selected) to count returning customers.

```
[Returning Customers] :=
COUNTROWS (
    CALCULATETABLE (
        VALUES ( <customer_key_column> ),
        VALUES ( <customer_key_column> ),
        FILTER (
            ALL ( <date_table> ),
            <date_column> < MIN ( <date_column> )
        )
    )
)
```

NOTE Remember that the first argument of the CALCULATE or CALCULATETABLE function is the expression that will be evaluated in a filter context modified by the filter arguments. Passing VALUES (<customer_key_column>) as a filter argument will keep the customers of the selected period in the filter context, once the filter over a different set of dates is applied. A possible bottleneck of the Returning Customers measure is that it applies a filter by date: if you are evaluating returning customers by month or year in a pivot table, the formula engine scans a materialized table including date and customer key. You might improve performance and reduce memory pressure by applying a filter over a month or year column instead of operating at the date level, possibly by denormalizing such a column in the fact table.

You can determine the number of lost customers by using the following calculation. The internal CustomerLostDate column sums the number of days since the last purchase of each customer, which defines when a customer is lost (the <days_lost_customer> marker). You filter only those customers who have a CustomerLostDate within the selected period, and no purchases in the selected period before the CustomerLostDate of that customer.

```
[LostDaysLimit] := <days_lost_customer> + 1

[Lost Customers] :=
COUNTROWS (
    FILTER (
        ADDCOLUMNS (
            FILTER (
                CALCULATETABLE (
                    ADDCOLUMNS (
                        VALUES ( <customer_key_column> ),
                        "CustomerLostDate",
                            CALCULATE ( MAX ( <fact_date_column> ) ) + [LostDaysLimit]
                    ),
                    FILTER (
                        ALL ( <date_table> ),
                        AND (
                            <date_column> < MIN ( <date_column> ),
                            <date_column>
                                >= MIN ( <date_column> ) - [LostDaysLimit]
                        )
                    )
```

```
                ),
                AND (
                    AND (
                        [CustomerLostDate] >= MIN ( <date_column> ),
                        [CustomerLostDate] <= MAX ( <date_column> )
                    ),
                    [CustomerLostDate]
                        <= CALCULATE ( MAX ( <fact_date_column> ), ALL ( <fact_table> ) )
                )
            ),
            "FirstBuyInPeriod", CALCULATE ( MIN ( <fact_date_column> ) )
        ),
        OR (
            ISBLANK ( [FirstBuyInPeriod] ),
            [FirstBuyInPeriod] > [CustomerLostDate]
        )
    )
)
```

You can obtain the number of recovered customers with a calculation that compares, for each customer in the current selection, the date of the last purchase before the period selected against the first date of purchases in the current period.

NOTE The formula engine performs an important part of the calculation, so the DAX expression performs the most selective test in inner FILTER functions in order to minimize the occurrences of the least selective comparisons, improving performance when the number of recovered customers is high.

```
[Recovered Customers] :=
COUNTROWS (
    FILTER (
        ADDCOLUMNS (
            FILTER (
                FILTER (
```

```
                    ADDCOLUMNS (
                        VALUES ( <customer_key_column> ),
                        "CustomerLostDate", CALCULATE (
                            MAX ( <fact_date_column> ),
                            FILTER (
                                ALL ( <date_table> ),
                                <date_column> < MIN ( <fact_date_column> )
                            )
                        )
                    ),
                    NOT ( ISBLANK ( [CustomerLostDate] ) )
                ),
                ( [CustomerLostDate] + [LostDaysLimit] ) < MAX ( <fact_date_column> )
            ),
            "FirstBuyInPeriod", CALCULATE ( MIN ( <fact_date_column> ) )
        ),
        [FirstBuyInPeriod] > ( [CustomerLostDate] + [LostDaysLimit] )
    )
)
```

Absolute Measures for New/Lost/Recovered/Returning Customers

Absolute template measures define the state of a customer (new/lost/recovered/returning) considering all the purchases ever made by the same customer.You can calculate the number of absolute new customers by counting how many customers had no transactions for any product before the period selected. In this case, you cannot use the difference between the customers in the current period and the returning customers.

```
[Absolute New Customers] :=
COUNTROWS (
    FILTER (
        ADDCOLUMNS (
            VALUES ( <customer_key_column> ),
            "PreviousSales",
                CALCULATE (
                    COUNTROWS ( <fact_table> ),
```

```
                    ALL ( <product_table> ),
                    FILTER (
                        ALL ( <date_table> ),
                        <date_column> < MIN ( <date_column> )
                    )
                )
            ),
            ISBLANK ( [PreviousSales] )
        )
    )
```

IMPORTANT Note that the only difference between measures of new customers and absolute new customers is an additional filter argument, which is highlighted in bold. If there are other attributes that you want to ignore for past transactions made by the same customer, you just include other ALL conditions on that table(s) in the filter arguments of the CALCULATE statement, removing filters on table/columns you want to ignore.

You can evaluate the number of absolute returning customers by adding ALL conditions in filter arguments of the Absolute Returning Customers measure, specifying the table/columns you do not want to filter in past transactions.

```
[Absolute Returning Customers] :=
COUNTROWS (
    CALCULATETABLE (
        VALUES ( <customer_key_column> ),
        VALUES ( <customer_key_column> ),
        ALL ( <product_table> ),
        FILTER (
            ALL ( <date_table> ),
            <date_column> < MIN ( <date_column> )
        )
    )
)
```

To calculate the number of absolute lost customers, you add ALL conditions (for tables/attributes you want to ignore in past transactions) in two CALCULATETABLE and CALCULATE filter arguments of the original Lost Customers expression. Look at the explanation of the Lost Customers measure for more details about its behavior.

```
[LostDaysLimit] := <days_lost_customer> + 1

[Absolute Lost Customers] :=
COUNTROWS (
    FILTER (
        ADDCOLUMNS (
            FILTER (
                CALCULATETABLE (
                    ADDCOLUMNS (
                        VALUES ( <customer_key_column> ),
                        "CustomerLostDate",
                            CALCULATE ( MAX ( <fact_date_column> ) ) + [LostDaysLimit]
                    ),
                    ALL ( <product_table> ),
                    FILTER (
                        ALL ( <date_table> ),
                        AND (
                            <date_column> < MIN ( <date_column> ),
                            <date_column>
                                >= MIN ( <date_column> ) - [LostDaysLimit]
                        )
                    )
                ),
                AND (
                    AND (
                        [CustomerLostDate] >= MIN ( <date_column> ),
                        [CustomerLostDate] <= MAX ( <date_column> )
                    ),
                    [CustomerLostDate]
                        <= CALCULATE ( MAX ( <fact_date_column> ), ALL ( <fact_table> ) )
                )
```

```
            ),
            "FirstBuyInPeriod", CALCULATE (
                MIN ( <fact_date_column> ),
                ALL ( <product_table> )
            )
        ),
        OR (
            ISBLANK ( [FirstBuyInPeriod] ),
            [FirstBuyInPeriod] > [CustomerLostDate]
        )
    )
)
```

Finally, you can count the number of absolute recovered customers (using the Absolute Recovered Customers measure) by adding ALL conditions (for tables/attributes to ignore in past transactions) in the filter argument of the only CALCULATE function included in the original Recovered Customers measure.

```
[Absolute Recovered Customers] :=
COUNTROWS (
    FILTER (
        ADDCOLUMNS (
            FILTER (
                FILTER (
                    ADDCOLUMNS (
                        VALUES ( <customer_key_column> ),
                        "CustomerLostDate", CALCULATE (
                            MAX ( <fact_date_column> ),
                            ALL ( <product_table> ),
                            FILTER (
                                ALL ( <fact_date_column> ),
                                <fact_date_column> < MIN ( <fact_date_column> )
                            )
                        )
                    ),
                    NOT ( ISBLANK ( [CustomerLostDate] ) )
```

```
                ),
                ( [CustomerLostDate] + [LostDaysLimit] ) < MAX ( <fact_date_column> )
            ),
            "FirstBuyInPeriod", CALCULATE ( MIN ( <fact_date_column> ) )
        ),
        [FirstBuyInPeriod] > ( [CustomerLostDate] + [LostDaysLimit] )
    )
)
```

Measures Implemented in Adventure Works

You can implement the measures of the New and Returning Customers pattern for the sample model based on Adventure Works after you create a column of Date data type (OrderDate) in the Sales table by using the following definition.

```
Sales[OrderDate] = RELATED ( 'Date'[FullDate] )
```

You can implement the measures of this pattern as follows.

```
[New Customers] :=
DISTINCTCOUNT ( Sales[CustomerKey] ) - [Returning Customers]

[Returning Customers] :=
COUNTROWS (
    CALCULATETABLE (
        VALUES ( Sales[CustomerKey] ),
        VALUES ( Sales[CustomerKey] ),
        FILTER (
            ALL ( 'Date' ),
            'Date'[FullDate] < MIN ( 'Date'[FullDate] )
        )
    )
)
```

```
[Lost Customers] :=
IF (
    NOT (
        MIN ( 'Date'[FullDate] ) > CALCULATE ( MAX ( Sales[OrderDate] ), ALL ( Sales ) )
    ),
    COUNTROWS (
        FILTER (
            ADDCOLUMNS (
                FILTER (
                    CALCULATETABLE (
                        ADDCOLUMNS (
                            VALUES ( Sales[CustomerKey] ),
                            "CustomerLostDate",
                                CALCULATE ( MAX ( Sales[OrderDate] ) ) + [LostDaysLimit]
                        ),
                        FILTER (
                            ALL ( 'Date' ),
                            AND (
                                'Date'[FullDate] < MIN ( 'Date'[FullDate] ),
                                'Date'[FullDate]
                                    >= MIN ( 'Date'[FullDate] ) - [LostDaysLimit]
                            )
                        )
                    ),
                    AND (
                        AND (
                            [CustomerLostDate] >= MIN ( 'Date'[FullDate] ),
                            [CustomerLostDate] <= MAX ( 'Date'[FullDate] )
                        ),
                        [CustomerLostDate]
                            <= CALCULATE ( MAX ( Sales[OrderDate] ), ALL ( Sales ) )
                    )
                ),
                "FirstBuyInPeriod", CALCULATE ( MIN ( Sales[OrderDate] ) )
            ),
            OR (
                ISBLANK ( [FirstBuyInPeriod] ),
```

```
                [FirstBuyInPeriod] > [CustomerLostDate]
            )
        )
    )
)

[Recovered Customers] :=
COUNTROWS (
    FILTER (
        ADDCOLUMNS (
            FILTER (
                FILTER (
                    ADDCOLUMNS (
                        VALUES ( Sales[CustomerKey] ),
                        "CustomerLostDate", CALCULATE (
                            MAX ( Sales[OrderDate] ),
                            FILTER (
                                ALL ( 'Date' ),
                                'Date'[FullDate] < MIN ( Sales[OrderDate] )
                            )
                        )
                    ),
                    NOT ( ISBLANK ( [CustomerLostDate] ) )
                ),
                ( [CustomerLostDate] + [LostDaysLimit] ) < MAX ( Sales[OrderDate] )
            ),
            "FirstBuyInPeriod", CALCULATE ( MIN ( Sales[OrderDate] ) )
        ),
        [FirstBuyInPeriod] > ( [CustomerLostDate] + [LostDaysLimit] )
    )
)

[Absolute New Customers] :=
COUNTROWS (
    FILTER (
        ADDCOLUMNS (
            VALUES ( Sales[CustomerKey] ),
```

```
            "PreviousSales",
                CALCULATE (
                    COUNTROWS ( Sales ),
                    ALL ( Product ),
                    FILTER (
                        ALL ( 'Date' ),
                        'Date'[FullDate] < MIN ( 'Date'[FullDate] )
                    )
                )
        ),
        ISBLANK ( [PreviousSales] )
    )
)

[Absolute Returning Customers] :=
COUNTROWS (
    CALCULATETABLE (
        VALUES ( Sales[CustomerKey] ),
        VALUES ( Sales[CustomerKey] ),
        ALL ( Product ),
        FILTER (
            ALL ( 'Date' ),
            'Date'[FullDate] < MIN ( 'Date'[FullDate] )
        )
    )
)

[Absolute Lost Customers] :=
IF (
    NOT ( MIN ( 'Date'[FullDate] )
        > CALCULATE ( MAX ( Sales[OrderDate] ), ALL ( Sales ) ) ),
    COUNTROWS (
        FILTER (
            ADDCOLUMNS (
                FILTER (
                    CALCULATETABLE (
                        ADDCOLUMNS (
```

```
                    VALUES ( Sales[CustomerKey] ),
                    "CustomerLostDate",
                        CALCULATE ( MAX ( Sales[OrderDate] ) ) + [LostDaysLimit]
                ),
                ALL ( Product ),
                FILTER (
                    ALL ( 'Date' ),
                    AND (
                        'Date'[FullDate] < MIN ( 'Date'[FullDate] ),
                        'Date'[FullDate]
                            >= MIN ( 'Date'[FullDate] ) - [LostDaysLimit]
                    )
                )
            ),
            AND (
                AND (
                    [CustomerLostDate] >= MIN ( 'Date'[FullDate] ),
                    [CustomerLostDate] <= MAX ( 'Date'[FullDate] )
                ),
                [CustomerLostDate]
                    <= CALCULATE ( MAX ( Sales[OrderDate] ), ALL ( Sales ) )
            )
        ),
        "FirstBuyInPeriod", CALCULATE ( MIN ( Sales[OrderDate] ), ALL ( Product ) )
    ),
    OR (
        ISBLANK ( [FirstBuyInPeriod] ),
        [FirstBuyInPeriod] > [CustomerLostDate]
    )
  )
 )
)

[Absolute Recovered Customers]:=
COUNTROWS (
    FILTER (
        ADDCOLUMNS (
```

```
            FILTER (
                FILTER (
                    ADDCOLUMNS (
                        VALUES ( Sales[CustomerKey] ),
                        "CustomerLostDate", CALCULATE (
                            MAX ( Sales[OrderDate] ),
                            ALL ( Product ),
                            FILTER (
                                ALL ( 'Date' ),
                                'Date'[FullDate] < MIN ( Sales[OrderDate] )
                            )
                        )
                    ),
                    NOT ( ISBLANK ( [CustomerLostDate] ) )
                ),
                ( [CustomerLostDate] + [LostDaysLimit] ) < MAX ( Sales[OrderDate] )
            ),
            "FirstBuyInPeriod", CALCULATE ( MIN ( Sales[OrderDate] ) )
        ),
        [FirstBuyInPeriod] > ( [CustomerLostDate] + [LostDaysLimit] )
    )
)
```

The only purpose of the initial IF statement in the measures for lost customers is to avoid evaluation for dates higher than the last date available in Sales, because the Date table contains more years than available data and a complete evaluation of lost customers for future dates would be useless and expensive.

More Pattern Examples

In this section, you will see a few examples of the New and Returning Customers pattern.

Customer Loyalty with Different Intervals Between Sales

Using a slicer, you can control the LostDaysLimit measure, which controls the evaluation of lost and recovered customers. This enables quick changes of the evaluation, trying different intervals between two sales to consider a customer as loyal. Figure 15-6 shows an example of the results obtained by defining a table (Days) containing a single column (Days Customer Lost) that is used to display the values in the slicer. The minimum value selected is the maximum distance between two sales before the customer is considered lost.

```
[DaysCustomerLost] := MIN ( Days[Days Customer Lost] )

[LostDaysLimit] := [DaysCustomerLost] + 1
```

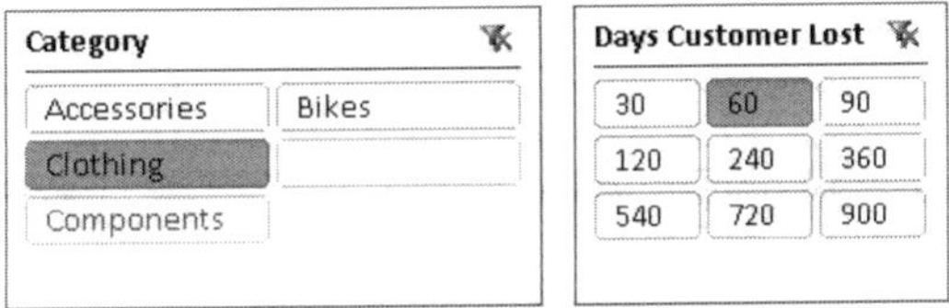

Row Labels	Customers	New Customers	Lost Customers	Returning Customers	Recovered Customers
2007	**2,867**	**2,867**			
July	153	153			
August	508	508	3		
September	536	516	150	20	
October	552	532	484	20	5
November	547	514	519	33	16
December	673	644	538	29	16
2008	**4,196**	**3,985**	**1,189**	**211**	**190**
January	632	572	555	60	46
February	633	581	612	52	32
March	642	599	616	43	28
April	683	628	636	55	41
May	699	633	631	66	51
June	771	687	663	84	62
July	346	285	683	61	45
Grand Total	**6,852**	**6,852**			

FIGURE 15-6 The Days Customer Lost slicer defines the number of days without sales before a customer is considered lost.

Sales Amounts of New, Returning, and Recovered Customers

You might want to filter a measure by considering only the new, returning, or recovered customers.

For example, a pivot table could display the Sales Amount of different types of customers, as shown in Figure 15-7.

Row Labels	Sum of SalesAmount	Sales New Customers	Sales Returning Customers	Sales Recovered Customers	Sales Loyal Customers
2007	**$293,709.71**	**$293,709.71**			
July	$14,468.20	$14,468.20			
August	$52,056.61	$51,918.67	$137.94		$137.94
September	$52,149.72	$48,709.83	$3,439.89	$191.26	$3,248.63
October	$54,595.17	$49,515.51	$5,079.66	$1,283.89	$3,795.77
November	$54,832.02	$47,418.84	$7,413.18	$2,973.29	$4,439.89
December	$65,607.99	$56,825.73	$8,782.26	$4,779.24	$4,003.02
2008	**$407,050.25**	**$338,594.92**	**$68,455.33**	**$52,726.27**	**$15,729.06**
January	$56,456.93	$46,400.46	$10,056.47	$6,023.08	$4,033.39
February	$56,995.90	$47,279.07	$9,716.83	$5,373.36	$4,343.47
March	$60,097.80	$48,386.32	$11,711.48	$7,535.24	$4,176.24
April	$62,673.58	$47,697.84	$14,975.74	$10,786.04	$4,189.70
May	$71,880.47	$54,649.76	$17,230.71	$11,826.20	$5,404.51
June	$65,200.93	$49,980.95	$15,219.98	$11,677.09	$3,542.89
July	$33,744.64	$20,529.23	$13,215.41	$9,253.73	$3,961.68
Grand Total	**$700,759.96**	**$700,759.96**			

FIGURE 15-7 The columns in the pivot table show the sales amount considering only the customers of the type described in the corresponding measure name (new, returning, recovered, and loyal).

You define the measure using a slight variation of the original pattern. Instead of counting the rows returned by a table expression that filters the customers, you use the list of customers as a filter argument in a CALCULATE expression that evaluates the measure you want.

```
[Sales New Customers] :=
CALCULATE (
    SUM ( Sales[SalesAmount] ),
    FILTER (
        ADDCOLUMNS (
            VALUES ( Sales[CustomerKey] ),
            "PreviousSales",
                CALCULATE (
                    COUNTROWS ( Sales ),
                    FILTER (
                        ALL ( 'Date' ),
```

```
                    'Date'[FullDate] < MIN ( 'Date'[FullDate] )
                )
            )
        ),
        ISBLANK ( [PreviousSales] )
    )
)

[Sales Returning Customers] :=
CALCULATE (
    SUM ( Sales[SalesAmount] ),
    CALCULATETABLE (
        VALUES ( Sales[CustomerKey] ),
        VALUES ( Sales[CustomerKey] ),
        FILTER (
            ALL ( 'Date' ),
            'Date'[FullDate] < MIN ( 'Date'[FullDate] )
        )
    )
)

[Sales Recovered Customers] :=
CALCULATE (
    SUM ( Sales[SalesAmount] ),
    FILTER (
        ADDCOLUMNS (
            FILTER (
                FILTER (
                    ADDCOLUMNS (
                        VALUES ( Sales[CustomerKey] ),
                        "CustomerLostDate", CALCULATE (
                            MAX ( Sales[OrderDate] ),
                            FILTER (
                                ALL ( 'Date' ),
                                'Date'[FullDate] < MIN ( Sales[OrderDate] )
                            )
                        )
```

```
                    ),
                    NOT ( ISBLANK ( [CustomerLostDate] ) )
                ),
                ( [CustomerLostDate] + [LostDaysLimit] ) < MAX ( Sales[OrderDate] )
            ),
            "FirstBuyInPeriod", CALCULATE ( MIN ( Sales[OrderDate] ) )
        ),
        [FirstBuyInPeriod] > ( [CustomerLostDate] + [LostDaysLimit] )
    )
)

[Sales Loyal Customers] :=
CALCULATE (
    SUM ( Sales[SalesAmount] ),
    FILTER (
        ADDCOLUMNS (
            FILTER (
                FILTER (
                    ADDCOLUMNS (
                        VALUES ( Sales[CustomerKey] ),
                        "CustomerLostDate", CALCULATE (
                            MAX ( Sales[OrderDate] ),
                            FILTER (
                                ALL ( 'Date' ),
                                'Date'[FullDate] < MIN ( Sales[OrderDate] )
                            )
                        )
                    ),
                    NOT ( ISBLANK ( [CustomerLostDate] ) )
                ),
                ( [CustomerLostDate] + [LostDaysLimit] ) >= MIN ( Sales[OrderDate] )
            ),
            "FirstBuyInPeriod", CALCULATE ( MIN ( Sales[OrderDate] ) )
        ),
        [FirstBuyInPeriod] <= ( [CustomerLostDate] + [LostDaysLimit] )
    )
)
```

Download sample workbooks for both Excel 2010 and 2013 on
http://www.daxpatterns.com/new-and-returning-customers

Note that you can easily create a corresponding SQL Server Analysis Services Tabular project starting from the Excel 2013 file

CHAPTER 16

Parent-Child Hierarchies

DAX does not directly support parent-child hierarchies. To obtain a browsable hierarchy in the data model, you have to naturalize a parent-child hierarchy. DAX provides specific functions to naturalize a parent-child hierarchy using calculated columns. The complete pattern also includes measures that improve the visualization of ragged hierarchies in Power Pivot.

Basic Pattern Example

Suppose you have an Agents table containing sales figures for each agent. The Parent column specifies the direct report of each agent, as you see in Figure 16-1.

Name	Parent	Sales
Bill		
Annabel		
Catherine	Annabel	32
Harry	Annabel	16
Michael	Annabel	8
Brad	Bill	
Julie	Bill	4
Chris	Brad	2
Vincent	Brad	1

FIGURE 16-1 Values in the Parent column reference the Name column.

You might represent relationships between nodes using a tree structure, where all nodes without a parent are roots of a hierarchy tree, as shown in Figure 16-2.

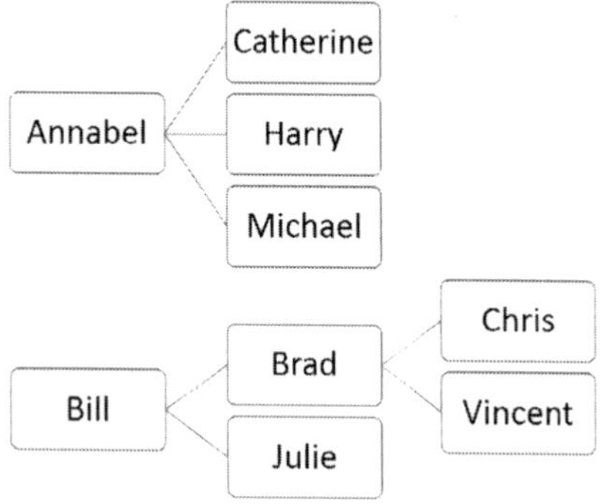

FIGURE 16-2 The hierarchy has two branches—one with two levels and one with three levels.

Your goal is to create one calculated column for each level of the hierarchy. To create the right number of calculated columns, you must know in advance the maximum depth of the hierarchy. Otherwise, you have to estimate it, because this number cannot change dynamically. Power Pivot and Analysis Services hierarchies have an intrinsic limit of 64 levels.

Figure 16-3 shows the resulting table with the naturalized hierarchy.

Name	Parent	Sales	Level1	Level2	Level3
Bill			Bill		
Annabel			Annabel		
Catherine	Annabel	32	Annabel	Catherine	
Harry	Annabel	16	Annabel	Harry	
Michael	Annabel	8	Annabel	Michael	
Brad	Bill		Bill	Brad	
Julie	Bill	4	Bill	Julie	
Chris	Brad	2	Bill	Brad	Chris
Vincent	Brad	1	Bill	Brad	Vincent

FIGURE 16-3 The naturalized hierarchy has one column for each level of the hierarchy.

You can create these columns in DAX by leveraging a hidden calculated column that provides a string with the complete path to reach the node in the current row of the table. The Path column in Figure 16-4 provides this content using the special PATH function.

```
[Path] = PATH ( Nodes[Name], Nodes[Parent] )
```

Name	Parent	Sales	Path
Bill			Bill
Annabel			Annabel
Catherine	Annabel	32	Annabel|Catherine
Harry	Annabel	16	Annabel|Harry
Michael	Annabel	8	Annabel|Michael
Brad	Bill		Bill|Brad
Julie	Bill	4	Bill|Julie
Chris	Brad	2	Bill|Brad|Chris
Vincent	Brad	1	Bill|Brad|Vincent

FIGURE 16-4 The Path column contains the result of the PATH function.

Each column that defines a level in the hierarchy uses the PATHITEM function to retrieve the proper value for that level, as shown in Figure 16-3.

```
[Level1] = PATHITEM ( Nodes[Path], 1 )
```

```
[Level2] = PATHITEM ( Nodes[Path], 2 )
```

```
[Level3] = PATHITEM ( Nodes[Path], 3 )
```

You define the hierarchy in the diagram view of the data model shown in Figure 16-5.

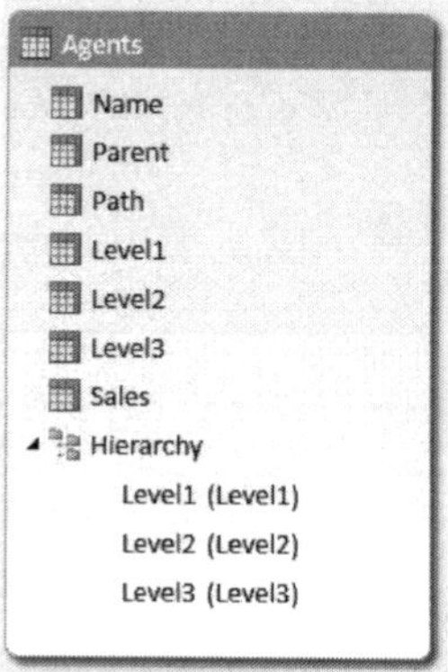

FIGURE 16-5 The Hierarchy heading includes the calculated columns created to naturalize the hierarchy.

You can navigate the resulting hierarchy in Excel as shown in Figure 16-6.

Row Labels	Sum of Sales
⊟Annabel	56
⊞Catherine	32
⊞Harry	16
⊞Michael	8
⊟Bill	7
⊟Brad	3
Chris	2
Vincent	1
⊞Julie	4
Grand Total	63

FIGURE 16-6 The Sum of Sales measure displays the total sales of all agents below the selected node in the hierarchy.

You can browse a pivot table and navigate this hierarchy down to the third level. If an intermediate node of the hierarchy has no children, you can still drill-down to an empty label, although this would result in a row of the pivot table with no description. You can avoid this behavior in Analysis Services Tabular by using the HideMemberIf property, and in Power Pivot by using the technique described in the complete pattern.

Use Cases

You can use the Parent-Child Hierarchies pattern any time you have a corresponding structure in your source data. This is a list of common use cases.

Profit and Loss Account Hierarchy

Most profit and loss statements have a native parent-child hierarchy for representing the list of accounts. When this is not the native representation in the data source, a parent-child hierarchy can be useful to show an alternative custom grouping of original accounts, such as in balance sheet reclassification.

Bill of Materials

A list of components of a product is usually a native parent-child hierarchy, because each component has other sub-components, with different levels of depth in different branches of the hierarchy. Calculations related to measures in a bill of materials are described in another dedicated pattern, Bills of Materials.

Organizational Structure

Company organizational structures are often represented as parent-child hierarchies. One of the limitations of parent-child hierarchies is that each node must have a single parent. Complex organizations that do not respect this constraint require more complex graphs, and mapping them to a parent-child hierarchy requires a normalization to a regular organization tree.

Complete Pattern

Suppose you have a Nodes table containing one row per node, with a ParentKey column that defines the parent of every node. The Transactions table has a many-to-one relationship with the Nodes table. You can see the two tables in Figure 16-7.

NodeKey	Name	ParentKey
1	Bill	
6	Annabel	
7	Catherine	6
8	Harry	6
9	Michael	6
2	Brad	1
3	Julie	1
4	Chris	2
5	Vincent	2

NodeKey	InvoiceNo	Amount	City
2	14001	200	Chicago
2	14002	200	Seattle
3	14003	300	Chicago
4	14004	400	Seattle
5	14005	500	Chicago
6	14006	600	Seattle
7	14007	600	Seattle
7	14008	600	Chicago
8	14009	400	Chicago
8	14010	400	Seattle
9	14011	300	Chicago
9	14012	300	Seattle

FIGURE 16-7 The Nodes table defines a parent-child hierarchy through the NodeKey and ParentKey columns.

You create a hidden HierarchyPath column containing the result of the PATH function, which provides a string with the complete path to reach the node in the current row of the table, as shown in Figure 16-8.

```
[HierarchyPath] = PATH ( Nodes[NodeKey], Nodes[ParentKey] )
```

NodeKey	Name	ParentKey	HierarchyPath
1	Bill		1
6	Annabel		6
7	Catherine	6	6|7
8	Harry	6	6|8
9	Michael	6	6|9
2	Brad	1	1|2
3	Julie	1	1|3
4	Chris	2	1|2|4
5	Vincent	2	1|2|5

FIGURE 16-8 The HierarchyPath column contains the result of the PATH function.

You naturalize the hierarchy by creating a hidden column for each level of the hierarchy. You have to define the maximum depth of the hierarchy in advance, planning enough levels for future growth. For each level, you populate the column with the node name of the hierarchy path at that level. You need to duplicate the name of the leaf node if the level is higher than the number of levels in the hierarchy path, which you obtain in the HierarchyDepth column using the PATHLENGTH function.

NodeKey	Name	ParentKey	IsLeaf	HierarchyPath	HierarchyDepth	Level1	Level2	Level3
1	Bill		FALSE	1	1	Bill	Bill	Bill
6	Annabel		FALSE	6	1	Annabel	Annabel	Annabel
7	Catherine	6	TRUE	6|7	2	Annabel	Catherine	Catherine
8	Harry	6	TRUE	6|8	2	Annabel	Harry	Harry
9	Michael	6	TRUE	6|9	2	Annabel	Michael	Michael
2	Brad	1	FALSE	1|2	2	Bill	Brad	Brad
3	Julie	1	TRUE	1|3	2	Bill	Julie	Julie
4	Chris	2	TRUE	1|2|4	3	Bill	Brad	Chris
5	Vincent	2	TRUE	1|2|5	3	Bill	Brad	Vincent

FIGURE 16-9 The HierarchyDepth column defines the level of the node in the current row.

In Figure 16-9 you can see the resulting column for the levels of the hierarchy, populated using the LOOKUPVALUE and PATHITEM functions. The hierarchy path is a string, but the LOOKUPVALUE has to match an integer column, so you need to cast the hierarchy path value to INT using the third argument of PATHITEM. The following formulas are used for the calculated columns in Figure 16-9.

```
[HierarchyDepth] = PATHLENGTH ( Nodes[HierarchyPath] )

[Level1] =
LOOKUPVALUE (
    Nodes[Name],
    Nodes[NodeKey],
    PATHITEM ( Nodes[HierarchyPath], 1, INTEGER )
)

[Level2] =
IF (
    Nodes[HierarchyDepth] >= 2,
    LOOKUPVALUE (
        Nodes[Name],
        Nodes[NodeKey],
```

```
        PATHITEM ( Nodes[HierarchyPath], 2, INTEGER )
    ),
    Nodes[Level1]
)

[Level3] =
IF (
    Nodes[HierarchyDepth] >= 3,
    LOOKUPVALUE (
        Nodes[Name],
        Nodes[NodeKey],
        PATHITEM ( Nodes[HierarchyPath], 3, INTEGER )
    ),
    Nodes[Level2]
)
```

In order to hide nodes duplicated at lower levels while browsing hierarchy in a pivot table, you create an IsLeaf calculated column, which contains a flag for nodes that have no children in the parent-child hierarchy, as you see in Figure 16-10.

```
[IsLeaf] =
CALCULATE (
    COUNTROWS ( Nodes ),
    ALL ( Nodes ),
    Nodes[ParentKey] = EARLIER ( Nodes[NodeKey] )
) = 0
```

NodeKey	Name	ParentKey	IsLeaf	HierarchyPath
1	Bill		FALSE	1
6	Annabel		FALSE	6
7	Catherine	6	TRUE	6|7
8	Harry	6	TRUE	6|8
9	Michael	6	TRUE	6|9
2	Brad	1	FALSE	1|2
3	Julie	1	TRUE	1|3
4	Chris	2	TRUE	1|2|4
5	Vincent	2	TRUE	1|2|5

FIGURE 16-10 The IsLeaf column marks as TRUE the nodes that have no children in the hierarchy.

The naturalized hierarchy duplicates leaf-level nodes that you do not want to display in a pivot table. In an Analysis Services Tabular model, you can hide these nodes by setting the HideMemberIf property with BIDS Helper (https://bidshelper.codeplex.com/wikipage?title=Tabular%20HideMemberIf). In Power Pivot, you have to build a DAX measure that returns a blank value for a "duplicated" node. You create two hidden measures to support such a calculation: BrowseDepth calculates the level of the hierarchy displayed in a pivot table, and MaxNodeDepth returns the maximum depth of the original parent-child hierarchy starting at the node considered. When BrowseDepth is higher than MaxNodeDepth, the node value should be hidden in the pivot table. You can see in Figure 16-11 a comparison of the BrowseDepth and MaxNodeDepth values returned for each node of the naturalized hierarchy.

Row Labels	BrowseDepth	MaxNodeDepth	Sales Amount Simple
Annabel	**1**	**2**	**3,200**
Annabel	**2**	**1**	
Annabel	3	1	
Catherine	**2**	**2**	**1,200**
Catherine	3	2	
Harry	**2**	**2**	**800**
Harry	3	2	
Michael	**2**	**2**	**600**
Michael	3	2	
Bill	**1**	**3**	**1,600**
Bill	**2**	**1**	
Bill	3	1	
Brad	**2**	**3**	**1,300**
Brad	3	2	
Chris	3	3	400
Vincent	3	3	500
Julie	**2**	**2**	**300**
Julie	3	2	
Grand Total	**0**	**3**	**4,800**

FIGURE 16-11 Nodes having BrowseDepth higher than MaxNodeDepth might not have data to display.

The Sales Amount Simple measure in Figure 16-11 displays blank when BrowseDepth value is higher than MaxNodeDepth.

```
[Sales Amount Simple] :=
IF (
    [BrowseDepth] > [MaxNodeDepth],
    BLANK (),
    SUM ( Transactions[Amount] )
)
```

If you display such a measure in a pivot table with default settings (hiding empty rows), you will see a result like Figure 16-12.

Row Labels	Sales Amount Simple
⊟Annabel	3,200
Catherine	1,200
Harry	800
Michael	600
⊟Bill	1,600
⊟Brad	1,300
Chris	400
Vincent	500
Julie	300
Grand Total	4,800

FIGURE 16-12 The pivot table hides nodes for which the Sales Amount Simple measure returns a blank value.

The Sales Amount Simple measure does not display a separate value for intermediate nodes that have values associated both with children and with the node itself. For example, in Figure 16-12 you can see that the value related to Annabel is higher than the sum of her children, and the same happens for the value related to Brad. The reason is that both Annabel and Brad have directly related transactions. You can show the value for these nodes by implementing a more complex test, checking whether a leaf node has related transactions. The final Sales Amount measure considers all of these conditions, and its result is shown in Figure 16-13.

```
[Sales Amount] :=
IF (
    [BrowseDepth] > [MaxNodeDepth] + 1,
    BLANK (),
    IF (
        [BrowseDepth] = [MaxNodeDepth] + 1,
        IF (
            AND (
                VALUES ( Nodes[IsLeaf] ) = FALSE,
                SUM ( Transactions[Amount] ) <> 0
            ),
            SUM ( Transactions[Amount] ),
            BLANK ()
        ),
```

```
            SUM ( Transactions[Amount] )
        )
    )
```

Row Labels	Sales Amount
⊟Annabel	3,200
Annabel	600
Catherine	1,200
Harry	800
Michael	600
⊟Bill	1,600
⊟Brad	1,300
Brad	400
Chris	400
Vincent	500
Julie	300
Grand Total	4,800

FIGURE 16-13 The Sales Amount measure displays values associated with intermediate nodes, such as Annabel and Brad.

Download sample workbooks for both Excel 2010 and 2013 on
http://www.daxpatterns.com/parent-child-hierarchies

Note that you can easily create a corresponding SQL Server Analysis Services Tabular project starting from the Excel 2013 file

About the Authors

Marco Russo and **Alberto Ferrari** are the two founders of SQLBI (http://www.sqlbi.com), where they regularly publish articles about Microsoft Power Pivot, DAX, and SQL Server Analysis Services Tabular.

They both provide consultancy and mentoring on business intelligence (BI), with a particular specialization in the Microsoft technologies related to BI. They have written several books and papers about these topics, with a particular mention of "SQLBI methodology" (http://sql.bi/methodology), which is a complete methodology for designing and implementing the back end of a BI solution; and "The Many-to-Many Revolution" (http://sql.bi/m2m), which is a paper dedicated to modeling patterns using many-to-many dimension relationships in SQL Server Analysis Services and Power Pivot.

Marco and Alberto are also regular speakers at major international conferences, such as TechEd, PASS Summit, SQLRally, and SQLBits.

Here are some of their latest books:

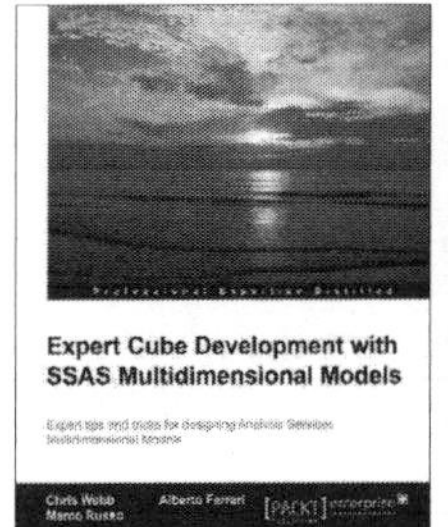

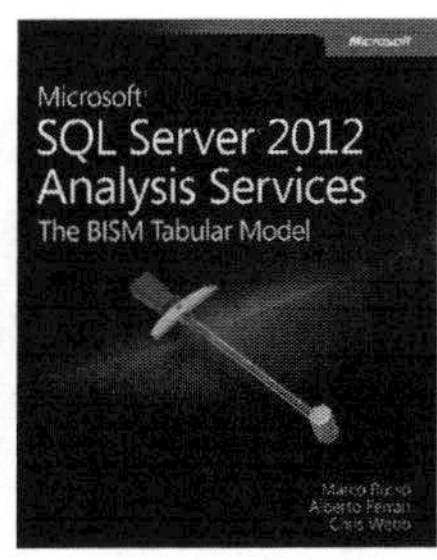

Made in the USA
Middletown, DE
12 March 2016